INTERNATIONAL TERRORISM
How Nations Respond to Terrorists

By

William L. Waugh, Jr.

University of Charleston Library
Charleston, WV 25304

DOCUMENTARY PUBLICATIONS
Salisbury, N.C., U.S.A.
1982

Copyright 1982 by Documentary Publications

All rights reserved. Inquiries should be addressed to:

Documentary Publications
Route 12, Box 480
Salisbury, North Carolina, U.S.A. 28144

ISBN 0-89712-136-8

Printed in the United States of America

10 9 8 7 6 5 4 3 2 1

DATE DUE

MAR 03 '90			
GAYLORD			PRINTED IN U.S.A

PREFACE

The approach to international terrorism used in this study is derived from the literature of policy analysis, particularly the literature dealing with the comparison of policy processes and the evaluation of policy choices. In many respects, the final product represents a summary of the literature on terrorism and, thus, should provide an introduction to that literature for students and observers of terrorist violence. Indeed, its major value may be in its development of a policy context into which can be fit the hundreds of psychological, legal, military, law enforcement, and political studies that have already been published.

While, in some cases, the discussion may seem overly simplistic to the expert, the study does recognize and explicate many of the fundamental conceptual and value conflicts that still influence analyses of and responses to international terrorist events. It does not assume that basic definitional conflicts have been resolved by analysts, governments, or commentators and, in that sense, it may serve as a useful reminder of the complex nature of terrorist violence and the subjective biases of subsequent analysis. It is also hoped that the discussion of fundamental conceptual frameworks, definitional conflicts, and value judgments, as well as the variety of satellite issues and spillover effects, will be of interest and benefit to persons directly involved in antiterrorist policymaking. Moreover, the policy analysis approach, by focusing on the functional nature of the violence and government interventions rather than on case or nation studies, does provide some new perspectives on the violent phenomena that governments face today and, for that reason, the analysis may be of benefit.

Undoubtedly, the analysis herein suffers from the same informational deficiencies evident in most nongovernmental analyses of international terrorism. The availability of government data is, understandably, limited. For that reason, no pretense is made of comprehensiveness or minute detail in the treatment of specific policy options. Acknowledgement, however, must be given the generosity and assistance of the following government analysts who contributed information to which I otherwise would not have had access: Mr. Edward Mickolus, of the U.S. Central Intelligence Agency; and, Mr. John C. Boehm, Jr., and Mr.

Lambert Heyniger, of the U.S. State Department's Office for Combatting Terrorism. Their assistance was invaluable.

Acknowledgement must also be given to the many mentors, colleagues, and friends who contributed so much to this effort. Dr. Walter Opello, Dr. Goberdhan Bhagat, Dr. Ronald John Hy, Dr. John W. Winkle (all of the University of Mississippi), and Dr. Richard Werking (of Trinity University, San Antonio), to mention but a few, deserve special credit. I, of course, am responsible for any deficiencies in the analysis.

TABLE OF CONTENTS

	Page
PREFACE	i
LIST OF TABLES	vii
LIST OF FIGURES	viii

Chapter

I. INTRODUCTION.	1
II. THE NATURE OF INTERNATIONAL TERRORISM	21
Terror and Political Terrorism.	25
International Terrorism	35
A Typology of International Terrorism	50
Spillover Terrorism	57
Integrated Internal Terrorism	60
External Terrorism.	63
III. CHALLENGE AND POLICY DEMANDS.	68
The Challenge of International Terrorism.	72
The Objectives of International Terrorists.	74
Ideological Objectives.	75
Strategic Objectives.	81
Tactical Objectives	90
Terrorist Strengths and Limitations	91
The Terrorist Potential	95
The Policy Imperatives and the Predicament	104
The Security Dilemma.	107
The Legitimacy Dilemma.	110
The Policy Predicament.	113
IV. THEORIES OF CHOICE AND RESPONSE	118
The Response Options.	125
Levels of Response.	125
Modes of Response	131
Preparation	135
Obstruction	137

        Containment 142
        Counteraction 144
        Answering 146
    Media of Response 149
    Theories of Response. 157
        1. Deterrence by Punishment. 158
        2. Deterrence by Denial. 166
    Policy Constraints and the Value
      Dilemma: A Summation 173

V. INTERNATIONAL HOSTAGE INCIDENTS 183
    Hostage Incidents and International
      Terrorist Violence. 186
    The Propositions. 192
    Concepts, Measures, and the
      Analytical Design 203
      Concepts and Measures 203
        Terrorist Demands (Tactical
          Objectives) 203
        Response to Demands 204
        Responding Governments. 205
        Types of International Terrorist
          Events 205
        Types of International Hostage
          Events (Terrorist Tactics) 206
        Hostage Safety. 207
        Nationality 207
      The Analytical Design 208
    Analysis of Data. 210
      Types of International Terrorist
        Events and Government Responses 210
      Challenges to Regime Authority and
        Government Responses. 213
      Government Responses and Hostage
        Safety. 217
    Conclusions 220

VI. CONCLUSIONS: AN OPTIMAL RESPONSE TO
     INTERNATIONAL TERRORISM?. 228

REFERENCES 244

SELECTED BIBLIOGRAPHY. 293

LIST OF TABLES

Table		Page
1.	International Hostage Incidents, 1968-1977.	191
2.	Types of International Terrorist Events and Government Responses (Percentages).	211
3.	Types of International Terrorist Events and Government Responses (Regression Analysis).	212
4.	Government Responses with Event Locations and Terrorist and Hostage Nationalities (Regression Analysis).	213
5.	Government Responses with Terrorist Demands (Tactical Objectives) (Percentages).	215
6.	Government Responses with Terrorist Demands (Tactical Objectives) (Regression Analysis).	216
7.	Government Responses with Types of Hostage Events (Terrorist Tactics) (Percentages).	216
8.	Hostage Safety with Government Responses (Percentages).	217
9.	Hostage Safety with Terrorist Demands (Tactical Objectives) (Regression Analysis).	218
10.	Hostage Safety with Types of Hostage Events (Terrorist Tactics) (Regression Analysis).	219
11.	Hostage Safety with Event Locations and Terrorist and Hostage Nationalities (Regression Analysis).	220
12.	Hostage Safety with Event Locations, Terrorist and Hostage Nationalities, Terrorist Demands, and Types of Terrorist Events by Government Responses (Partial Correlation Analysis).	222

LIST OF FIGURES

Figure		Page
1.	Typology of Terrorism (Mickolus)	49
2.	Permutations of International Terrorism	53
3.	Types of International Terrorism	56
4.	Hierarchy of Terrorist Tactics by Levels of Organizational Competence	97
5.	The Process of Terrorism and the Loci of Government Action	134
6.	An Elementary Typology of Direct Responses and Some Variations	147

INTERNATIONAL TERRORISM
How Nations Respond to Terrorists
A Comparative Policy Analysis

CHAPTER I

INTRODUCTION

Few subjects have generated as much controversy in world politics as has international terrorism. Terrorist violence carries with it a tremendous amount of emotional baggage -- decried as an unconscionable "crime against humanity" by those attacked or threatened and defended as a justifiable tactic of warfare against an oppressive regime by those sympathetic to the goals of the terrorists. The question of whether terrorist violence can be justified by the political ends sought has created a major bifurcation within the arenas of international dialogue.

The United Nations, for example, has been prevented from taking decisive action to reduce the incidence of such violence by the deadlock over whether terrorism is "just" when used against an "unjust" regime. No nation has openly advocated or supported terrorist violence for its own sake, without regard for the motivations or goals of the terrorists. The difficulty of determining the "justness" of terrorist violence involves a political question for which there is no one answer and on which there is never likely to be consensus. The most common cliche of terrorism literature and discussion is the statement that one man's terrorist is another man's freedom fighter or hero. For that reason, a part of the United Nations membership, primarily the developing nations, has sought a narrow definition of international terrorism to preserve the legitimacy/legality of terrorist violence by national liberation movements. The developed nations, on the other hand, have sought a broad definition which would outlaw virtually all forms of international terrorist activity -- "because," as Ambassador Anthony Quainton of the U.S. Department of State declared to a special U.N. committee on international terrorism in March of 1979, "the acts themselves violate the basic principles of human decency."[1]

The violation of "principles of human decency" may well be the raison d'etre of terrorist violence. Certainly the mass media have responded to, or exploited, the morbid curiosity of their international audiences.[2] Who could fail to respond to the graphic accounts of mutilations and torture, rape and killing, arson and bombing, and other forms of violent destruction? Indeed, the spectacle is impossible to ignore. Whatever the political perspectives of the audience, terrorism will elicit a response. That is the nature of the beast -- the response is all important.

Introduction

From the point of view of the political group using terrorist violence, the tactic represents a means of gaining international recognition for its cause while, at the same time, costing little in terms of personnel and equipment. The violence is also a means of demonstrating the inability of the target government to maintain order. Few governments are not vulnerable to terrorist activity and few governments can afford the price of not responding to the disruptions of public order that terrorism engenders. Terrorism, by most definitions, is after all violence for effect.

From the point of view of the government that has been subjected to terrorist attack, the effects of terrorism present several problems, in addition to the actual or potential loss of life. Perhaps most important, the incidence of terrorist violence is a direct challenge to that government's ability to maintain civic order -- hence, the acts present a challenge to the government's claims of legitimacy. Failure to respond effectively may be a signal to the terrorist organization, other political opponents, and the citizens as a whole that the government lacks the power or the will to maintain order. This challenge is particularly difficult to answer when the attacks extend beyond, are launched from, or are committed outside of the territory of the target government.

International terrorism, then, creates special problems. The lack of territorial jurisdiction precludes the traditional police, internal security, responses that are appropriate for domestic bombings, murders, and other violence. This is not to say that governments cannot use force outside of their own borders. The experiences of the Israeli raid on the Entebbe, Uganda, airport in 1976 and the West German rescue operation at the Mogadishu, Somalia, airport in 1977 indicate the contrary. However, the lack of clear jurisdiction complicates the government's ability to define the terrorist acts as criminal or psychotic and, thus, not representing legitimate political competition. The audience, as well as the foreign jurisdiction, inhibits the target government's ability to define and control the event.

For the government that is forced to respond to acts of international terrorism, as an innocent victim of circumstances rather than as the target of the violence, there are slightly different problems. When the responding government is faced with acts of violence perpetrated by terrorists from another country, on victims that may also be foreign, for political ends for which it has no direct influence, the choice of how to respond is more complex than it would be if it were the target of the violence. The partisanship of the responding government's citizens in the struggle being waged within its territory, the sympathy of the government for one side or the other, and the need to eliminate terrorist disruptions in order to prevent and discourage similar acts by indigenous forces are some of the considerations that will influence the choice of response. The responding government can be forced to take sides in the larger struggle between the target government and the terrorists and, thus, be branded as an ally or co-conspirator by the opposing side. This aspect of international terrorism is analogous to the controversies over the status of "neutral" and "nonaligned" nations in past international, inter-nation, conflicts. The more clearly political the act, the more clearly political the government's response to it can be interpreted.

Hostage situations, as in the Entebbe and Mogadishu events, involve more clearly articulated demands, therefore, are more clearly political, and present even less clear alternatives for government response than do terrorist faits accomplis, such as assassinations or bombings. With the hostages to consider, the responding government, as well as the government that is the ultimate target of the violence, has to weigh the potential costs in human lives against the costs that might result if the terrorists were encouraged to commit further acts of violence and if the government were shown to be ineffectual.

Terrorist violence does, however, present the responding and target governments with opportunities to demonstrate their strength of will and control. Terrorist activity can provide a reason for the display of military and paramilitary forces, dissuading other opposition groups from similar acts of violence. Terrorist violence can also provide the responding and target governments with a convenient issue around which popular support can be rallied, assuming that the terrorists do not already enjoy or are endangering their popular support.

It is the weighing of the humanitarian considerations against the practical, law and order, considerations that determines the governments' responses to terrorist acts. In those terms, the study of how governments respond or how they should respond to terrorist violence involves the determination of the major legal, political, and humanitarian considerations that impact the decision-making processes, as well as the potential or probable costs of the alternative responses. While those factors -- national policies, the constraints upon policy choice, and the costs of alternative policies -- are the focus of this study, attention must also be paid to the perceptual, and definitional, ambiguities which have acted to confuse government policies, terrorism studies, and journalistic interpretations of terrorist events.

If the lines of definitional battle were clearly drawn, governments could respond to international terrorism by means of systems of bilateral and multilateral agreements. There is little international consensus upon what constitutes "terrorism," however. Policies are based upon individual, national, interpretations of terrorist violence, with few governments enjoying broad popular consensus upon their own interpretations. As a consequence, even within nations like the United States, "terrorism" assumes a very ambiguous meaning, denoting violent tactics utilized by a movement or group that does not enjoy wide popular sympathy. The pejorative connotations of the term dictate its application to foes rather than to friends.

The difficulty of arriving at a definition of terrorism, not to mention international terrorism, then, is of paramount importance in both policy-making and research efforts. The United Nations, for example, has been more successful in adopting conventions against the hijacking of airliners than it has been in the reduction of other international political violence. This relative success, at least in part, can be attributed to the unambiguous nature of the aerial hijacking offense. Attempts to prohibit broader categories of international violence have been met with much more resistance. The 1972 U.S. Draft Convention on Terrorism, a case in point, failed to be adopted by the United Nations membership because of "an unnecessary confusion among states as to what [it] . . . sought to control and, more importantly, what it did not prohibit."[3]

The definitional problem cannot be pushed aside; it complicates a policymaking environment already convoluted by a multiplicity of national and subnational actors. The large number of actors that can be involved in international terrorist events, in addition to other unique aspects of international terrorist events, can be illustrated by an account of one of the aerial hijackings mentioned earlier.

On October 13, 1977, four terrorists seized control of Lufthansa Flight 181 after the plane left Palma, Majorca, on a scheduled flight to Frankfurt, West Germany. The flight, with its eighty-two passengers and four crew members, began a five-day, 6000-mile ordeal, with stops in Rome, Larnaca (Cyprus), Bahrain, Dubai, Aden, and finally Mogadishu (Somalia). The four terrorists, two of whom spoke Arabic, claimed to be members of a previously unheard of group called the "Society Against World Imperialism" and demanded the release of eleven imprisoned members of the Baader-Meinhof group in West Germany and two imprisoned Palestinian terrorists in Turkey. On the fourth day of the hijacking, the terrorists executed the Lufthansa pilot -- possibly to lend credibility to their threats to blow up the plane and the hostages if their demands were not met. On the fifth day, sixty West German commandos stormed the plane, killing the terrorists and freeing the hostages without serious injuries to the hostages or the commandos.[4]

The governments of West Germany, Turkey, Majorca (Spain), Italy, Cyprus, Bahrain, Dubai, Aden, and Somalia were directly affected by the hijacking, as were the governments whose citizens were held hostage by the terrorists (including the U.S.). Crete (Greece) and Iran were also affected in that a plane or planes carrying West German commandos reportedly landed in each prior to the action in Somalia. American, French, and Israeli news services were involved when they were asked to withhold information concerning the commandos' progress in catching up with the hijacked plane.[5] Five days of news media coverage involved a multinational audience; millions of people all over the world awaited the fate of Flight 181. The impact of the hijacking was global.

For the government of West Germany, the hijacking of Flight 181 presented humanitarian, legal/political, and logistical problems. The initial success of the terrorists in taking control of the flight was a dangerous precedent, proof of the vulnerability of such flights. The humanitarian problem of how to effect the release of the eighty-six hostages was further complicated by the presence of passengers of other than West German nationality, requiring the consideration of the other nations in the selection of the West German response.

Even more nations were involved directly in the West German action. Turkey, as well, was responsible for the decision of whether to comply with the terrorists' demands. The nations on whose territories the hijacked plane landed had to be consulted. There were legal and political problems involved in the movement of the West German commandos to the site of the rescue operation, as well as the logistical problems attendant with the transfer of men and equipment.

The medium of response, the commandos, was available prior to the hijacking. The unit, Border Protection Group 9, had been set up in 1972, after the massacre of Israeli athletes at the Munich Olympics, and had undergone five years of training with weapons and techniques specifically designed for such hostage situations.[6] The experiences of the Israeli commandos during the 1976 raid on Entebbe airport were also important lessons in the West German training. Now the West German experiences in Mogadishu are being used to train anti-terrorist units in more than a dozen other nations.[7] The attitudes of many nations toward terrorist violence, particularly international terrorist incidents, are evidently changing.

The hijacking of Flight 181 may well mark a watershed in the determination of government response policies toward international terrorist violence. The day that the rescue was effected in Mogadishu, the U.S. State Department issued a statement summarizing U.S. policy toward such acts and reaffirming the U.S. resolve to "make no concessions to terrorist blackmail because to do so would merely invite further demands."[8] Similar reactions were evidenced by other nations, and, on November 3, the United Nations General Assembly issued an appeal to its member states to take a united stand against aerial hijackings. In making the appeal, the General Assembly, at least temporarily, broke a long-standing deadlock over whether such acts of international terrorism are justifiable. The greatest impact of the hijacking, however, was the lesson inherent in the West German success -- terrorists could be beaten at their own game.

Introduction

In terms of the range of responses available to governments faced with hostage-holding terrorists, the experiences of the Mogadishu rescue, and the Entebbe rescue which preceded it, have encouraged governments to take stronger measures against terrorist violence. Indeed, the increased propensity of governments to adopt strict "no ransom" policies and to respond to terrorist violence with uncompromising severity has spawned a controversy over the efficacy of such inflexible positions.[9] The proponents of "no ransom" or no negotiation policies argue that the denial of success will dissuade terrorists from making further demands and the capture or killing of terrorists will, at least, prevent those terrorists from committing more acts of violence.

The arguments for more flexible response policies are based upon a variety of orientations toward terrorist violence, in addition to the orientations of those persons or groups that are sympathetic to the ends sought by the terrorists. There are critics of uncompromising policies who base their arguments upon the sanctity of human life and the unjustifiability of governmental, as well as anti-governmental violence. Another group bases its opposition to inflexibility on the experiences of civil authorities in negotiating with criminal, non-political, captors and the apparent effectiveness of negotiations in preventing unnecessary deaths and injuries in the resolution of hostage incidents.[10] Additional criticism may be found among those students of revolutionary violence and change who suggest that social, political, and economic adjustments or reforms could best alleviate the root causes of terrorism and, thus, provide more lasting reductions of terrorist violence.[11]

Regardless of the orientation toward terrorist violence or the policy toward terrorism preferred, the action by the West German commandos proved that techniques could be developed to combat international terrorism and that international cooperation could greatly facilitate the implementation of those techniques. Whether the West German response to the hijacking of Flight 181 has been an important lesson which can be used to resolve future hostage incidents has not been proven, however.

While the efficacy of the West German action was convincingly demonstrated at Mogadishu, the hijacking also provided a warning that the terrorists themselves were expanding their own cooperative efforts. The hijacking of Flight 181 was not the first time that terrorist violence has been perpetrated by a multinational group, but it is indicative of the trend in international terrorist events toward mixed terrorist groups and mixed demands. The fact of increased cooperation and coordination among terrorist organizations, even crossing ideological lines, is now well-documented.[12] As one article has stated the problem, the advent of modern international terrorism means that "an operation can be planned in Germany by a Palestinian Arab, executed in Israel by terrorists recruited in Japan, with weapons acquired in Italy but manufactured in Russia, supplied by an Algerian diplomat financed with Libyan money."[13] That is, in fact, a description of the attack on Lod airport, near Tel Aviv, by three Japanese terrorists in May of 1972. As a result of that attack, twenty-four persons were killed, including sixteen Puerto Ricans on pilgrimage to the Holy Land, and seventy-six were wounded.[14] This new aspect of international terrorism has given further impetus to the efforts to develop multinational structures and procedures for combatting terrorism.

Although the hijacking of Flight 181 was more spectacular than most of the previous aerial hijackings, probably the greatest stimulus that it has given efforts to curb international terrorist activity has been psychological. Indeed, terrorism, in general, and international terrorism, in particular, have become almost commonplace during the last two decades; or, at least, they have been so publicized that they have come to be accepted as familiar facts of our political lives. The recent attacks have demonstrated that almost no one is immune from terrorist attack -- tourists, shoppers, business agents, and government officials alike are vulnerable. The violence of terrorism which had previously been confined to a few unstable nations, having little international impact, has now become a concern of most nations. Terrorism is an international problem that is likely to remain with us in the next decades, particularly after the Palestine Liberation

Organization's apparent success in being recognized as the representative of the Palestinian peoples.[15]

This study will attempt to bring together the policy questions, challenges and imperatives, that have been raised by different forms of international terrorism and the policies that have been and are being implemented by the governments that have experienced international terrorist attacks. The analysis will be conducted in four parts, concluding with the consideration of the question of whether there is one "optimal" response to all acts of international terrorism.

The analysis will focus first on the nature of international terrorism as a threat to societies and governments and, in keeping with the policy focus of this study, a new typology of international terrorist events will be developed to conform to the perspectives of the responding governments. The second major part of the analysis will be the identification of the challenges presented by international terrorist events to governmental authority and the necessary goals or imperatives of response policy choice.

The third section of the analysis will center on the choice of a response policy, including the range of response options that may be available to governments, the major theories or schools of thought about how governments can best respond, the domestic and international constraints on policy choice, and the value dilemmas and trade-offs inherent in policy selection.

The range of direct responses to terrorist demands will be ordered in an elementary typology, and the loci of government response will be illustrated on a model of the process of terrorism. The purpose of this analytical approach is to generate some expectations concerning the impacts of perceptual and situational variables on response policy choice.

The final part of the analysis will be an adjunct to the three-part theoretical treatment of international terrorism and government responses. International hostage incidents will be examined to test some of the propositions developed concerning the influences on and impact of response selection and the "fit" between the theoretical framework, the typologies, and actual terrorist events.

The approach utilized in this study was derived from the literature on policy analysis, especially that part of the literature that has indicated the need for theory or paradigms to provide framework and foundation for decision-making and other policy studies. As stated by John Blair and Steven Maser, "The unavailability of theory has confounded the interpretation of empirical research and fueled the debate surrounding the choice of policy."[16] As a beginning, normative models are needed to provide guides for policymaking, a serious limitation of empirical models.[17]

To that end, this study also represents a marriage of convenience between the normative and empirical approaches to international relations and comparative political research and the empirical approach to policy analysis. Nonetheless, it is hoped that the combination will help overcome the more serious limitations inherent in each approach used alone.

In the first two analyses, those of the nature of international terrorism and of the policy predicament in which responding governments find themselves, the analytical approach will be largely normative. The objective of these analyses is to identify and define the nature and challenge of international terrorism, to provide a foundation upon which more indepth studies can be based -- not to attempt to construct a "general theory" of terrorism or to arrive at a "one best way" to combat international terrorism.

The third analysis, that of the theories of response and the policy choice, will attempt to bridge the gap between the normative theories of how governments should respond to international terrorism and the practical alternatives actually available given the domestic and international constraints upon policy choice. The definition of the policy environment will remain, of necessity, in relatively general terms. Governments, understandably, do not release the full details of their anti-terrorist procedures. Nonetheless, it is expected that the framework of trade-offs and constraints will facilitate the descriptive analyses of past terrorist events and the development of some expectations about what kinds of terrorist violence are likely to occur in the future and how governments are likely to react.

The final major analysis, that of international hostage incidents, will include a variation of what has been called "policy impact analysis" and, in a much broader sense, cost-benefit analysis in the literature,[18] as well as an analysis of some of the perceptual and situational variables in policy choice. To a very limited degree, the influence of government responses to hostage events on the most visible and immediate indicator of policy impact, hostage safety, will be measured, both in terms of the direct relationship between the two concepts and in terms of the mediating influence that government responses may have on the impacts of other variables on hostage safety. While the analysis will not show whether the government response policies were successful in the long-term, it will indicate whether the cost-benefit trade-offs that were anticipated are realistic.[19]

In short, the analytical approach will be an attempt to bridge the gap between the so-called "pure" and "applied" policy studies.

Several caveats, however, must be noted about the use of policy analysis in general, policy impact analysis in particular, and the variation of both used in this study. Some forms of policy analysis, particularly those that deal with policy choice and policy or program effectiveness, have been controversial because of their potential to be prostituted to the interests of the analysts and/or the policymaking authorities. The potential for misuse has also been pointed out in other forms of political analysis, but policy analysis has generated considerably more concern over its potential to be used to promote the personal policy preferences of the analysts or to justify or legitimate the preferences of the policymakers. The likelihood of inadvertent misuse is at least somewhat lessened by the multinational, comparative nature of this study with its focus on the relative costs of several different policy alternatives. But, the danger of becoming a "legitimator" of government or elite preferences will require care in the analyses. Elliot Feldman stated the problem as such:

> The political scientist, in opting for the role of independent analyst, takes on two responsibilities. First, he undertakes to analyze what the objectives of the policy are, and he measures, with the policy maker's own criteria, whether the policy succeeds or fails. This responsibility corresponds to the policy analyst's role in making the policy maker live up to his own pretensions.
>
> The second responsibility concerns global analysis -- that is, analysis outside the terms of the policy maker. In this responsibility,

the policy analyst undertakes to reject incrementalism by exploring a policy problem in its broadest context, thereby seeking to appreciate its systemwide applications. The terms of analysis are not of the policy maker, nor of the policy analyst, but rather of the political system. A given policy may succeed while it betrays the system within which it is set. The policy analyst must be responsible for measuring both the policy's success within its own terms and within a global context.[20]

Compliance with Feldman's second "responsibility" of the analyst role will require that this study recognize the inherent bias of the approach in favor of the governments responding to international terrorist violence.

There is a decided and intended status quo bias. The justifiability of international terrorist violence, or any such armed opposition for that matter, is not accepted as a major consideration of this study. The status of the terrorists is presumed to be unjustifiable, hence illegal or illegitimate, as defined by the responding governments. Terrorist violence is not considered to be a manifestation of legitimate political opposition.

The assumption of that bias in the definition of the problem of international terrorism may be the single most distinguishing characteristic of this study vis-a-vis other studies of the problem. There have been policy-oriented studies of terrorism in the past, and they will be considered in this work, but previous studies have not attempted to use the perspective of the responding governments to define and typologize the terrorist events. In fact, most of the previous studies have been prescriptive, taking terrorism as a given, often undefined or inconsistently defined, and suggesting one or another desirable policy choice.

With the bias in mind and with the corresponding responsibility to reconsider that bias at the conclusion of this study accepted as necessary, this analysis will consider the nature of international terrorism, the challenge that international terrorism presents to government authority, the major theories of response and the policy choice, the impact of policy upon the resolution of international hostage incidents, and the question of whether there is an optimal response to international terrorism. In doing so, it is hoped that the study can cut through the definitional confusion that has impaired policymaking and research on the phenomena of international terrorism and can provide a new perspective on the problem of international terrorism.

CHAPTER II

THE NATURE OF INTERNATIONAL TERRORISM

The study of the problem of international terrorism and anti-terrorist policymaking has suffered greatly from the emotive quality of the terror phenomena and process. Analysts of the impacts of terrorism upon individuals, societies, governments, and the international community as a whole, as well as of terrorist philosophies and techniques, can be lost in the labyrinth of conflicting orientations and arguments. Social-political-economic studies of revolution and internal war, psychological profiles of both terrorists and their victims, journalistic accounts of individual terrorist acts, romanticized biographies of famous or infamous terrorists, legalistic treatises on terrorism and political violence, military manuals on counter-insurgency, and humanitarian denounciations of the theories and tactics of terrorist violence present conflicting evidence of the problem and conflicting points of view on how it can be resolved.

For many, particularly journalists, the label of "terrorism" is applied to "almost any violent, asocial act."[1] In recent years, the term has come to be associated with the spectacle of international terrorist violence, often with little differentiation made between the acts of criminals with no political goals and those of terrorists seeking political ends. That is, however, not to say that the terrorists are not criminals because that is, in fact, how they are labelled by the affected governments in most cases. The point is that criminals are not necessarily terrorists. Promiscuous use of the label "terrorist" has acted to confuse both popular opinions and government policies concerning the phenomena of terrorist violence, and journalists alone cannot be expected to bear the brunt of criticism for the confusion.

History has also confused the distinction. Many of the national liberation movements of the post-World War II period have been romanticized in the years since their victories (or defeats). The success of the movements has overshadowed their violence -- time has erased, at least in part, the memory of their excesses. The once-feared revolutionary terrorists have become, in some cases, "respectable" and, in some instances, national heroes and international cult figures. Menachem Begin of Israel, Che Gueverra of Cuba, and Ho Chi Minh of Vietnam are cases in point.

The unsuccessful or partially successful revolutionary terrorists, on the other hand, have not been as fully vindicated by time. The "atrocities" (another emotive word) committed by the Mau Mau in Kenya and the Hukbalahaps, Huks, in the Philippines, for example, have not been so quickly erased from the memories of their audiences. The Mau Mau and the Huks waged unsuccessful war -- the legacies of which have been left to interpretation by unsympathetic historians.

Time has not yet tempered the popular perceptions of contemporary terrorists, however. Their violence is too fresh a memory or too real a threat for many. The terrorist violence of today finds less sympathetic appeal in the graphic and grisly journalistic accounts of the events than it may in the history books. The audio-visual media, as well, make the acts more real and more abhorent for the viewing audiences than do the printed media for their readers.[2] As noted by James Rosenau, the morbid curiosity of the audiences that are not directly affected by the violence of the acts may well have an effect on the audiences' attitudes, sympathies and antipathies, toward the acts and the actors.[3]

Emotions profoundly affect the responses to terrorism. For a large portion of the audience such violent behavior is beyond their comprehension, beyond their experience and understanding. For those people, terrorism is abhorent, abnormal, and psychotic. Some academic and government analysts have the same difficulty in seeing beyond the violence of the acts and in considering the motivations and objectives behind the actions. Albert Parry, for example, has branded all terrorists as "abnormal," psychopathic or sociopathic.[4]

Certainly, the sympathizers and supporters of movements or groups using terror tactics would not agree that all terrorists suffer from psychological disorders -- nor do most of the analysts of terrorist violence.[5] The point is, however, that the audiences frequently associate violence with disorder, particularly audiences acculturated to shun violence within their own social and political processes. Within such a context, terrorist violence can be viewed as symptomatic of mental illness -- rather than simply criminal or political behavior.

The student of terrorist violence, the analyst rather than the participant, has to contend with these variances in orientation as they are reflected in the growing body of writing dealing with the phenomena of terrorism. As a result of the variances, a comprehensive definition of "terrorism" has been elusive. Indeed, a comprehensive definition may be impossible according to several of the leading authorities on terrorist violence. Paul Wilkinson, for example, has interpreted the persistent confusion about the definition of terrorism to mean that:

> These ambiguities and contradictions should warn us against any premature general theory or model of the causes, inception and development of terrorism. For in reality there are many terrorisms, each calling for different theories, models and approaches from the scholar seeking to relate these phenomena to other dimensions of political change. Therefore the primary tasks must be: to clarify and refine the concept of political terrorism; to establish a working typology of political terrorism; and, most difficult of all,

to relate terrorism to other modes of violence and to the basic political values, structures and processes of liberal democracy.[6]

J. Bowyer Bell has given an even more pessimistic view of the likelihood that the confusion can be sorted out by analysts with his statement that " . . . any study of terrorist activities must be largely qualitative and, since conventional academic approaches do not work in this field, dependent on less than rigorous sources."[7]

Nevertheless, there has been much academic work dealing with the "many terrorisms," including international terrorism, despite the ambiguities. While a comprehensive definition may be impractical, or even impossible, at this time, a functional definition and working typologies are certainly possible. The functional definition to be used in this study can be found among those currently being used by academic and government analysts. The definitions and typologies will also provide a foundation for the typology of international terrorism that is to be constructed.

Terror and Political Terrorism

It is not necessary to indulge in a complete review of the literature on terrorism in order to delineate and clarify how the term is to be used here. There are, in fact, several good reviews and analyses available.[8] It is useful, however, to use several of the major conceptualizations and typologies from the literature in order to make clear the focus and scope of this study. But, first, a fundamental distinction must be made concerning the use of the terms "terror" and "terrorism."

The distinction was made quite simply by Thomas P. Thornton in these terms:

> The word "terror" has two meanings. The basic one is an induced state of fear or anxiety within an individual or group of individuals. It is sometimes called "subjective terror." Derived from this meaning is the use of "terror" to describe the tool that induces the state of being terrified. This tool is variously called "terror," "objective terror," and "terrorism." Although it would be convenient to distinguish simply between terror (the psychic state) and terrorism (the tool), this distinction is not advisable, for frequently "terrorism" and "terror" are used interchangeably to denote objective terror...[9]

Terror as a tool is the subject of this study and, although both terms will be used, ample clarification will be given when "subjective terror" is meant.

To avoid undue confusion in the use of the term "terrorism" at this point, it is also necessary to offer a tentative definition, subject to further clarification

The Nature of International Terrorism 27

later. A large part of the difficulty in discussing terrorism is due to its familiarity. Rather than seeking a rigorous definition, many analysts and writers have simply taken the attitude that they know it when they see it and so do their readers. Notwithstanding that attitude, there are several aspects of terrorism that are consensually supported:

> 1. Terrorism involves[10] the use or threat of extraordinary violence.
>
> 2. Terrorism is goal-oriented action (i.e., terrorists have goals and objectives beyond the creation of destruction, injury, and death).
>
> 3. The aim of terrorism is its psychological impact on an individual or individuals apart from its immediate victims.
>
> 4. The victims of terrorism are chosen for their symbolic, rather than instrumental, value.

Those aspects of terrorism can be summed up in this definition: "Terrorism is political, goal-oriented action, involving the use or threat of extraordinary violence, performed for psychological rather than material effect, and the victims of which are symbolic rather than instrumental."[11] The meaning of "extraordinary violence" and the political nature of terrorism are to be considered in the following pages, nonetheless the definition will provide a basis for the discussions to follow.

Beginning, then, with the tentative definition of terrorism and the distinction between terror as a psychological state and as a tool or tactic, it is possible to consider the process whereby terrorism, the instrumental means, is used to induce the state of terror.

The process of terrorism described by Eugene V. Walter in his study of political violence among primitive African societies and the concept of terror as a process has been implicit or explicit in most of the studies of terrorist violence. The process is also explicit in the writings of many of the theorists of terrorism.[12] For Walter, the term "terrorism" was used as an "equivalent to 'process of terror,' . . . a compound with three elements: the act or threat of violence, the emotional reaction, and the social effects."[13] Terrorism, then, according to Walter, involves three actors or groups of actors: the users, the victims, and the targets of the violence. The relationships among these actors Walter called the "system of terror."[14] The conceptualizations of Walter are not complex and often they are not very clear, but they are helpful. His description of the group or class within which the "process of terror" is confined, the target group, as the "zone of terror" requires considerable broadening to be transferred from the context of a small African village or tribe to the context of the international community. Nevertheless, the two additional concepts of "regime of terror" (the violence used by the powerholders or authorities against their opponents) and "siege of terror" (the violence used by the opponents of the incumbent authorities)[15] are more easily transferred.

The conceptual framework of Paul Wilkinson introduces a new element into the picture of terrorism given by Walter, i.e., the distinguishing characteristic of terrorist objectives. Wilkinson first delineates between what he calls "political terrorism" and other forms of terrorism, including: "criminal terrorism," the "systematic use of acts of terror for objectives of private material gain"; "psychic terrorism," the use of terror for "religo-magical" objectives; and "war terrorism," the use of terror tactics in the conduct of a war (usually between two nations.)[16]

Wilkinson's identification of the various forms of terrorism is useful to this study to the extent that it facilitates the elimination of those types of terrorism that are not to be considered. Certainly, Wilkinson's concept of "psychic terrorism" does not conform to the usual perceptions of international terrorism -- unless, of course, a violent conflict can be determined to be primarily religious in nature. Moreover, the concepts of "criminal terrorism" and "war terrorism" may be matters of perspective. The likelihood that governments will define terrorism used by challengers to their authority as "criminal" behavior and that the challengers, in turn, will defend their use of terroristic violence as necessary to the conduct of their "war" against the government or other authorities has been noted earlier. The differentiation between those two forms of terrorism and political terrorism, then, is not as easy as the definitions would suggest.[17]

Political terrorism is the general type of violence with which this study is concerned, but even that category encompasses several distinctly different kinds of political violence. Wilkinson identifies three subtypes of "political terrorism" -- revolutionary, subrevolutionary, and repressive. "Revolutionary terrorism" and "subrevolutionary terrorism" are distinguished by the ultimate objectives of the terrorists and are conceptualized much like Walter's concept of "siege of terror" and Thornton's concept of "agitational terror," i.e., as terror used against the powerholders by their opponents.[18] "Revolutionary terrorism" is very close to the popular perception of terrorism in general, particularly among those analysts and publics who are not inclined to be sympathetic to the use of violence as a means of realizing political objectives. Even some so-called experts have the tendency to use the terms "revolutionary terrorism" and "political terrorism" synonymously. As a result, a number of analysts have felt the need to attack that misconception. Ted Robert Gurr, for instance, has warned against the use of such a biased view as can be found in the definition of political terrorism as "a destructive revolutionary strategy in which sustained campaigns of violent action are directed against highly visible public targets."[19] Certainly such acts or campaigns may be appropriately considered as political terrorism, but it is not necessary that the acts have revolutionary objectives or that the targets of the violence or threats be "highly visible" or public.

By contrast, Alexander Dallin and George Breslauer define "political terror" in quite a different way -- as the "arbitrary use, by organs of political authority, of severe coercion against individuals or groups, the credible threat of such use, or the arbitrary extermination of such individuals or groups."[20] Dallin's and Breslauer's concept is similar to Wilkinson's third subtype of political terrorism, "repressive terrorism," defined as "the systematic use of terroristic acts of violence for the purposes of suppressing, putting down, quelling, or restraining certain groups, individuals or forms of behavior deemed to be undesirable by the repressor."[21] The repressive violence described by Wilkinson could easily fit the uses of terrorism within a revolutionary terrorist organization itself to maintain discipline. The definition, however, was intended to describe such violent, repressive measures as used in the coercive operations of state, police, military, prison or prison camp, slave control, ideological, or counter-insurgency authorities,[22] that is, by the incumbent authorities or their agents. Wilkinson's seeming focus on the objectives of the terrorists in his three-fold typology is really a focus on the actors involved in the process of political terrorism.

It is clear that terrorism can be used as a political tool by both governments and their challengers. And, the use of terrorism by nongovernmental groups to support the status quo, including government authority, has also been noted by analysts. J. Bowyer Bell, for example, has included "vigilante terror" in his typology of terrorism, citing such organizations as the Ojo por Ojo (Eye for an Eye) group in Guatemala and the Ku Klux Klan in the U.S. as illustrations.[23] This form of terrorism too could be included within Wilkinson's definition of "repressive terrorism," particularly since it may be impossible to determine the extent of official support of or tolerance for such groups.

The importance of the actors involved in the system of terror, as Walter called it, is manifest in the confusion concerning the concept of political terrorism. Indeed, the nature of the actors involved in the violence is crucial to a discussion of political terrorism and the determinant of whether such acts can be considered international terrorism. Who, then, are the actors?

The three principals mentioned by Walter (and noted earlier) are the terrorists, their victims, and the targets of the violence. The first group, the terrorists, has been found to be comprised of revolutionary (and subrevolutionary) groups, governments and their agents, or nongovernmental vigilante groups. It must also be noted that many, if not most, of the definitions of political and revolutionary terrorism in the literature indicate that the terrorists are part of an organization, not isolated individuals. In fact, several scholars have stated that political terrorism is always carried out by a group.[24] Consistent with that view, Wilkinson maintains that revolutionary terrorism involves groups, but that subrevolutionary terrorism may not.[25] This distinction may be helpful later in determining the nature and the extent of the threat presented by terrorist activity.

The second group of actors, the victims, may well be the major determinant of whether an act of violence is in fact terrorism rather than military action. As was stated in the tentative definition of terrorism offered earlier, the victims of terrorist violence are selected for their symbolic value rather than their instrumental value. As expressed by J. Bowyer Bell: "The victims are not the targets, only the means."[26] Here too some clarification is needed.

The victims may be a part of a larger target group such as members of the government structure, the police, the military, a minority group, or the national elite. The victims may also be such inanimate objects as public buildings, private homes, communications or transportation facilities, public monuments, or party headquarters. Edward Hyams has characterized terrorist attacks on the government, its agents, or facilities as "direct terrorism" and attacks on the government's constituents to destroy confidence in the regime as "indirect terrorism."[27] That dichotomy, however, does not take into consideration the possibility that the victims of terrorist violence may not be related to the terrorists or the intended targets.

Of particular importance and impact are the incidences of international terrorism in which some or all of the victims are entirely innocent of any association with the real targets of the violent attacks and should be, by all international rules of warfare, properly considered as noncombatants and legally protected from such violence. These innocent victims may not be located within a narrowly defined "zone of combat," such as being within the national territory or even of the nationality of the target group or the terrorists. What is clear is that terrorist violence "involves some measure of threat directed at those beyond the scope of the immediate act that has been perpetrated."[28]

The job of the analyst or policymaker, given the indirect and limited nature of the violence, has been summed up by Thornton in the following:

> Since a terrorist act is public and thus meant to have a propaganda effect and since the victim is usually physically eliminated and therefore not in need of being propagandized, there is a <u>prima facie</u> requirement that the analyst of terrorism look for the real target of intent. When he locates this target, he will not only be better able to counter the propaganda effect of the act, but he also may be able to take measures to reduce the incident of terrorism by protecting targets that have high symbolic contents, rather than

those that may be of purely utilitarian value. Lacking a knowledge of the target of intent, his chances for taking purposeful counteraction are extremely small.[29]

The threat, the violence, is directed at a target audience -- a "resonant mass" according to Thornton.[30] The target may be a government, the constituency of the government, or some portion of either collective; and, for the terrorism to have the impact that the terrorists seek, it must influence the behavior of the target audience. The threat must be communicated.

That process of communication involves more actors in the process of terrorism, the news media (unless, of course, the terrorist violence is so visible to the target audience that the media are not needed to carry the message, such as in Walter's African communities). In addition to the media's participation in the process, more actors may become involved, especially if the violence or its effects cross national boundaries.

International Terrorism

From one to many government and media actors, as well as a variety of terrorists, may be involved when the use or resolution of political terrorism extends beyond the territorial jurisdiction of one nation. The "international" character or impact of such violence requires further qualification of the concept of political terrorism.

The interpretations of international terrorism in the literature vary greatly, including such vague definitions as "the threat or use of violence by private persons for political ends, where the conduct itself or its political objectives, or both, are international in scope."[31] Aside from the narrowness of the political terrorism aspect of the definition, the distinction drawn between those acts of terrorism that are "international in scope" and those that are not does not provide enough definitional precision to permit unambiguous classification of the acts. The definition would equally suit such violent phenomena as internal wars which involve the insurgent use of sanctuaries outside of the territorial jurisdiction of the regime that is being attacked or the intervention of foreign civilians in an ostensibly internal war. It can be argued that most uses of violence in domestic political conflicts may have international consequences. According to George A. Kelly and Linda B. Miller: " . . . only conceptually can there be an 'internal' war . . ."[32] If that is true, the definition of international terrorism must be more precise.

The United Nations Ad Hoc Committee on International Terrorism has encountered the same difficulties. The committee's 1973 report to the General Assembly included the following definitions of international terrorism: "any threat or act of violence committed by a person or group of persons on foreign territory or in any other place under international jurisdiction against any person with a view to achieving a political objective" (this definition was offered by the representative from Haiti) and any "heinous act of barbarism committed in the territory of a third state by a foreigner against a person possessing a nationality other than that of the offender for the purpose of exerting pressure in a conflict not strictly internal in nature" (this definition was offered by France).[33] Again, the definitions are somewhat vague concerning the nature of the violence itself, particularly France's use of the phrase "heinous act of barbarism." The Haitian definition could also be taken as a description of international war. Despite the problems with the determination of the nature of political terrorism, both definitions included the qualification that the acts involved the use of violence on foreign territory.

Greater specificity can be found in the definitions of international terrorism given in the Ad Hoc Committee's 1977 report to the General Assembly. Folke Persson, the representative from Sweden, for example, said that "acts which should be characterized as acts of international terrorism were acts committed by individuals or by private groups or organizations in the territory of a third country or which in some other way affected the interests of a third country, for instance by being directed against a national of a third country or against property situated in, or belonging to, a third country."[34] The question of the nature of the violence was not addressed, rather the definition was primarily focused on the location, the victims (property or persons), and the consequences of the violent acts.

The elements of the definition related to the international character of the violence can be summed up by the qualifications that the acts:

    1.   be committed in the territory of a third state,

    2.   be directed against a national of a third state,

    3.   be directed against property in a third state,

    4.   be directed against property belonging to a third state (but, presumably, not located in that state), or

    5.   "affect the interests" of a third state.

There are still some difficulties with such a definition, even assuming that a reasonable description of political terrorism was attached. It is relatively clear that, when an act of terrorism is committed on foreign territory, whether against an individual, a group of individuals, or property, the act should be characterized as international terrorism. However, the question of whether an act of violence "affects the interests" of a third state is not at all clear in some cases. The vagueness of that qualification would allow that domestic political violence in Venezuela is international terrorism when it affects the flow of oil to Venezuela's foreign clients or that similar violence in another Third World state is international terrorism when it affects that state's support for the U.S. or the Soviet Union.

The qualifications concerning attacks on foreign nationals or property may also be problematic. Again assuming that the "terrorism" aspect of the definition were adequate, there is some difficulty in determining the "political" nature of the acts of violence. Within the state in which the acts are committed, the objectives of the terrorist organizations will identify the acts as "political" in nature. For the third party states, those whose nationals or property were attacked, the acts may not be imbued with a political character. Indeed, the attacks may have little more significance than the mugging of a tourist. That is not to say that the acts would necessarily be ignored by the third party states, rather the states may view the problem as basically a common violation of domestic criminal law for which the host government has legal, i.e., territorial, jurisdiction and responsibility for prosecution of the offenders.

The kidnappings of American business agents in Latin America are cases in point. Terrorist organizations have used the foreign "exploiters" to realize huge ransoms from their own governments. To the extent that the violence has an impact in boardrooms far beyond the borders of the host state, the acts are international. To the extent that foreign diplomatic missions and governments become involved in the resolution of the crises, the acts are international. Nonetheless, American business agents and, undoubtedly, business agents of other nationalities have been left largely to their own devices when attacked in foreign states, albeit with some warnings and suggestions from their own governments' diplomatic missions.

There may be no easy solution to the inclusion or exclusion of acts of violence directed at foreign nationals or property in a definition of international terrorism, except for the attacks on foreign diplomatic personnel and facilities. It is necessary to note the ambiguous nature of that type of violence, however, particularly since broad interpretations of international terrorism are common.

An example of a broad interpretation can be found in an article by Brian Jenkins of the Rand Corporation. Jenkins stated that:

> The most simple definition of international terrorism comprises acts of terrorism that have clear international consequences: incidents in which terrorists go abroad to strike their targets, select victims or targets because of their connections to a foreign state (diplomats, local executives or officers of foreign corporations), attack airliners in international flights, or force airliners to fly to another country.[35]

Jenkins went on to explain that expansion of the definition of international terrorism by saying that:

The Nature of International Terrorism 41

International terrorism may also be defined as acts of violence or campaigns of violence waged outside the accepted rules and procedures of international diplomacy and war. Breaking the rules may include attacking diplomats and other internationally protected persons, attacking international travel and commerce, or exporting violence by various means to nations that normally would not, under the traditional rules, be considered participants in the local conflict.[36]

Several questions arise in this broad definition.

First, Jenkins' inclusion of attacks on foreign business agents using the wording "executives or officers of foreign corporations" may be significant. It is uncertain whether an international character would be attributed to similar acts directed against less visible, less important foreign travelers or businessmen. Part of the answer may be that less visible victims are not often chosen as targets by terrorist groups. But, the question arises concerning whether the more visible corporate representatives are singled out because of their visibility within the host state, their symbolic value as representatives of "exploitive" foreign economic interests, their instrumental value in attracting an international audience, their value as targets less likely to cause the alienation of the terrorists popular support within the host state, the likelihood that they may be viewed as subversive agents of the foreign government or a mixture of some or all of these reasons. To what extent, then, can the violent acts be construed as direct attacks on the foreign government? Or, can the attacks be viewed simply as convenient, and profitable, extensions of terrorist campaigns against the host regime (and, more properly characterized as domestic terrorism)?

Second, the part of Jenkins' definition that refers to the attacks upon and diversions of international flights also requires closer scrutiny. Skyjackers of all types are routinely labelled "terrorists"; however, many skyjackings for political reasons fail to fit the usual definitions of terrorism. Skyjackings motivated exclusively by the desire for political asylum are cases in point.

In the same article in which his definition of international terrorism appeared, Jenkins states that: "Terrorism is violence for effect, not only, and sometimes not at all, for the effect on the actual victims of the terrorists."[37] In reality, skyjackers seeking political asylum alone often use the threat of violence, or violence itself, reluctantly -- no "terror" is intended as a ploy to achieve political ends, except to the extent that the skyjacker wants to force the pilot to fly to a particular location and to dissuade the passengers and crew from interferring. The violence is not directed at a target group outside of the aircraft. In fact, skyjackers seeking political asylum may jeopardize their claims of legitimate political necessity for their threats of violence when a hostage, or anyone else, is killed or injured as a result of the action. West Germany, for instance, has tried and imprisoned Czech skyjackers who sought political asylum, although the prison terms were quite short and probably were intended as an excuse not to extradite the skyjackers. On the other hand, West Germany has returned skyjackers to Czechoslovakia when their actions have resulted in the death of a hostage.

The third and final question raised by Jenkins' definition concerns the violation of "accepted rules of international diplomacy and war" by terrorists. The existence of such "rules" is not an issue, rather those that support terrorist activity or, at least, sympathize with terrorist aims would raise the question of <u>who</u> has "accepted" the rules. The present conventions proscribing certain kinds and targets of violence in war and diplomacy owe their historical development and adoption to the colonial and imperialist powers of the pre-World War II periods, although those states no longer dominate the large colonial empires that they once did. The rules were made by these nations, the defenders of terrorism would maintain, to formalize and protect their traditional patterns of interstate relations and warfare -- to maintain the status quo, as long as the status quo suits their own purposes. Even among the "civilized" states there have been gross violations of the "rules." What recent war has gone without charges that one or more of the participants were violating the Geneva Conventions" The "rules" find imperfect support and adherence at best.

Terrorists and their sympathizers would contend that the "rules" have been developed to prevent challenges to incumbent authority, that the rules exploit the military weaknesses of revolutionaries by requiring that they wage wars within certain parameters, confining their attacks to the strongest buttresses of the incumbent regimes. In any case, the many states that have achieved independence since World War II were not party to those conventions adopted before. Moreover, the challengers to authority, the freedom fighters of today, were not parties either.

Notwithstanding the arguments in defense of the formal conventions that guide diplomacy and war among "civilized" states, as well as the laws which prohibit most forms of violence in domestic political conflicts, the arguments of the terrorists and revolutionaries must be considered. The arguments must be considered to the extent that they illustrate the need to determine the constraints within which the terrorists operate, i.e., the "rules" of their brand of warfare.

Despite the aforementioned issues raised by his definition, Jenkins is not alone in the liberal use of the labels "terrorist" and "international terrorist." In fact, Jenkins' definition is narrower than most. Liberal uses are common in the international terrorism literature, although it is evident that policymakers are aware of the difficulties inherent in such loosely applied labels.

That policymakers are cognizant of the distinctions between terrorist and nonterrorist violence has been amply evident in the recent international efforts to suppress the violence. For example, the European Convention on the Suppression of Terrorism, ratified in November of 1976, included a reservation concerning acts precipitated by an individual's or a group's desire to escape repressive governments, i.e., political asylum-motivated acts.[38] That same reservation, to protect those persons forced to flee government oppression, has been common to most of the international efforts to combat international terrorism, albeit it has been perhaps less common in those efforts initiated by the U.S. Suffice it to say at this point that the controversial issues of political asylum and international extradition involve complex legal arguments that still do not enjoy consensus among international jurists or national policymakers.

The positions taken by governments on these issues, including the issue of violence directed against foreign business agents, may have a profound effect on the governments' reactions to the violent acts. How the governments perceive the violence is more important than the motivations or objectives of the individuals or groups that commit the violent acts. It may even be that violent attacks on foreign business agents will be viewed as international terrorism by the home governments of the victims and as criminal, non-political, violence by the host governments (or vice versa) -- with each responding according to its own interpretation. Similarly, skyjackers seeking political asylum may be viewed differently by each of the governments involved.

Policy, or response, may be the only reliable indicator of which interpretation of the violent acts that the governments are using. Broad policy orientations can certainly be determined from the definitions of international terrorism given by the policymakers and government analysts, but even those definitions may be inconsistent. The Jenkins' definition, for example, was cited in a similar form by Louis G. Fields, Jr., an assistant legal advisor in the U.S. Department of State, in an address to a symposium on January of 1979.[39] Despite that citation, in September of 1978, Ambassador Anthony C. E. Quainton, then Director of the U.S. Department of State's Office for Combatting Terrorism, had identified the most widely used definition within the U.S. government as: " . . . the threat or use of violence for political purposes when such action is intended to influence the attitude and behavior of a target group wider than its immediate victims and its ramifications transcend national boundaries."[40] The definition used by Quainton appeared in a 1976 U.S. Central Intelligence Agency study by David L. Milbank which went on to explain that the violence becomes international terrorism when its "ramifications transcend national boundaries as a result, for example, of the nationality or foreign ties of its perpetrators, its locale, the identity of its institutional or human victims, its declared objectives, or the mechanics of its resolution."⁴¹

The Milbank-Quainton definition is somewhat more general than that of Jenkins. The second definition does not insist on the inclusion of all skyjackings in the category of international terrorism, for instance. It is also interesting to note that Milbank, in the 1976 study, used the portion of Jenkins' description of international terrorism that states the terrorist objective of having an effect on an audience wider than the immediate victims of the acts.⁴² What seems to have happened is that Fields used the second portion of Jenkins' definition, as cited earlier, and Milbank used a different portion; both avoided the first portion and both used portions that carried different orientations to the violence. Fields focused on the legal aspects of international terrorism and Milbank focused on the targets of the violence.

Milbank also offered a dichotomy of international terrorism based upon the types of terrorists, identifying those acts "when carried out by individuals or groups controlled by a sovereign state" as "international terrorism" and those acts "when carried out by basically autonomous non-state actors, whether or not they enjoy some degree of support from sympathetic states" as "transnational terrorism."⁴³ The distinction is clear, although the terminology is somewhat confusing given the usual connotations of the adjective "international." Nevertheless, the dichotomy is now in common usage, as can be noted by the titles of many of the articles and books cited previously.[44]

Edward Mickolus has developed the classification a step further by coupling it with the same types of domestic terrorism and has expanded Milbank's definition of international terrorism as well. Mickolus' typology is based on two attributes of terrorist violence: (1) whether the terrorists are government controlled or directed and (2) whether there is direct involvement of nationals of more than one state. The typology is summed up in Figure 1.

The typology is clear, although there still can be some confusion about the narrow interpretation of "international," as noted earlier. Differentiating among the types, Mickolus defined international terrorism (including transnational terrorism) as:

> The use, or threat of use, of anxiety-producing extranormal violence for political purposes by an individual or group, whether acting for or in opposition to established governmental authority, when such action is intended to influence the attitudes and behavior of a target group wider than the immediate victims and when, through the nationality or foreign ties of its perpetrators, its location, the nature of its

institutional or human victims, or the mechanics of its resolution its ramifications transcend national boundaries.[45]

FIGURE 1: TYPOLOGY OF TERRORISM (MICKOLUS)

		Direct Involvement of Nationals of More Than One State?	
		Yes	No
Government Controlled or Directed?	Yes	International	State
	No	Transnational	Domestic

SOURCE: Mickolus, "Trends in Transnational Terrorism," in <u>International Terrorism in the Contemporary World</u>, ed. Marius Livingston (Westport, Conn.: Greenwood Press, 1978), p. 45.

The distinction was then made between "international" and "transnational" terrorism, depending on whether the terrorism is directed or controlled by a government. The Mickolus definition does emphasize the psychological objectives of terrorism and the "extranormal" character of its violence more than did the Milbank definition;[46] therefore, it will be the definition to be used here.

The Mickolus typology, however, only distinguishes between two forms of international terrorism and the distinction is often unclear in actual terrorist events. What is needed is a typology of international terrorism with more explanatory power that will encompass the relationships of all the affected governments to the violent events. That is the next task of this study.

A Typology of International Terrorism

It may be true that in analyzing political terrorism "[t]he key factor becomes the relationship between initiators, victims, targets, objectives, and goals."[47] However, the actor not mentioned by Vaughn Bishop in that statement and crucial in the resolution of international terrorist events is the government that is forced to respond to the violent acts. That government may not be the target of the violence. Indeed, the responding government may be otherwise unrelated to the victims, the targets, or the terrorists. International terrorism involves more than one government and presents different problems for each of the affected governments.

The government that has jurisdiction over the location of the terrorist event or finds itself host to fugitive terrorists clearly has different responsibilities and imperatives than does the government that views the events from the outside or seeks to apprehend the fugitives. It may well be that the government will respond by offering asylum or sanctuary to the terrorists, either officially or tacitly, or that the government will arrest or detain the terrorists. Either way, the initial response to the terrorists, apart from the responses to the act itself (e.g., police or military mobilization and evacuation of the site of the violence) is made by the government having legal, i.e., territorial, jurisdiction over the location of the event or the terrorists.

By the same token, the government that is forced by the necessity of self-defense to respond to terrorist violence is faced with distinctly different challenges and constraints than is the government that is reacting on the basis of territorial jurisdiction alone. When a government finds that its own nationals are involved in the violence and/or that it is the target of the violence, the situation becomes more complex. The responding government has to answer challenges, in this case, to its own authority and responsibility as the ultimate guarantor of civic order. The dangers are more distinct and the threats less easily disregarded. In short, the location of the violent act or the terrorists and the nationalities of the victims, terrorists, and targets are important factors in the determination of the initial parameters of government response.

This does not mean that governments cannot respond to terrorist acts committed outside of their own borders, only that territorial jurisdiction takes precedence. There are possibilities for government response to external events or to terrorists outside of that state's borders, as the Entebbe and Mogadishu rescues attest. But, as stated by Manuel R. Garcia-Mora:

> It has long been an unquestioned postulate of legal theory that criminal jurisdiction is essentially territorial and that a state has very wide powers to exercise jurisdiction over nationals and aliens for unlawful acts committed in whole or in part within its territory.[48]

States, then, have primary jurisdiction within their own borders. Even so, if governments opt to exercise their jurisdiction in ways inconsistent with the wishes of the other affected governments, such as by dealing leniently with the terrorists (e.g., like the governments of Algeria and Libya have done in the past by offering sanctuary) or by seeming to offer aid and support to the terrorists (e.g., like Uganda did during the Entebbe affair), other governments might respond.[49] Other governments may also respond if the government having territorial jurisdiction defers to the actions of another, such as Somalia did in allowing the West German commandos to handle the terrorists at Mogadishu. The focus of this study is on the government or governments that ultimately react.

The objectives and goals of the terrorists, as well as the strength and popular support of the terrorist organization, are factors in the determination of the degree of challenge presented to the targets of the

The Nature of International Terrorism   53

violence, but the responding government may not be so affected. These factors are more relevant to the government that is the target of the attack or is responsible to the targets. The factors may impact the ultimate selection of a response policy, but the territorial jurisdiction of the responding government and the nationalities of the actors involved are crucial to the initial selection of viable policy alternatives.

Given these two primary variables in policy selection, the permutations of international terrorist violence (from the perspective of the responding government and assuming that no government will respond to events in which it is not involved) are illustrated in Figure 2 below.

FIGURE 2: PERMUTATIONS OF INTERNATIONAL TERRORISM

	Location	Primary Terrorist Nationality	Primary Victim Nationality
1.	Internal	Foreign	Foreign
2.	Internal	Foreign	National
3.	Internal	National	Foreign
4.	External	Foreign	National
5.	External	National	Foreign
6.	External	National	National

The configuration of actors involved in terrorism conducted by terrorists against victims of the same nationality and within their home state may also be considered international terrorism by the affected government when the terrorists are supported or directed by a foreign government; and, similarly, acts committed in a foreign state by foreigners against foreigners may also be viewed as "international in scope" when the violence indirectly affects or is emulated in other states. Neither of these two contingencies is within the scope of the definition used here.

The assumption of the perspective of the responding government also solves the difficulty of determining whether a group is actually "foreign." That status is determined by the respondent.

Additionally, there are several other factors which must be clarified. First, the events are not always confined to one location. The government that has territorial jurisdiction when the event takes place may lose that jurisdiction when the terrorists flee. This is frequently the case with single-phase terrorism, i.e., shootings, bombings, or arsons. The jurisdiction may also shift from one state to another during dual-phase terrorist events, such as kidnappings, skyjackings, and other hostage incidents.[50] Dual-phase terrorism is generally more complex, although it does offer the responding government more time to consider alternative policies. And, it may also be that the events take place outside of the usual jurisdiction of any government, e.g., on the high seas or in the "high skies," with the

The Nature of International Terrorism   55

initial jurisdiction being claimed by the government whose nationals or carrier (ship or airplane) are involved.

Second, many terrorist events involve groups of terrorists of mixed nationality. However, even in such cases, the predominant nationality can be determined usually by the evident target of the terrorists' demands or threats. During the initial phases of the events, though, it may be somewhat difficult to make that determination without prior intelligence concerning the make-up of the group. In the case of the 1972 attack at Lod airport, near Tel Aviv, by Japanese Red Army terrorists that was conducted in support of the Palestinian cause, the determination of nationality may certainly confuse the issue. But it is likely that Israel reponded to that event in much the same way it would to any other foreign attack. Again, here, the responding government's perception of the composition of the terrorist group is more important than its actual composition.

Third, similarly, the victims may also be of mixed nationality. In this case, there is also means of determining the dominant nationality. One way is by considering the relative proportions of each nationality represented by the victims. Because most of these cases would involve skyjackings, the origin of the airplane would likely be the deciding factor, but this determination should also allow the government with the largest number (or even a significant number) of nationals on the airplane to react as if it's nationals were the primary victims. Government perceptions are the deciding factor.

Given these clarifications and the permutations of international terrorism illustrated in Figure 2, three primary types of international terrorism, based on the perspectives of the responding government can be identified. The three types are displayed in the modification of Figure 2 below.

FIGURE 3: TYPES OF INTERNATIONAL TERRORISM

		Location	Terrorist Nationality	Victim Nationality
1.	Spillover Terrorism	Internal	Foreign	Foreign
2.	Integrated Terrorism	Internal	Foreign	National
		Internal	National	Foreign
3.	External Terrorism	External	Foreign	National
		External	National	Foreign
		External	National	National

The types are based on the responding governments' jurisdictions and responsibilities.

Spillover Terrorism

The principal characteristic of spillover terrorism is the use of violence by foreign nationals against foreign individuals or property.[51] The terrorist threat is not directed at the responding government, and the responding government is not directly involved in the political conflict, except to the extent that it is responsible for the protection of foreigners traveling or residing within its territory, and their property, and for the maintenance of public order.

The following are examples of spillover terrorism:

(1) On February 10, 1970, three Arab terrorists attacked a bus and a lounge containing passengers of an El Al flight at a Munich, West Germany, airport. The passengers were in the process of reboarding their Tel Aviv to London flight. The terrorists, unable to stop a bus that was ferrying passengers from the lounge to the aircraft, threw hand grenades into the bus and the lounge. One Israeli was killed and eleven others injured in the blasts. All three terrorists, one Egyptian and two Jordanians, were captured by West German police and charged with murder. The following day, two Jordan-based terrorist organizations claimed responsibility for the attack, the Popular Front for the Liberation of Palestine and the Action Organization for the Liberation of Palestine.[52]

West Germany was the responding government, but not the primary target of the attack (although the terrorists may have chosen Munich as the site of the violence because of West German support for Israel). The terrorists and the victims were in transit through German territory.

(2) On July 21, 1973, a Moroccan believed to have been a member of the Palestinian Black September organization was killed by two gunmen in Lillehammer, Norway, 115 miles north of Oslo. Six persons, three Israelis, one South African, one Dane, and one Swede, were arrested by Norwegian police in connection with the killing and were charged with being accessory to the murder and spying for Israel. All were believed to be members of the Israeli counterterrorist organization, Wrath of God. All but one, an Israeli, were convicted and sentenced to prison terms.[53]

Again, the responding government was not the target of the attack. All the terrorists and the victim were foreigners in Norway. The larger Arab-Israeli conflict had simply spilled over into Norway, and Norway responded by means of its criminal laws against such violence. The complicating factor, however, was the evidence that the terrorists were agents for the state of Israel.

(3) The Yugoslavian ambassador to Sweden was assassinated by Croatian terrorists in April of 1971. The two terrorists were arrested, tried, and sentenced

The Nature of International Terrorism

to life imprisonment by Swedish courts, along with accomplices who received lighter sentences. Yugoslavia reproached Sweden for its failure to control the Croatian emigre organizations within Sweden and warned that further problems might endanger their diplomatic relations.[54]

The Swedish government was presented with a <u>fait accompli</u> in this case, but the violence perhaps could have been anticipated, if not prevented, had Sweden acted to control the Croatians operating within Swedish territory. Having territorial jurisdiction over the offense and the offenders, Sweden had to bear almost complete responsibility for responding to the violence.

In each of the preceding three cases, the responding government was not directly involved in the fundamental political conflict. The question of involvement is often not so clearcut, however. For example, the violence committed by South Moluccan groups in the Netherlands has presented unique problems for the Dutch government. The South Moluccan attack on the Indonesian Embassy in December of 1975 forced the Dutch government to respond to action directed at an outside government primarily but committed by residents of the Netherlands. By contrast, the South Moluccan terrorists' seizure of the Dutch train in May of 1977, while essentially involving the same target, also involved demands on the Dutch government.[55] The status of the terrorists is a crucial determination which will become even more evident in the discussion of the second form of international terrorism, integrated internal terrorism.

Integrated Internal Terrorism

The distinguishing characteristic of integrated internal terrorism is the difference in the nationalities of the terrorists and the victims, one group being indigenous to the host state. The responding government may or may not be the target of the terrorist threat. In dealing with this type of terrorism, the responding government has the twin responsibilities to protect the lives and property of its own constituents and of foreign nationals within its territory. The government may abrogate either of these responsibilities, but each will likely be considered in the selection of a response.

The following are examples of integrated internal terrorism:

(1) On November 22, 1968, a bomb exploded in the Jewish section of Jerusalem. Twelve persons were killed, ten Jews and two Arabs, and fifty-five were injured. Thirty Arabs were held for questioning, after five hundred had been initially picked up for questioning by the Israeli police. Responsibility for the bombing was claimed by the Popular Front for the Liberation of Palestine that same day.[56]

The history of the conflict between the Israeli government and the Palestinian organizations that regularly use terroristic violence supports the assumption that all or most of the violence directed against Israeli citizens is perpetrated by exogenous Palestinian groups. Certainly, it is likely that at least some of the violence is committed by Palestinians living in Israel, but it is unlikely that Israel bases its response upon that determination of where the terrorists originate. As noted earlier, the question of nationality becomes somewhat blurred in the cases of the Palestinian peoples. In any case, this incident can be viewed as an attack on Israeli nationals (Jewish and Arab) by foreign terrorists.

(2) On April 22, 1971, a bomb exploded in the offices of the Soviet trading agency, Amtorg Trading Corporation, in New York City. No one was injured in the blast. The authorities suspected Jewish Defense League responsibility for the act, and those suspicions were confirmed in September of 1972 when a member of that organization pleaded guilty to involvement in that incident.[57]

This case involved an attack by an American group on a foreign target in the U.S. Diplomatic protests and apologies followed the violence, with the Soviet Union protesting because of the U.S.'s failure to protect the Soviet facilities. While the target of that attack was a foreign state, the following example is one in which the responding government is the primary target.

(3) On May 11, 1972, a series of explosions at the headquarters of the 5th U.S. Army Corps in Frankfurt, West Germany, killed one U.S. officer and injured thirteen others. Responsibility for the bombings was claimed by the "Petra Schelm Command" of the "Red Army Faction" with references to the activities of the U.S. in Vietnam.[58]

Despite the references to Vietnam, the Rote Armee Fraktion (Red Army Faction) was essentially a West German terrorist organization (better known as the Baader-Meinhof group) with indigenous goals and targets. The selection of foreign targets is a useful device to avoid alienating the terrorists' home public while, at the same time, demonstrating the strength of the terrorist organization and the inability of the target government to maintain order. The attack on the U.S. Army facility was only one of many targets bombed by terrorists in West Germany during May of 1972 including a U.S. Army facility in Heidelberg and numerous West German targets.[59]

The attacks on internal targets, whether foreign or indigenous, present relatively clear alternatives to the responding government. While the degree of challenge to the host government's authority may vary greatly, from the relatively slight challenge offered by spillover terrorism to the comparatively large challenge offered by the terrorism used by foreign organizations against the government or its constituents. The freedom of action that the host government enjoys within its own territory greatly simplifies response.

Response is more complex when the terrorists commit their violence outside of the territory of the affected government, escape from the territory of the affected government, or initiate the violence outside of the affected government. That is the case with external terrorism.

External Terrorism

The distinguishing characteristic of external terrorism is that the terrorists are located or the act is committed outside of the territory of the target government, i.e., in the jurisdiction of another government. To respond to such attacks, the target government must either seek the consent and cooperation of the government having jurisdiction or deal with the legal and political ramifications attendant with having its agents operate outside of its borders. In the example given of the killing of the Moroccan national in Norway, for instance, the terrorists presented a _fait accompli_ to the Moroccan government; but, in many cases, the affected governments may be presented with different opportunities to react. The skyjacking that set the stage for the West German rescue of its nationals at Mogadishu allowed adequate opportunity for West German officials to formulate a response. Morocco could only protest; West Germany could respond directly. The difference between the acts of terrorism was that the "one-phase" act committed in Norway precluded Moroccan response, and the "dual-phase" act that culminated in Somalia did not preclude West German response. The latter type of terrorist violence offers more opportunities for external response, although campaigns of terror comprised of many separate acts of "one-phase" terrorism might also provide opportunities to the governments reacting to events outside of their borders.

The Entebbe rescue and the Israel air strikes against Palestinian bases in Lebanon and Jordan are examples of external responses. The killing of the suspected Black September organization member in Norway (if, in fact, committed by agents of the Israeli government) is an example of a preemptive or retaliatory response to the Black September organization's activities. More frequently, however, the governments having territorial jurisdiction permit the target governments to respond. Just as Somalia deferred to and cooperated with the West German government during the Mogadishu affair, host governments routinely wait for the target governments to respond to terrorist demands before they take action to resolve the crises themselves.

It must also be noted that governments frequently respond indirectly, internally, to acts of external terrorism by increasing pressure on domestic terrorist organizations, e.g., increasing surveillance of or arresting members of the terrorist organization still within the government's territorial jurisdiction.

The above categorization of international terrorist acts is not without ambiguities. Some incidents of terrorist violence prove very difficult to fit into categories. The explosion of a letter bomb in the British embassy in Washington, D.C., on August 27, 1973, is such a case. The secretary of the military attache was severely wounded in that blast. The letter bomb was one of a series of such bombs sent by the Irish Republican Army to British embassies overseas (bombs were later intercepted at the British embassies in Paris and Lisbon). Despite the fact that the explosion occurred in the U.S., the letter bomb was believed to have been delivered to the embassy from England by British military transport and, thus, was not vulnerable to U.S. detection. Moreover, the terrorists were beyond the jurisdiction of the U.S. when the explosion occurred (as well as before). Britain responded to the bombings by increasing efforts in England to apprehend the bombers.[60] The location of the violence was less important than the location of the terrorists in the determination of which government should respond.

Despite the difficulties that arise with incidents like the letter-bombing, the categorization does focus attention on the responses to individual acts of international terrorism by individual governments. Each act of terrorist violence can be interpreted differently by the governments involved. Moreover, should the terrorists (particularly those engaged in international hostage incidents) escape the jurisdiction of the host government, the categorization can also be inverted with the acts of internal integrated terrorism becoming external terrorism (or vice versa).

This preliminary look at the nature of terrorism, political terrorism, and international terrorism and the typology will be expanded upon in the following chapters. It is not possible to capture the meaning of international terrorism in a few pages -- perhaps it is not possible to capture the meaning of such violence at all. International terrorism means something different for each person and government touched by the violence, be they perpetrater, target, victim, respondent, reporter, or spectator of the event. The violence is for effect, and the perspective is all important.

The typology is predicated on the perspectives of the responding governments with the acts categorized according to the governments' jurisdictional relationships to the acts, the victims, and the terrorists. This typology will provide an initial framework for the illustration of the challenges presented by international terrorist events, the constraints on response policy choice, and the ultimate selection of a government reply to terrorist violence. The possession, or lack, of territorial jurisdiction certainly provides a starting point for the identification of viable policy alternatives, and the next task is to clarify the nature of the challenge to government authority presented by international terrorist events. The focus is now on the targets of the violence.

CHAPTER III
CHALLENGE AND POLICY DEMANDS

International terrorism presents many faces to participant and spectator publics. Every act transmits different cues, communicates different dangers, and incites different reactions; and, thus, the interpretations of each terrorist deed vary widely, even among the governments most directly infected by the violence. Truly, there are "many terrorisms."

The proximity of the violence and the relationship of the audience to the primary actors have considerable impact on how governments, as well as nongovernmental participants and witnesses, respond. These factors define the nature of government involvement in the events and the initial parameters of government response.

Beyond those basic attributes of terrorist events, the perceptions of the danger implied in the violence assume paramount importance in the response choice. Affected governments are not equally threatened, and, clearly, the first step in measuring the threat being faced by a government is to determine the relationship of that government to the target of the violence. In other words, is the government itself the target, are its constituents the targets, or is a foreign government or people the actual target? What are the challenges being communicated?

Normally, terrorist attacks against a foreign target will convey very little threat to the incumbency of a third party government, although the attacks may endanger, injure, or kill nationals of that government. Such are the cases with terrorist campaigns that have spilled over into the government's jurisdiction from another state (i.e., spillover terrorism) and campaigns that are conducted outside of the government's jurisdiction but involve the victimization of the government's nationals or agents (i.e., external terrorism).

If the government is, in fact, the target of foreign or domestic terrorists, the threat becomes more serious. The challenge produces a new set of imperatives, urgencies, that must be taken into consideration in the government's choice of a response. What, then, is the breadth of the terrorist challenge? Does the violence endanger the very existence of the sociopolitical structure, place into jeopardy the social or political roles of some components of that structure (e.g., the dominance of an elite group, the incumbency of specific officials, or the pursuance of certain policies), or simply disrupt public order and represent a challenge amenable to resolution by the traditional law enforcement agencies? In short, how great is the challenge to incumbent authority?

The policy predicament that the responding government finds itself in is greatly influenced by the context of the conflict, as well as the breadth of the terrorist challenge. Wilkinson has described the relevant contextual variables as:

> 1. <u>the nature of the terrorist movement</u> -- ideology, strategic aims, tactical objectives, size and social base, weaponry and financial resources, leadership, discipline, technical and organizational competence, and internal and external allies;
>
> 2. <u>the condition of the target state and/or community</u> -- internal stability, form of government, degree of popular will to resist terrorism, competence of leadership at various levels of administration, economic and military resources and capabilities; and
>
> 3. <u>the influence of the international environment</u> -- the nature and degree of influence or direct or indirect intervention by external states in the conflict, opposition or support of foreign-based ideological, ethnic or exile groups for parties in the conflict, influence of terrorist pressure and propaganda on international opinion and on international organizations, the influence of international opinion and organizations on the course of the terrorist conflict, indirect effects of other

international crises and involvements on the target state and its military, diplomatic and economic capabilities.[1]

Wilkinson went on to suggest that internal factors such as the amount of popular support enjoyed by the terrorists and the effectiveness of government responses "tend to be far more important" in dealing with domestic terrorism, particularly popular support.[2] In focusing on the jurisdictional imperatives and constraints of responding governments, the degree to which international terrorism presents threats comparable to those of domestic terrorist activities becomes particularly relevant to the study of government responses. The fact that international terrorist events often do not present a "clear and present danger" to the governments in whose territory the acts are committed may, at least in part, explain the reluctance or inability of those governments to respond effectively or even decisively. By contrast, there is seldom any reluctance to respond to domestic terrorism in a decisive manner.

In light of that distinction between the acts of terrorism that do not present serious dangers to responding governments and those that do, the analysis of government responses must be predicated on the degree of challenge that the authorities face. Indeed, the response should be predicated on that challenge. With that in mind, the policy predicament precipitated by international terrorist campaigns will be considered in terms of: (1) the challenge of terrorism -- the terrorists' objectives, strengths and limitations, and potentialities; and, (2) the policy imperatives -- the extent to which the terrorist challenges are inconsistent with the authority maintenance and security functions of the affected governments. The challenge and the imperatives will provide a foundation for the discussion of response policy alternatives and choice.

The Challenge of International Terrorism

A frequent description of political terrorism is that it is a "weapon of the weak."[3] Certainly, the number of people killed or injured in terrorist incidents, particularly international incidents,[4] suggests that the threat of terrorism is not as grave as one would surmise from the reaction to the violent acts. The response would seem to be out of proportion to the costs. Why, then, if terrorists are weak and the destruction is comparatively slight, has the public and official outcry been so great? Is there, in fact, a serious threat posed by international terrorists?

That question has elicited a variety of answers from analysts. Walter Laqueur, for instance, has concluded that terrorism "tends to be ineffective" and that "compared with other dangers facing mankind, it is almost irrelevant."[5] Several other analysts have concluded that terrorism alone has not caused the downfall of a regime.[6] Perhaps terrorism, as we are familiar with it, is not an imminent threat to societies, governments, or the world community.

However, other analysts do not find solace in the apparent weakness of terrorist organizations. Marius Livingston, for example, has taken issue with Laqueur's opinion that terrorism elicits responses disproportionate to its effects. Livingston contends that "the significance of international terrorism does not lie in the number of lives taken or the amount of destruction inflicted; it lies in the number of lives threatened and in the amount of fear and terror generated."[7] Ted Robert Gurr has expressed a similar evaluation of terrorism and suggested that the duration of a terrorist campaign is a better measure of the terrorist threat than are the number of casualties or the amount of physical destruction.[8] The crucial impact of terrorism is psychological rather than physical, according to both analysts.

If the primary impact is psychological rather than physical, does this mean that terrorism is not an effective weapon? According to Edward Hyams, the answer to that question is "no." Hyams' assessment is "quite the contrary, for at all epochs and in all parts of the world governments have, in fact, repeatedly been forced by terrorists to change their policies, and in some cases have been overthrown by terrorism."[9] Crozier, too, has found that terrorism has proven to be a "useful auxiliary weapon" -- "decisive" in Palestine from 1944 to 1948, successful in Egypt from 1954 to

1959, and important in many of the other post-World War II national liberation struggles.[10] And, David Rapoport maintains that political terrorism has been used successfully by groups with more limited objectives, such as the terror used by the Sons of Liberty to intimidate and punish agents and supporters of the King in colonial America and the terror used by the Ku Klux Klan to counter the Reconstruction policies imposed on the South after the Civil War.[11] Indeed, the weaknesses or limitations of international, as well as domestic, terrorists are only relevant within the context of what the terrorists are attempting to achieve.

Evidently, the assessment of terrorism as a "weapon of the weak" requires qualification. Terrorist objectives determine the strengths and limitations of their violent methods and underlie their potential for success.

The Objectives of International Terrorists

The objectives sought by the terrorists are crucial factors that must be considered in the selection of a response to the violence. To deny terrorists their goals, governments must first determine what those goals are and then determine whether the goals are incompatible with regime and societal values. Basic to those determinations is the need to distinguish between the long-term, ideological objectives of the terrorists and the short-term, strategic and tactical objectives.

The stated and unstated objectives of terrorist organizations vary considerably. Some groups appear to be motivated by very narrow political goals, largely compatible with the existing sociopolitical order of the target society, while others represent broad revolutionary goals almost totally antithetical to the existing sociopolitical arrangements. In addition, the ultimate or ideological (in the broadest sense of the term) goals of terrorist organizations are distinct from the mid-range strategic and immediate tactical objectives of their violent campaigns.[12] Some or all of those objectives may not be expressed clearly; but, if terrorist campaigns are viewed as rational applications of violence for political ends, the objectives at all levels are important factors in measuring the terrorist challenge to authority. Furthermore, the incompatibility of the objectives with government authority defines the imperatives of government response.

Ideological Objectives

Virtually all terrorist organizations offer some ideological justification or objectives for their violence, albeit the revolutionary rhetoric of many often obscures more than it reveals about their ultimate aims. Despite the frequent lack of clarity, terrorists find it necessary to provide "normative context" for their actions by "endowing the brutality of terrorism with social meaning."[13] The terrorist has to convince the audience that his (or her) use of extreme violence is unavoidable and, in fact, appropriate to the pursuit of the organization's political goals.[14]

Despite the strong ideological content of terrorist demands and actions, ideological orientations have generally been neglected as variables.[15] The importance of the ideological trappings of terrorist organizations cannot be easily dismissed, however. Just as liberal democratic governments and publics seem to react emotionally to any sort of violence that even appears to be motivated by Marxist doctrine, the perceived ideological bases of a terrorist organization may have a profound impact on how governments respond to its violence.

As well as impacting the choice of a response policy by an affected government, the ideological orientations of terrorist groups may affect the propensity for other governments to become involved in the conflict.[16] Foreign governments and publics may give assistance to the government that is facing an ideological threat that the foreign government or public finds particularly abhorent. Inversely, foreign actors may become involved in conflicts when their opposition is to the target government rather than the terrorists. And, as has been evident in the inability to arrive at an international consensus on combatting terrorism, the propensities of governments and publics to cooperate in the suppression of terrorist violence has been influenced by the ideological orientations of the active terrorist groups.

The greatest impact of ideological factors, however, may be in terms of the groups' "legitimacy potentials," i.e., their potentials to attract mass support.[17] Herein lies the real danger of incumbent authorities and, perhaps, the primary determinant of the terrorists' success or failure.

Terrorist ideologies have not been as amenable to analysis as have other variables of terrorist violence. There are several reasons for the resultant lack of study. First, terrorists often do not provide clear statements of their ultimate aims or guiding principles. That may be due to the terrorists' lack of a clear ideology or their pursuit of multiple objectives. Second, the terrorists may deliberately misrepresent their objectives. Some may not advertise their true objectives for fear of alienating mass or foreign support; or, false objectives may be stated in order to attract support. In some cases, the need to attract a diverse following may cause the terrorist organization to publicize very vague statements of goals.[18] And, in a few cases, terrorist organizations may operate under cover names to prevent the alienation of support, such as the Black September group's operations on behalf of Al Fatah.[19] In such cases, the group may not profess ideological objectives or may profess objectives much more extreme than those of the parent group. In any event, the false, nonexistent, or vague statements of terrorist objectives makes the study of ideological influences extremely difficult.

Third, the terrorists' objectives may be interpreted by their opponents in such a way as to subvert the terrorists' potential for popular support, such as the branding of political terrorists as common criminals, "communists," "revisionists," or puppets of a foreign government. The vulnerability of terrorist causes to misrepresentation is related directly to the amount of control the target government has over the dissemination of information concerning the violence. Foreign audiences in particular may be misled as to the ideological and popular bases of terrorist organizations. That may be one reason that terrorists choose to perform their violent acts for international, rather than domestic, audiences.

In any case, the ideological objectives of terrorist organizations have not been dealt with adequately by analysts. And, notwithstanding the lack of consideration of ideological variables, the possibility that some terrorist groups simply do not have broad ideological goals cannot be overlooked. Gurr's study of political terrorism in the 1960s, in fact, concluded that only eight percent of the terrorist acts and campaigns during that period had explicit and primary goals of seizing power or implementing a revolutionary ideology.[20] Moreover, recently, analysts have noted a trend away from the traditional ideological bases that characterized terrorist organizations during most of the post-war period and toward more nihilistic, anarchistic, and ethnic bases.[21]

Because of the difficulty involved in typologizing the ideological variables, attempts to draw parallels among and comparisons between terrorist ideologies have been few. Nonetheless, the classification schemes offered in the literature do reveal some agreement on three basic categories, apart form pathological and other nonpolitical groupings: ethnic, nationalistic, and ideological.[22] Ideological movements are difficult to group because each seems to follow a unique interpretation of one of the traditional ideologies. The problems attendant with the development of a classification is amply evident in Crozier's typology. Crozier has categories for orthodox communist (Moscow-oriented), extreme right-wing, ethnic and nationalist, and revolutionary left groups. The latter category seems to be a "catch-all," because it includes such disparate ideological groups as Trotskyists, anarchists, Maoists, "Guevarists," and "miscellaneous leftists."[23] However, there is little reason to believe that the terrorists so classified would have more than a very superficial ideological resemblance. Therefore, the classification scheme is awkward at best.

A much more useful typology, based on the objectives sought by the terrorists, has been offered by Edward Mickolus. He classifies international terrorist organizations into eight categories: territorialists, national revolutionaries, global anarchists, criminal gangs, psychotics, hoaxes, cover names, and vigilantes.[24] Although this typology eliminates the need to differentiate among the seemingly infinite number of leftist organizations, it does not consider the terrorist groups that seek more limited objectives, such as the alteration of a specific policy or the removal of a particular official.

The necessity of developing a typology with adequate breadth to permit analysis of all terrorist ideological bases is manifest in the apparent successes of certain terrorist movements. It is important to know what distinguishes the successful terrorist from the unsuccessful. Similar objectives may signal similar strengths, weaknesses, and potentialities.

According to Wilkinson, ideology determines the size of the terrorists' base of popular support, with nationalist, autonomist, and secessionist (i.e., territorial) groups enjoying more support than nihilist and anarchist groups.[25] The projected ideological orientations of the terrorists profoundly affect their abilities to attract domestic and foreign support. Terrorists with ready-made constituencies, such as ethnic, religious, or racial minorities, have a distinct advantage -- particularly if the minority feels that it is maltreated or ignored by the incumbent regime. Violent action can bring together such a community.[26]

The history and success of national liberation struggles since World War II has also created an interest in and sympathy for terrorists pursuing campaigns of violence to achieve "self-determination." The sympathy and support given the ideological groups is difficult to gauge, as is the support given vigilante groups. The context of the struggle determines the success or failure of the latter two groups.

In any case, the ideological (ultimate aim) underpinnings of the terrorist organizations do influence their abilities to realize their goals and their potential to attract support and sympathy from domestic and foreign audiences. That influence, however, may be mediated by other political factors, such as government action or the visibility of the terrorists' constituencies.[27]

Strategic Objectives

For the most part, there is consensus among analysts concerning the mid-range or strategic objectives of terrorist activity. Six general themes reoccur in the literature, indicating that terrorists may seek a variety of goals, individually or concurrently. Those principal objectives are:

1. Organizational objectives
2. Publicity objectives
3. Provocation objectives
4. Disruption objectives
5. Punishment objectives
6. Instrumental objectives.

Organizational Objectives

Terror is frequently used within terrorist organizations to enforce discipline and used outside the organizations to build the morale of the members and their sympathizers.[28] In some cases, terrorist violence may be used to cement the "bonds of organization" -- as a ritual "blood-letting" -- to insure that the members of the organization cannot renounce or leave the organization at a later date.[29]

The use of terror by the organization against its own members may even be greater than the use of terror against the external targets. Crozier, for example, has suggested that three of every five victims of terrorism are on the terrorists' side. Crozier went on to suggest that this type of terrorism is a "fairly precise indicator of the amount of public support the group has; if many group members fall victim to the organizational terror, support is very low."[30]

Publicity Objectives

Communication is essential to the process of terror, and the communication of the terrorists' cause to domestic and international audiences involves the transmittal of two primary messages. The first is a "positive indoctrination campaign" seeking popular sympathy and support, and the second is a negative campaign of intimidation.[31] It is the first, the propaganda, message that is the subject here.

The publicizing of the terrorist cause is intended to arrouse the admiration of their audiences, demonstrate the seriousness of their cause, advertise the strength and resolve of their organization and its members, and/or stimulate emulation by potential supporters.[32] All these purposes are designed to encourage domestic and/or foreign support.[33] The competition is for the allegiance or, at least, the compliance of the target audience.[34]

International terrorism, in particular, lends itself to the publicizing of the terrorist cause. The use of "armed propaganda" or "propaganda of the deed" can attract large audiences, especially when the victims are highly visible -- thus, the frequency of attacks on foreign diplomats and businessmen and other foreign targets.[35] The massacre of the Israeli athletes at the 1972 Olympics in Munich, for instance, attracted an audience estimated to be around 500 million.[36] Despite the international outcry, the violence increased recognition of the Palestinian cause. Two years later, the head of the Palestine Liberation Organization was accorded the ceremonial reception of a head of state at the United Nations.[37] However ugly the violence, the publicity may prove beneficial to the terrorists.

Provocation Objectives

The provocation of government officials to overreact to terrorist violence is one of the primary objectives of terrorism. The purpose is to push the government into instituting repressive countermeasures that will also affect the movement and livelihoods of previously uninvolved citizens, thus undermining the government's own popular support.[38] Foreign support for the incumbent authorities may also be adversely affected by the countermeasures taken by the regime.[39]

As well as alienating the government's domestic and foreign support, Brian Crozier concludes that the provocation of an extreme counterterrorist campaign can "force a rising spiral of official expenditure in arms, lives and money, resulting in public clamour for the abandonment of counteraction."[40] Most important, however, is the possibility that governments will be encouraged to abridge their constitutional guarantees of individual and collective civil liberties -- to deny the very bases of their own claims to represent legitimate authority and to reduce government responses to the same level of "extraordinary" or "extralegal" violence as used by the terrorists.[41]

Disruption Objectives

The degree of disruption sought by the terrorists may vary greatly, from a relatively brief interruption of regime or societal function to the complete collapse of the social, political, and/or economic structures. The objective is to demonstrate the incumbent authorities' inability to maintain civic order by directly or indirectly interrupting (e.g., by provoking repression) the normal processes of social, political, or economic interaction. The resultant disruption of the public's everyday life may alienate a significant portion of the population and cause the polarization of public sympathies and support as segments of the population are attracted to the terrorists' movement.[42]

An even more serious threat to civic order can be envisioned, as well-- the collapse of the rule of law. This extreme objective has been associated with the more anarchist and nihilist terrorist organizations. The object of their activity, according to Thomas P. Thorton, is to:

> . . . disrupt the inertial relationship between incumbents and mass. In order to do this, the insurgents must break the tie that binds the mass to the incumbents within the society, and they must remove the structural supports that give the society its strength -- or at least to make those supports seem irrelevant to the critical problems that the mass must face. This process is one of disorientation, the most characteristic use of terror . . .[43]

Based on the analyses of Martha Crenshaw Hutchinson, the resultant disorientation of the populace may lead to more extreme and critical breakdowns because:

> Terrorism affects the social structure as well as the individual; it upsets the framework of precepts and images which members of society depend on and trust. Since one no longer knows what sort of behavior to expect from other members of society, the system is disoriented. The formerly coherent community dissolves into a mass of anomic individuals, each concerned only with personal survival.[44]

Taken to its logical conclusion, then, the process of disruption can lead to the polarization of society, as a segment of the population remains loyal to and supportive of the government and another aligns with alternative authority structures, possibly the terrorists; and, ultimately, to the atomization of society, as the populace becomes more and more disoriented. It is not likely, however, that many terrorist groups would seek the extreme state of disorientation because, among other things (e.g., limited objectives), it would not be certain that the terrorist organization would be chosen as an alternative authority structure.[45]

Punishment Objectives

This objective is simply to punish specific government agents and private citizens for noncompliance with terrorist demands, although punishment can also be directed against foreign governments and businesses for their dealings with the target government or some other target group.[46] The messages conveyed are that the individuals, whether domestic or foreign and whether government agents or private citizens, cannot escape retribution when they fail to give in to terrorist demands and that the authorities are unable to prevent the violence. The "sanctions" imposed by the terrorists demonstrate their power and the vulnerability of their targets.[47]

Instrumental Objectives

To some extent, terrorists may also use their violence against the agents of incumbent authority as part of a generalized attack upon the regime, although this "military" use of violence is seldom a principal means of achieving the terrorists' broader objectives. The elimination of strategically placed officials or military leaders may be used to damage the morale of the authorities and the public,[48] but attempts to reduce significantly the opposition's security or military forces will be futile. After all, terrorist organizations by definition are unable to mount sustained military operations. It is necessary to note, however, that some terrorist organizations may have the potential to become large-scale, mass-supported insurgent organizations with the capacity to launch military operations.

Because many analysts have concluded that terrorist organizations do not possess the capacity to conduct military operations, the literature offers less support for the inclusion of instrumental objectives in a list of terrorist goals than it does for the preceding objectives. It is likely, nonetheless, that terrorists use instrumental targets to demonstrate their power and their potential to become large-scale movements. The similarities of their attacks to actual military operations provide more convincing evidence of their intentions and capabilities than do less direct attacks. Instrumental objectives seldom provide the primary impetus for terrorist attacks, though.[49]

Obviously, the aforementioned objectives are not always discretely pursued. Several strategic objectives may be sought with each act or threat of violence. Moreover, strategic objectives may be pursued indirectly. International terrorism frequently provides an indirect means of influencing the target government, particularly when the target government has used repressive countermeasures to force the terrorists out of the government's territory (e.g., by making the costs of terrorist operations too great for the organizations to bear[50]).

Terrorists may attempt to influence the target government by interferring with its economic relations with foreign governments or companies, causing the flight of foreign capital[51] or the termination of foreign economic assistance.[52] The disruptive impact of the violence may extend well beyond the boundaries of the state in which the acts are committed. Richard Clutterbuck goes so far as to suggest that terrorists may hope that their attacks on foreign, international, corporations will cause recessions in the foreign countries, as well as frustration in the target state.[53] Interruptions in the extraction or shipment of crucial raw materials or foodstuffs may indeed have such an impact on foreign markets, but not all economic relations are that critical.

For the target state, the interruption of economic activities may create dire problems. Terrorism's impact on a country's tourist industry alone may be highly disruptive to its domestic economy and politics.[54] For that reason, the projection of violence outside of the target state can be a useful device for terrorist organizations. Indeed, foreign victims may put more pressure on the target government than would domestic casualties.[55]

By broadening the zone of combat to include foreign victims, whether innocent of any involvement in the conflict or "guilty" of lending sympathy or support to the target government or group (or simply being indifferent to the terrorists' cause), the terrorists may be able to improve their chances of realizing their ideological and strategic objectives. Similarly, the pursuit of short-term, tactical objectives serves to strengthen the terrorists' position.

Tactical Objectives

Specific concessions and/or logistical gains are frequently sought by terrorists in order to maintain or escalate their campaigns of violence, their pursuit of political ends. Hostage incidents (i.e., kidnappings, barricade episodes, and skyjackings), for example, have generally been conducted for the purposes of securing ransom monies or supplies, the release of political prisoners, the publication of terrorist manifestos or the issuance of some other form of terrorist statement, and the guarantee of safe passage or political asylum.[56] Armed attacks, robberies, and break-ins, on the other hand, have frequently been used to procure supplies, such as arms, money, medical stores, explosives, and food. In some cases, armed attacks have been used to rescue imprisoned or detained terrorists and to create diversions.

These immediate objectives of terrorist organizations seldom generate the confusion that the ideological and strategic objectives do. The pursuit of these objectives provides indicators of the strengths and vulnerabilities of the terrorist organizations, as well. Both the conduct of the violent attacks and the subject of the demands give indications of the terrorists' potential. Moreover, a government's inability or unwillingness to counter these limited designs may be a signal of its own weaknesses.

Still, the ideological, strategic, and tactical objectives of the terrorists are insufficient indicators of whether governments are faced with credible threats to their authority. The objectives only serve to show the terrorists' intentions and the general compatibility of those intentions with the ideology, policies, personnel, and function of the incumbent regime. The next aspect that must be considered is the capacity of the terrorist organization to carry out its designs.

Terrorist Strengths and Limitations

The persistence of terrorist challenges to domestic and foreign governments and publics attests to the perceived efficacy of terror tactics. Notwithstanding that perception or its validity, the choice of terrorism, domestic or international, as a principal means of challenging incumbent authority is a tacit admission of political and/or military weakness. The terrorists are acknowledging that they lack the political support (and patience) necessary to use the legally constituted channels for effecting political change or, if such channels are not available, they lack the military resources necessary to launch a general attack against their target. And, by opting for the use of terror tactics rather than other political means, the terrorists (whether government agents or nongovernmental groups) accept the limitations of the tool as well as its inherent advantages.

The very nature of terrorist organizations gives them advantages over more conventional opposition groups. The tactic is characteristically utilized by small, clandestine groups[57] which are difficult to uncover and apprehend. Moreover, the small size of the organizations facilitates the maintenance of secrecy and discipline, as well as the unobtrusive creation of support structures such as underground sanctuaries and supply caches.

Terrorist organizations are particularly difficult to expose in liberal democratic societies where the terrorists enjoy the same freedom of movement and communication as does the rest of society. Indigenous terrorist groups are virtually invisible in democratic societies; unless, of course, there are obvious ethnic, racial, or linguistic differences between the terrorists and the people within their operational environment. Foreign terrorists, on the other hand, may have more difficulty in securing logistical support and avoiding discovery -- hence the frequency of terrorist attacks on facilities in which foreigners would not be conspicuous, such as international airports.[58]

The small size of the organizations also dictates that the attacks offer few risks of capture, injury, or death to the terrorists and require the expenditure of minimal resources. Terrorism is, therefore, characteristically low-level violence, and the impact of such violence is necessarily limited. The nature of the targets also limits the violence. Attacks on public officials, for instance, may be of questionable value to the terrorists because an assassinated official will simply be replaced[59] or the act may be too dangerous to attempt because of government security. Thus, a viable target is a vulnerable one[60] -- which often means that an innocent person is a preferable victim.

In addition to its impact on the choice of victims, the small size of terrorist organizations often means that the terrorists have limited personnel resources and expertise. Those limited resources are reflected in the repetitious nature of the violence -- the preference for particular victims and means of destruction.[61] Few groups display an extensive repertoire of violence.

Despite the economy of effort and resources involved in low-risk violence, terrorists have to contend with the negative reactions of nongovernmental publics, including the public that the terrorists may be attempting to win over to their cause, to prolonged uses of seemingly senseless violence. According to Ernst Halperin, terrorists run a higher risk of being branded as "criminals" if they cannot elevate their violence to a military level, i.e., the "propaganda yield" of low-risk operations dissipates over time unless the terrorists can show visible results in their campaigns.[62]

Results have to be realized fairly quickly, particularly if the level of violence is escalating. Speed is essential because, according to David Milbank's findings:

> The record suggests that no group can long sustain a high intensity campaign of terror without running against some very serious practical problems in terms of (1) depletion of resources, (2) factional divisions, (3) erosion of international sympathy or support, or (4) more vigorous countermeasures (at least at the national level). In short, while the internal dynamics of a campaign of terrorist violence tend to create pressures for escalation, the process would appear to be to some degree self-limiting.[63]

If, in actuality, high intensity terrorist campaigns are "self-limiting," terrorists will have to either restrain their impulses to escalate the level of violence or gamble on their abilities to increase the destruction to a level high enough to assure a speedy victory. The first course may also be self-limiting to the extent that concrete results may not be attainable when the projected threat is not reinforced by actions.

The second course, the gamble, is more risky, but it does carry the greatest promise of rewards. The problem with escalation is that the terrorist organization may lack sufficient personnel and logistical support to launch high-risk operations and sufficient resources to maintain the campaigns. Arms, supplies, personnel, expertise, and, at least, some popular (domestic or international) support are necessary ingredients for successful terrorist operations. The ability to escalate the violence is a measure of the revolutionary potential of the terrorist organization.

The Terrorist Potential

The elevation of the level of violence from very low-level, low-risk actions (such as bombings) to high intensity, even military, operations is beyond the capabilities of most terrorist organizations -- but, not beyond the capabilities of all. In view of that potential, though low probability, for escalation, governments must assess the risk of increased violence.

Organizations that do have the capacity to raise the level of violence can utilize either of two strategies: (1) to increase the destructiveness of each act of violence or (2) to redirect the violence toward instrumental targets and wage a guerrilla war against the regime and/or its constituents.

The destructiveness of terrorist violence has been and is undergoing rapid change as the technology of war has become more sophisticated. Terrorists have replaced their pistols with small automatic weapons and their large, cumbersome bombs with high explosive or incendiary grenades and plastic explosives.[64] The technology accessible to terrorists has come to include small surface-to-air missiles (SAMs) and armor-piercing anti-tank rockets, both with ultra-sophisticated guidance systems.[65] And, even more destructive weapons may be made available to terrorists through sympathetic or sponsoring governments or raids on military and police installations. The rapid evolution of the destructive potential of military hardware has made even the smallest terrorist organization exceedingly dangerous and impossible to ignore.

Moreover, the terrorists' access to the most advanced military weapons portends even more extraordinarily destructive acts in the future. Bowman H. Miller and Charles A. Russell, for example, have developed a hierarchy of terrorist tactics to illustrate the levels of competence and operational sophistication exhibited by terrorist organizations. That hierarchy is shown in Figure 4 below.

Miller and Russell indicated that the choice of particular tactics by the terrorists would depend upon: "the group's capabilities, weapons, general support apparatus, cadre experience, unique skills, operating environment, target pool, government countermeasures, level of sophistication, clandestine havens, and external support."[66] The hierarchy may have some utility as a measure of terrorist capabilities, but as a continuum, it is suspect. Although mass destruction is at the top of the scale, it can be carried out by relatively unsophisticated organizations. It does not require sophistication to pour chemicals into a city's water supply. By suggesting a progression from one level of expertise or tactics to another, the hierarchy also fails to take into consideration the differences in terrorists' objectives. One tactic may be very appropriate or effective in one instance, within the context of one political conflict, but very inappropriate in another; the contextual differences may not be a reflection of the terrorist organization's competence or sophistication. It is not uncommon, for example, for terrorist groups to avoid taking human lives,[67] preferring instead to take hostages so that the blame for deaths can be shifted to their opponents or restricting the violence to the destruction of property. In any case, the terrorists' objectives are very crucial factors in their choice of tactics and victims.

FIGURE 4: HIERARCHY OF TERRORIST TACTICS BY LEVELS OF ORGANIZATIONAL COMPETENCE

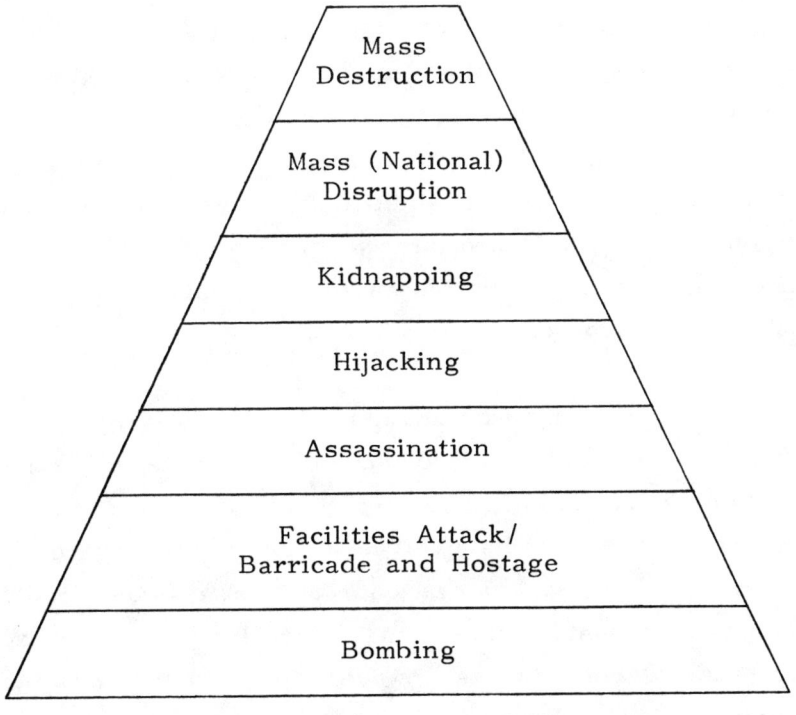

Source: Miller and Russell, "The Evolution of Revolutionary Warfare: From Mao to

Marighella and Meinhof," in <u>Terrorism: Threat, Reality and Response</u>, pp. 193-194.

The concern that terrorists will be capable of and use mass destruction to realize their political objectives is manifest in the discussions of terrorist access to nuclear devices. Analysts, journalists, government officials, and fiction writers are now wrestling with scenarios of nuclear blackmail.[68] The likelihood that terrorists will steal or build nuclear devices is debatable, although their capability to do so is less subject to doubt.

One analyst who discounts the possibility that terrorists will use nuclear devices is Brian Jenkins of the Rand Corporation. Jenkins suggests that terrorists seldom seek to kill great numbers of people because large numbers of deaths would only alienate the popular support that the terrorists seek. Therefore, nuclear terrorism, or any other form of mass killing for that matter, would be counterproductive.[69]

Similarly, Ernest Evans concludes that the escalation of terrorist violence to the level of mass destruction is restrained by several factors: (1) terrorists normally have little interest in large-scale killing, (2) the enlargement of destruction would alienate terrorist support internationally, and (3) the terrorists' constituents would be subjected to reprisals.[70] But, there are other analysts who express fears that nuclear terrorism might become a reality, particularly if a terrorist group is sufficiently fanatical, irrational, or desperate.[71]

Whether a terrorist group will use the threat or the actuality of nuclear destruction to achieve its ends it a question for which there is no answer at present. Nonetheless, the potential for mass destruction certainly exists. The fact that there were 175 threats or acts of violence directed against U.S. nuclear facilities between March of 1969 and March of 1976 and ten attacks on Western European nuclear facilities (eight attacks with explosives) between 1969 and 1975 is not encouraging.[72] The expression of a credible threat to kill hundreds or thousands of people would certainly draw the attention of mass audiences to the terrorists' cause, even though the use of mass destruction itself might be counterproductive.

The second means of increasing the level of violence and the challenge to authority is perhaps the more difficult to achieve and, at the same time, the more advantageous. To mobilize sufficient resources to launch military operations against a target group or government demands more substance than most terrorist organizations possess. To acquire the requisite weapons, personnel, and financial and material resources, the terrorists must attract significant domestic or foreign support. The attraction of popular support, the "sine qua non of victory in modern warfare,"[73] is the distinguishing characteristic between terrorists and guerrilla "soldiers," between terrorist violence and civil war.

Governments, therefore, cannot dismiss lightly the possibility that a terrorist organization enjoys the support of or has the potential to mobilize large segments of the population. Indeed, analysts have frequently contended that terrorism is but one stage in the development of a dissident group's capacity to wage full-scale revolutionary war. The literature on terrorism, internal war, and revolution abounds with hypothesized continuums of revolutionary conflict.[74]

The view of terrorism as part of a continuum of political violence, preceding guerrilla warfare and large-scale civil war, probably enjoys the greatest currency in the literature. According to this view, at the point where the terrorists begin to direct their attacks primarily against the military forces of the regime, the term "terrorist" begins to lose its applicability. The tactics used may continue to involve the intent to create an atmosphere of terror, but the targets are primarily instrumental rather than symbolic. The violence becomes more focused, less seemingly indiscriminant, and terror is no longer the primary goal of the combatants. The terror resultant in the succeeding stages of the conflict has been termed "epiphenomenal terror" by Wilkinson, denoting "those random but often extremely deadly acts of large-scale terror which occur in the course of major outbreaks of intra-specific violence such as international and civil wars and mass insurrection."[75]

The propensity of organizations to decrease their use of terrorist tactics as their strength and popular support increases is evident in most of the continuums of revolutionary violence and has been noted by several analysts. Crozier, for example, has described that inverse relationship as a "barometer of revolutionary success," with the use of terrorism declining as the group's strength and confidence increase and increasing again if the group's strength declines. Crozier went on to suggest that the use of terrorism is also an indicator of the popular support, or its lack, that the terrorists enjoy.[76]

As terrorist organizations attract mass support, terrorism becomes an inappropriate weapon; Edward Weisband and Damir Roguly have offered an explanation for that relationship, saying that:

> For violence to have impact, it can never be its own reward; when effective, terrorism pulls violence out of the realm of war and into the world of politics. But politics has rules, patterns of normative interaction, do's and don't's of legitimate conduct. In the beginning it is the terrorists' task to violate norms of civilized conduct. Yet terrorism is fundamentally a psychological strategy and must point to a way of resolving the conflict.

> If terrorist violence appears wanton, it threatens to lose the support, or at least the respect, it is seeking to gain. Thus the terrorist irrevocably comes face to face with a tortuous self-contradiction: as he becomes more successful, he must become more responsible. He is left to live with the painful tension of responsible violence, that is, calculated, disciplined and permeated with politics. As he wins recognition through violence, he must place limitations on the use of violence.[77]

The renounciation of international terrorism by the Palestine Liberation Organization in January of 1975 would seem consistent with Weisband's and Roguly's explanation.[78] The recognition of the PLO as the legitimate representative of the Palestinian people by the United Nations and the majority of its membership has guaranteed the PLO forums for less violent confrontation and, thus, made it more difficult for the PLO to justify acts of international terrorism. That is not to say, however, that the PLO has renounced the use of violence altogether.

The recognition of the PLO as the spokesman of the Palestinian people and the status accorded to Yasir Arafat by the United Nations may be indicative of a different challenge to the international community than simply violence. The recognition of terrorist, or former terrorist, organizations as legal entities, in essence governments-in-exile, by the international community may prove to challenge the legal status of nation-states. The creation of sovereignty without territory would set a precedent amenable to claims of sovereignty by countless other organizations and peoples, from Latvian exiles to leftist student organizations.[79] Perhaps too little attention has been paid to the international implications of such recognition.

Apart from the possible negative impact that international terrorism might have on the status of nations in the present international system, the challenges presented to individual governments by internal and external acts of terrorist violence are myriad. The physical and psychological consequences of terrorist violence offer challenges to government authority and process which vary considerably, dependent upon the terrorists' objectives, strengths and limitations, and potentialities. Governments cannot dismiss the challenges casually, without first assessing their magnitude -- or, the consequences may prove deadly.

Governments must consider what the terrorists are attempting to do, how capable they are of achieving those objectives initially, and under what circumstances they will be able to increase the level of violence and the magnitude of the challenge. Terrorist organizations that have very limited objectives or are very weak and possess little potential for growth can be dismissed almost casually. The law enforcement agencies of most nations can adequately combat that terrorist threat. But groups that possess great strength or potential for strength cannot be as easily dealt with by law enforcement agencies. The threat that they present must be responded to more cautiously, less mechanically.

Governments must defend themselves, defend their authority and legitimacy and their personnel.

Policy Demands and the Predicament

The terrorist challenge (i.e., objectives, strengths and limitations, and potentialities) forms but one side of the policy selection equation. The other side of the equation includes the counter-objectives (values), strengths, and vulnerabilities of the target group or government. Target values, strengths, and vulnerabilities are also unique, dependent on a complex system of societal and regime variables (e.g., ideology, political and economic stability, popular and foreign support, strength of will, leadership, and resources). Despite the variability of the context of the conflict, however, there are certain fundamental policy imperatives that underlie the exigencies created by terrorist violence.

The challenge offered to responding governments by international terrorism, as well as domestic, is principally dependent on the extent to which the violence undermines regime authority. The imperatives of government response, therefore, are determined by both the terrorists' objectives and their capacity to realize those objectives. The basic elements of a response strategy, then, must be the maintenance of public order and regime legitimacy, the foundations of regime authority.

The ultimate selection of a response to terrorist violence must be predicated on a strategy to (1) defend the individuals, property, and institutions subject to the government's jurisdiction, as well as the values (ideological foundations) of the regime and society, and (2) reaffirm the government's monopoly of the use of legitimate violence (i.e., government authority).

The imperatives of defending society and its social, economic, and political institutions, including the constitution that bestows legitimacy on government authority, require that the response policy adopted accomplish several primary objectives:

1. Protect the population, including foreign nationals residing in or traveling through the government's jurisdiction, and its property from terrorist violence;

2. Protect government agents, civilian and military, from terrorist violence;

3. Deny the terrorists the requisite resources to maintain or escalate their violent campaigns;

4. Minimize and, ultimately, eliminate terrorist interference with the normal processes of social, economic, and political interaction;

5. Minimize government interference with the normal processes of social, economic, and political interaction in its counterterror operations; and,

6. Define the nature of the political conflict, in particular the legal status of the terrorists.

These objectives are based on the necessities for the government to provide security for its constituents and agents, discourage the continuance and escalation of terrorist campaigns, and reduce the likelihood that terrorism will have its desired impact. In short, the counter-objectives of the government can be achieved by manipulating the relationships among victims, targets, and terrorists.

Like terrorist objectives, the objectives or imperatives of government response may be pursued simultaneously. The policy predicament that governments frequently find themselves in, however, is when the pursuit of one set of objectives interferes with the pursuit of another. Most commonly, governments face a choice between the security of their constituents (and personnel) and the preservation of their political institutions. The temptation to abridge the civil rights of citizens in order to control the violence of terrorists is a strong one. The transformation of Uruguay, for example, from one of the most democratic of Latin American governments to a repressive military regime attests to the dangers inherent in that policy predicament. It does no good to protect the institutions from terrorist threats only to have them subverted by government counter-terror. In the case of Uruguay, the tradeoffs have proven costly. Domestic security was purchased with reduced regime legitimacy. The response was not appropriate to the challenge.

The Security Dilemma

What becomes readily apparent to government officials, analysts, victims, observers, and terrorists alike is that all governments and societies are vulnerable to terrorist violence to some degree. Small, dedicated, and skilled bands of terrorists can commit acts of political violence in even the most repressive of societies, despite the restriction of movement and communication and the reduced access to weapons in such societies. The flexibility afforded terrorist organizations in their selection of victims, because they are not restricted to instrumental targets, precludes entirely effective security measures. Moreover, the technological advances of modern societies have made the media of social, economic, and political interaction extensive, fragile, and, thus, susceptible to violent interruption, particularly by terrorists with ultra-sophisticated weapons and tactics.

The tremendous vulnerability of modern societies to terrorist violence is causing increasing concern among analysts. The difficulties that governments encountered in their efforts to prevent bombings at airports, as well as skyjackings, illustrates the predicament in which governments find themselves. Airports cannot be made fully secure without severely curtailing the movement, the liberties, of the public utilizing (indeed, in the proximity of) the airport facilities.[80]

Even less public facilities are difficult to protect from possible terrorist attack. Several analysts and government officials have expressed concern that oil and natural gas facilities may be targeted by terrorists, for example. In fact, the Alaska Pipeline has already been sabotaged on several occasions. The cut-off of gasoline, heating oil, and natural gas that might result from a major attack or series of attacks on refineries, pipelines, transportation lines, extracting facilities, and storage areas could result in enormous hardships in the U.S. or other nations. The physical costs of such destruction would be compounded by the social and economic costs (not to mention the political costs of the violence).[81]

While the physical costs of terrorist violence may be tremendous, the social, economic, and political costs are potentially more threatening to the target government and society. The disruption of the very fabric of society may result from unabated violence. The structures and processes of societal interaction may collapse, if the violence is permitted to escalate and it is apparent that there are no authority structures capable of arresting the spread of chaos.

Social collapse, however, would be an extreme, and unlikely, result of political terrorism. Such a cataclysmic alteration of societal function would be preceded by less severe change, in all likelihood; but, the potentiality of collapse should be recognized nonetheless. Peter Knauss and D.A. Strickland call this potentiality the "terror within terrorism," meaning:

> . . . the root fear that official and unofficial violence will someday, somehow, lead to the complete breakdown of society and that the brutish state of nature which Hobbes told us lurks just beneath the surface of the political order, will reclaim us.[82]

That fear can become more real to individuals when terrorist violence and government ineffectuality destroy the stability of their expectations of behavior. Individuals become confused and disoriented when caught between competing claims of the government and the terrorists to represent legitimate authority and civic order, as well as the competing definitions of the political struggle in progress.[83]

It is not likely that terrorism alone would create such a fragmentation of society, but it does make clear the necessity for governments to try to maintain a sense of stability, if not security, among their constituents. Basic to that idea of stability is the principle that the government has a monopoly of the use of legitimate violence.[84]

The Legitimacy Dilemma

Terrorists disregard the constraints that societies and governments place on the use of violence and attempt to supplant the authority, the monopoly of the use of legitimate violence, of the incumbent regime.[85] However, if the terrorists are acting for or in support of the incumbent regime, their violence does not supplant existing authority structures as much as it reinforces that authority by extralegal means.

The distinction between the legitimate and illegitimate uses of violence, i.e., the uses of "force" by authorized agents of the state and "violence" by challengers to that authority, is an important one.[86] Terrorism, by definition, means the use of extraordinary, extralegal, violence. Governments, as well as individuals or groups, can use violence illegitimately. Terroristic violence is not sanctioned by the rule of law. Even among the most repressive states, the laws do not expressly permit the use of violence by the government in an arbitrary, ostensibly indiscriminate fashion. The distinction, according to Wilkinson, it that: " . . . it is only meaningful to perceive certain behavior as terroristic if our conceptions of normalcy incorporate the idea of a peaceful order under the rule of law, free from terror and fear."[87] The government is charged with the responsibility of protecting that order -- that is basic to the authority of the state.

Also, basic to the authority and legitimacy of the state is the principle that the values implicitly and explicitly represented by the government are derived from a "natural order." The government seeks to defend the "natural order" that its authority represents, and the terrorists seek to regain the "natural order" destroyed or perverted by the incumbent authorities. The existence of a "natural order" and the need to maintain it once found or restore it once lost underlies much of the classical philosophical discussion concerning the justifiability of tyrannicide, rebellion or revolution ("just wars"), and, more recently, terrorism.[88]

It is that "natural order" on which the competing claims to represent legitimate authority are based. Nonetheless, the "state will normally defend itself, whatever its degree of legitimacy, or of public acceptance."[89] It is not a question of legal or moral right as much as it is a question of self-defense because "nations maintain their credentials in the last resort by maintaining their monopoly over the means of violence."[90]

Challenges to that monopoly cannot be long tolerated, without jeopardizing the legitimacy of the state. Governments must respond, must maintain order, when challenged by domestic and international forces.

That is the most important imperative that governments must recognize. Violence must be subdued, lest it become an accepted, an ordinary, mechanism for conflict resolution.[91]

The reduction or elimination of violence, however, must be accomplished through several means, dependent upon the compatibility of the terrorists' larger objectives with those of the incumbent authorities. There can be little room for compromise and accommodation if the ideological objectives of the terrorists and the authorities are diametrically opposed. In fact, Wilkinson finds that these basic objectives are not negotiable at all.[92] The importance of the ideological goals of the opponents, therefore, should not be underestimated.

The mid-range strategic and short-range tactical objectives of terrorist organizations can be mitigated by government response, however. Government responsibility for domestic security and order provides ample justification for government action and is represented by a system of law enforcement and criminal justice administration structures. The mandate for and media of response are in place.

Governments must assess the risks inherent in their responses, including the risks that might result from noncompliance with legitimate or reasonable grievances as well as those that might result from compliance with illegitimate demands. The response must be calculated to maximize the values most supportive of the state, including its ideological foundations. The imperatives of maintaining social order and regime authority must be balanced and tradeoffs must be minimized.

The Policy Predicament

The policy imperatives of maintaining security and government authority are interrelated, but not necessarily mutually inclusive. Direct attacks on government authority by domestic or foreign terrorist organizations present clear dangers. The imperative of authority maintenance requires that government officials react to such violence unequivocally, particularly if the terrorists display a capacity or potential for high-level violence. The challenge to authority must be met.

Terrorist attacks, however, may disrupt security or public order without offering a serious threat to the maintenance of government authority. Indeed, spillover terrorism does not represent a direct challenge to authority, although frequent or prolonged attacks may demonstrate the government's inability to respond to violence effectively. The real danger, then, lies in the possibilities that spillover terrorism or more domestically oriented violence may be encouraged by the government's apparent ineffectuality and, thus, the authority of the regime will lose its credibility.

Integrated internal terrorism may or may not present a challenge to government authority. To the extent that domestic terrorists single out foreign victims to give added emphasis to their propaganda messages and to involve foreign audiences in the conflict, the challenge to authority that they offer may be significant. The fact that the victims are foreign nationals, or property, may be largely incidental to the terrorists' campaigns against their own government. To the extent that foreign terrorists operate against a government's constituents, the challenge to authority is less clear. The importance of determining the real, or primary, target of the violence is especially manifest with this type of terrorist activity.

External acts of terrorism that are directed against the government or its constituents present the least clear dangers to authority. To the extent that popular opinion may lean heavily toward an external response, such as compliance with terrorist demands or a military rescue of hostages, the government may seem to be abdicating its responsibility in the eyes of a portion of its constituents if it does not act. In fact, external terrorism may exacerbate already unstable internal politics and, if directed against agents of domestic commercial interests, may precipitate internal economic crises. But, those exigencies would be somewhat remote. In the vase majority of cases, the challenge to domestic order and authority from external terrorism is much less than that of internal terrorism.

The urgency of government response, therefore, is determined by the degree of challenge to government authority. External violence is generally less threatening than internal, and spillover terrorism less threatening than integrated internal terrorism. However, notwithstanding those generalizations, fragile or unstable domestic circumstances may make all forms of terrorism perilous to incumbent authority.

In any case, the choice of a response policy necessitates assessment of the elemental threat. It also requires that the response chosen be commensurate to that threat. The challenge has to be met, but an underraction will be ineffectual and an overreaction may be exactly what the terrorists seek.

The fundamental predicament that terrorism presents is the problem of balancing challenge and response. Certainly, the abridgement or destruction of institutions and relationships that the government has the responsibility to secure should be avoided; unless, of course, the very existence of the social and political order is at stake. The curtailment of civil liberties, for instance, may be accepted as necessary by the populace if the threat of violence is perceived to be intolerable and other countermeasures have proven fruitless or inadequate. But, if those qualifications have not been met, public support will likely be alienated by restrictive, repressive counterterror efforts.

The response must be calculated to preserve or even engender popular support while, at the same time, neutralizing the disruption of order and the challenge to authority. The importance of popular support cannot be overestimated. For that reason, the extent to which governments can define the conflict to protect their own bases of legitimacy and to deny or redirect the terrorists' counterclaims is crucial. Definition of the status of the terrorists, the validity of their grievances, and the relationship of the violence to government authority is the fundamental prerequisite to government action.

The competition is for the minds of men, the support or at least the acquiescence of the population. To the extent that the terrorists present a credible challenge to authority, the government must defend itself. The challenge must be eliminated or, at minimum, discredited. To the extent that the terrorist violence is not threatening to regime authority, the government must act to restore public order. Security and authority are critical to the maintenance of the state.

To meet the challenge, governments must assess the degree of threat. They must determine what the terrorists hope to gain and how capable they are, or might become, of realizing those objectives. At the same time, governments must consider their own vulnerabilities and the potential costs of unmitigated violence. The response choice should be tailored to the circumstances, premeditated to insure minimal interference with regime and social values and functions while reducing the incidence of and propensity for violent conflict. To that end, several courses of action may be taken, and it is to the choice of a response that we now turn.

CHAPTER IV
THEORIES OF CHOICE AND RESPONSE

After a government recognizes the potential for international terrorist activity, the selection of a policy to deal with the violence is a complex and controversial undertaking. The initial consideration is the government's jurisdictional responsibilities, including an evaluation of the government's relationships to the primary actors: the victims, the terrorists, and the targets of the violence. These factors define the government's involvement in the terrorist violence and provide the basic parameters for government action; namely, the need and the opportunity to respond.

The next step is an assessment of the threat that the terrorist activity represents to government authority, public order and regime legitimacy. This assessment is not an easy task because the perceptions of the threats offered by terrorist organizations vary considerably, even among the persons and governments most intimately involved in the violence. Indeed, the challenges to authority that the terrorists appear to be trying to communicate may differ significantly, even within the same organization, and may or may not be consistent with the terrorists' real objectives, their strengths, or their potentialities.

While the imperatives for government action may vary, depending on what the terrorists are seeking to achieve, the problems that authorities may encounter in their efforts to protect constituents, limit the impact of terrorist violence, and define the nature of the conflict will be greatly influenced by the domestic context of the violence and the government policymaking. The degree to which societies and regimes are vulnerable to terrorist attacks varies greatly. The ability of societies to absorb violence, to endure the uncertainty of terrorist campaigns and to accept the reality of casualties, without succumbing to the disruptive influence of the violence varies tremendously. Some societies are too unstable to permit even low levels of political violence, while others exhibit greater tolerance for violent behavior and greater resilience in the aftermath of crises.

Apart from those levels of sensitivity to and tolerance for terrorist activities among societies and regimes, there are distinct variations among governments in their capacities to regulate violent behavior. The variance is, at least in part, a function of the political, economic, military, and social resources available to the government. But, it is also a function of the government's ability to use its resources effectively, i.e., the sophistication of its administrative processes and its leadership, and the commitment of its constituents and leaders to the resolution of the conflict.

Domestic stability, resilience, tolerance, resources, commitment, administrative skills, and leadership, therefore, are crucial internal factors in the selection of a response to terrorist violence. Additionally, external variables such as the involvement of foreign governments in the conflict, the support or opposition given the terrorists and the government by international public opinion, and the stability of the international political order may impact the selection of a response. The importance of societal, regime, and international constraints on the selection of national policies is particularly evident in antiterrorist policymaking when the effects of the response, as well as the violence itself, may extend well beyond the boundaries of the responding state.[1]

Based on the multiplicity of constraints on policy choice dictated by societal and regime needs and international interests, the range of policy options available to the responding government may be severely limited. What is clear, nonetheless, is that the government, at minimum, must offer some resistance to the violence, although that resistance may be more verbal than physical. Unattended or uncontained violence is a threat to public order, even if the government sympathizes with the terrorists.

For purposes of clarity, it is also necessary to consider one possible policy alternative that is beyond the scope of this study. The focus here is on reactive policies or responses to terrorist activity, but there are two major approaches to political violence that governments can take. The first approach is the adoption of prophylactic measures to forestall the use of terrorist violence in domestic conflicts or to discourage the importation of violence by foreign terrorists. The second approach, the one that will be considered in this analysis, is the adoption of curative or palliative measures to eliminate or reduce the incidence and impact of terrorist violence once begun. In other words, governments can direct their attentions to either (1) the causes of terrorist activity and alleviate the conditions that give rise to such violence or dissuade potential terrorists from using violence within the government's jurisdiction or against its constituents or agents by supporting such an alleviation of conditions; or, (2) the violence itself and eliminate or minimize the damage and the challenge to authority. Each of the two approaches may be adopted simultaneously, but the distinction is important.

That distinction between the two approaches represents the essential disagreement that has characterized United Nations debate on how to deal with international terrorism on an international level. The Third World states generally support the adoption of measures to alleviate the conditions that precipitate international terrorist violence, and they perceive those conditions to be racism, colonial domination, and economic exploitation of Third World peoples by the industrialized states. The Western states, on the other hand, support the adoption of measures to outlaw international terrorist violence and, thereby, to facilitate national efforts to eliminate or reduce the incidence of terrorism.

Although it is beyond our focus, it is clear that the better course would be to preclude terrorist violence altogether, to alter the conditions that precipitate violent dissent. But, that could mean the use of repressive policies to suppress terrorist causes rather than a genuine alleviation of undesirable social, political, or economic conditions to preempt challenging causes. Moreover, some of the "causes" (in the sense of the antecedent conditions for political violence) may not be rectifiable. Quite apart from the possibilities that terrorism may be a product of psycho-medical disturbances, such as personality disorders, biochemical imbalances, diseases, drugs, or even fluctuations in barometric pressure,[2] there are many variables in the environments of individuals and collectivities that cannot be manipulated -- at least, not with any assurance that the manipulation will have its desired effect. Psycho-social and cultural variables, too, may be difficult to manipulate. The possible effects of such things as childrearing roles, generational conflicts, cultural predispositions to use violence ("warrior" cultures or extreme individualism) are not easily determined or modified.[3]

Although most subjective variables are difficult to isolate and control, there are possibilities that some may be amenable to change in order to reduce the likelihood of social and political violence. The impact of individual and collective alienation, boredom, senses of inefficacy, frustration, relative deprivation, nationalism, and desires for autonomy, for example, may be ameliorated by alterations in a society's objective social, political, and economic conditions and relationships.[4] Economic inequalities can be reduced, segregationist policies can be terminated, political participation can be expanded, educational opportunities can be made more nearly equal, ethnic minorities can be given greater autonomy, colonial peoples can be given independence, and so on. To some extent, these "causes" of terrorism can be mediated by social and political action.

The question, however, is whether the government responsible for the conditions is capable or willing to do so. The roots of terrorist, or potential terrorist, anger and frustration may not be factors that the government can realistically change. Intolerance (ethnic, religious, racial, or any other), overpopulation, economic development or underdevelopment, etc., are variables that even the most capable of governments have difficulty manipulating. Moreover, desires for complete independence or autonomy, just like challenging ideological orientations, will not be consistent with the values of the state or its most influential elites in most cases. And, if the government acquiesces to those desires, demands, it could mean the destruction of the state or, at minimum, revolutionary change.

Nevertheless, the aforementioned generalizations concerning the "causes" of terrorist violence do not mean that the government should not attempt to understand and correct problems, if to do so would not jeopardize the government's own existence and function and the social order. On the other hand, the generalizations do mean that the government may not be able to change the precipitating conditions for violence. That inability to change conditions may be due to a lack of control over particular phenomena or an unwillingness to disrupt the status quo by redistributing wealth, political power, social status, or some other value. In any case, whether the government decides to rectify problems that might generate political violence or to suppress them, it should recognize the potential for violence before it erupts.

Having failed to prevent the outbreak of political violence, governments have to turn their attentions to the management of the crises attendant with the violence. That is not to say, however, that the "causes" of terrorism can then be ignored. It still will be necessary to recognize the origins of the violence in order to deal with it effectively, albeit the violence itself will likely exacerbate the political conflict making it more difficult for the government to accommodate even legitimate terrorist demands.

Notwithstanding that complication, our next steps will be to consider (1) the range of response alternatives available to reactive governments, which will be ordered in a model of the system and process of terrorism and an elementary typology of direct response alternatives; (2) the major theories of how governments should respond to international terrorist violence; and (3) the primary domestic and international constraints on policy choice and the relationships among costs and benefits inherent in the selection of a response policy.

The Response Options

The obvious first step in the process of responding to international terrorist violence is the recognition of the need and the opportunity to respond. The next steps are to determine and implement an appropriate response, based on the responding government's affective orientation toward terrorist violence, its peculiar domestic and international circumstances, and an assessment of what the terrorists are attempting to achieve and how capable they are of realizing those objectives. Whether realistic or not, given the responding government's own unique social, political, and economic situation, incumbent authorities can react to terrorist violence (1) on several levels, (2) by several modes, and (3) with several media.

Levels of Response

The levels of response that governments will adopt will depend on which aspects of the violence that they are concerned with. They can react to the phenomenon of international terrorism, their potential involvement in terrorist events, the acts of violence themselves, the process of terrorism, and the content of terrorist challenges. Each of these aspects of international terrorism may be approached individually or concurrently.

Whether involved in international terrorist violence or not, governments can attempt to influence the operational environments of terrorist and responding governments in an altruistic fashion. That is, governments can engage in international dialogues and domestic debates and in the codification of conventions and resolutions that will proscribe, limit, facilitate, or encourage international terrorist activity. In doing so, the governments are afforded the opportunity to express their own definitions of (affective orientations toward) and willingness to tolerate such violence, as well as to elicit formally the same from the international community and its member states.

In terms of the governments' own self-interests, in anticipation of and preparation for their involvement in international terrorist events, incumbent authorities can attempt to manipulate the international and domestic context of the violence to their own advantage or to the advantage of those with whom they sympathize. Assuming that the affected government is disposed to offer resistance to terrorist actions or desires, such manipulation may consist of attempts (1) to precondition constituents and foreign publics and governments to deny the legitimacy of terrorist violence and to support the legitimacy of government actions; (2) to reduce the vulnerabilities of the society and regime; (3) to erect legal barriers to terrorist operations to facilitate the detection, apprehension, and punishment of terrorists; and, (4) to prepare the government's media of response (e.g., counter-terrorist forces, administrative and logistical support structures, and command and control agencies). Such manipulation may also include the encouragement of foreign governments to take the same precautions and to act to reduce the likelihood that terrorists will target diplomatic or commercial agents or facilities within their jurisdictions.

If the affected government supports or is sympathetic to the actions of particular terrorists or terrorists in general, the manipulation of the environment could be designed to facilitate terrorist activity. But, that would not eliminate the need to prepare for the potentiality of terrorist attacks within that government's own jurisdiction.

Once the violence has been perceived to be imminent or has begun, governments can focus on tactical operations to counter terrorist activity. They can act (1) to determine the nature and location of specific attacks before they occur (i.e., to gather intelligence), (2) to obstruct terrorist operations by securing likely targets, (3) to contain the violence within as small an area as possible, and (4) to resolve the crises as soon as possible. Responding only on the level of the acts themselves is essentially the same as responding to common criminal activities. In both cases, law enforcement agencies generally respond by attempting to anticipate, obstruct, contain, and resolve the crises with a minimum amount of damage and loss of life. The advantage of such mechanical, nonpolitical responses to violent events is that it permits the government to deny or, at least, to ignore the validity of the terrorists' (or criminals') motivations.

While responses to isolated and limited acts of violence can be relatively mechanical, responses to frequent or very intrusive violence cannot be so perfunctory. Such violence may signal problems potentially more dangerous than the violence itself, such as a credible challenge to regime authority. Countering campaigns of violence (like crime waves) requires much greater expenditures of government resources, greater attention to terrorist intentions and capabilities, and greater understanding of the process of terrorism.

It is necessary to recognize that terrorism cannot be prevented by physical security measures alone.

There are too many potential targets for terrorist violence, and the expense of securing more than a few of them would be prohibitive. Therefore, affected governments must anticipate the effects that the terrorists seek to achieve and act to limit the impact of the violence. Physical containment is one means of limiting its impact, but the containment of the threat that the terrorists are attempting to communicate is another. Government control or influence over the dissemination of information about the terrorists and their acts generally permits some manipulation of the communication process. Terrorism is, after all, a process of communication.[5]

Part of the task of containing the impact of terrorist violence is to counteract the content of the terrorist challenge, i.e., the terrorists' short- and long-term objectives. That requires an assessment of the social and regime values that might be contravened if the terrorists are successful.

To the extent that the terrorists' ideological goals are not inconsistent with the authority maintenance imperatives of the incumbent authorities, the government may find the conflict amenable to resolution by nonviolent means. If, however, the values of the terrorists and the regime are not compatible, peaceful resolution of the conflict becomes a less tenable option -- although a negotiated settlement may be necessary if the terrorists command significant popular support or show great potential for the elevation of the level of violence.

The terrorists' strategic objectives represent more immediate challenges to public order and regime legitimacy. The terrorist goals of gaining publicity and support; disrupting social, political, and economic interaction; punishing noncompliant civilians and government agents; provoking a government overreaction; eliminating instrumental targets; and, providing for their own organizational needs (e.g., discipline and logistical support) are more problematic. It is necessary for the government to act to obstruct, contain, and counteract the violence issued for those purposes, although the publicizing of the terrorists cause, in itself, may not pose an immediate danger to regime authority.

Similarly, acts of violence designed to secure the terrorists' short-term, tactical objectives do not pose immediate dangers to authority. The threats implicit in terrorist operations to gain ransom monies, the release of prisoners, supplies, the publication or broadcast of terrorist messages, or safe passage are only serious within the context of their contribution to the realization of the terrorists' larger objectives. Bombings, murders, arson, and other one-step acts of terrorism generally do not present immediate dangers, either.[6] That is not to say, however, that these acts should be dismissed as unimportant -- rather, it is to say that terrorists may achieve their lower level objectives without realizing their ideological ones or endangering the existence of the regime or the society against whom the violence is directed. Nonetheless, it is to be expected that governments will be more amenable to some of those lower level demands than they will be to others. Granting one or several terrorists safe passage out of the country, for instance, is not as serious a breach of government authority as freeing terrorists who have been imprisoned, rightly or wrongly, by the regime's judiciary processes.

It is clear that the preceding discussion does not cover all the possible actions that governments can take when faced with international terrorist events. The discussion, nonetheless, does illustrate the different levels of responses.

Modes of Response

While it is certainly conceivable for governments to ignore terrorist violence altogether, that is seldom a viable alternative. Even if the government sympathizes with or supports terrorists operating within its jurisdiction, at least a pretense must be made of offering resistance to the terrorist activity. That resistance may be to the violent acts themselves rather than to the process of terrorism or the content of the terrorists' challenge to authority, i.e., the terrorists objectives (apart from the tactical objectives of committing violence and escaping). Such resistance may be simply to contain the violence within a particular area to insure that it does not spread and that persons not otherwise involved in the conflict do not inadvertently wander into the zone of combat. The use of government troops by Uganda to seal off the Entebbe airport during that 1976 crisis, the use of revolutionary guards in Iran to seal off the American embassy during the 1979-1981 hostage crisis, and the use of Somalian troops during the Mogadishu skyjacking in 1977 to seal off that airport illustrate the lowest levels of resistance to international terrorism activity. In the first two cases, government support for the actions of the terrorists was indicated;[7] but, in the third case, the Somalian government used its troops to stabilize the situation and to isolate the violence and, then, deferred to the West German government's response.

In any case, the assumption being followed here is that governments will offer at least some resistance to international terrorist violence within their own jurisdictions based on their imperatives to maintain public order. That resistance may be (1) active, in the sense that the government will attempt to eliminate the terrorist activity, or (2) passive, in the sense that it will only seek to confine the violence to particular areas or targets. But, resistance will be offered nonetheless.

Theories of Choice and Response   133

The modes of action that responding governments may adopt, like the levels of response, frequently overlap and several may be subsumed in the general process of preparation for terrorist violence. Nevertheless, the range of strategic countermeasures from which governments will choose once international terrorist activity has begun or appears imminent can be categorized generally as efforts to prepare for, obstruct, contain, counteract, and answer terrorist threats.[8] The loci of these efforts are indicated in Figure 5, within the context of the system and process of terrorism.

First, Figure 5 illustrates the system and process of terrorism, including (a) the commission of the violent acts, (b) the communication of the threat to the target group, (c) the communication of the terrorist message to domestic and international audiences, (d) the communication of the threat to the government that ultimately will respond, and (e) the direct response, the feedback, from the government to the terrorists. Second, Figure 5 indicates the locations at which responding governments may interrupt and counteract the process of terrorism by means of (1) preparing for terrorist activity, (2) obstructing terrorist operations, (3) containing the physical impact of the violence, (4) containing the communication of the terrorist threat and propaganda message, (5) counteracting the propaganda content of the terrorist challenge, and (6) answering the specific demands of the terrorists.[9]

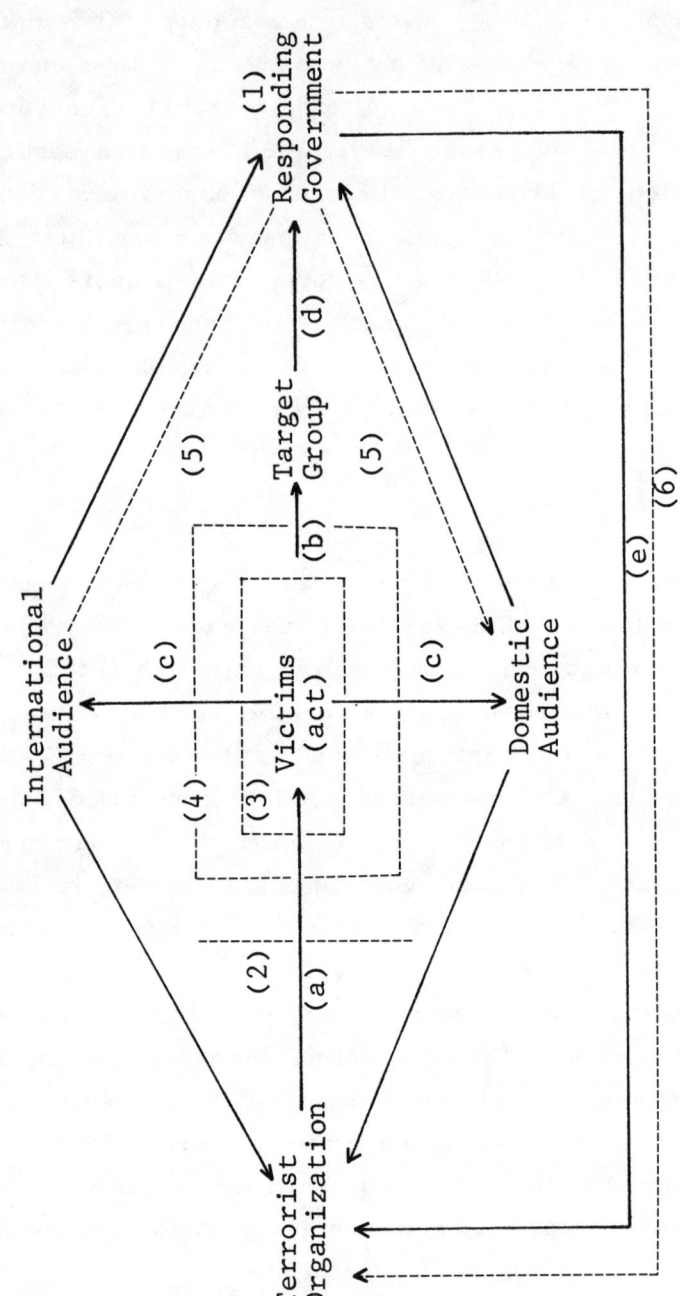

FIGURE 5: THE PROCESS OF TERRORISM AND THE LOCI OF GOVERNMENT ACTION

Key: ----- denotes government action
      ——— denotes the process of terrorism

Preparation

The strategies formulated, the precautions taken, the means of response designated or created, and the resources committed in anticipation of terrorist activity are generally predicated on intelligence data gathered from a variety of sources. Such sources may include direct observation,[10] the analysis of past terrorist events,[11] evaluations of known terrorist personalities,[12] studies of known terrorist organizations,[13] private citizens, cooperative governments,[14] terrorists who have been captured or have defected from their organizations, and surveillance or infiltration of actual or potential terrorist groups. By means of such information, authorities may be able to determine the credibility of terrorist threats;[15] when, where, and how terrorists are likely to strike; the vulnerabilities of terrorist organizations; and, the identities, locations, resources, objectives, sizes, etc., of terrorist groups. Information is the key to successful counterterrorist operations.[16]

Despite the crucial role of intelligence, complete information is not possible, even under the best of circumstances. Nevertheless, as the completeness of intelligence increases, the probability of an effective and appropriate response to terrorist violence improves. Response policies can be tailored more easily to the weaknesses of the terrorists and take fuller advantage of the strengths of the society and regime, if sufficient information is available. Response mechanisms can be in-place and operational. It may even be possible to apprehend terrorists before they commit their violence or, at minimum, to predict likely targets and strengthen their defenses. In other words, prior information permits a government to set its agenda of response, allowing it to focus its resources where and when they will do the most good to obstruct terrorist operations,[17] contain the impact of violence, counteract the content of terrorist threats and propaganda, and answer specific terrorist demands.

The question is how far governments should go in their intelligence gathering. Strother and Methvin have suggested that special grants of power should be made to law enforcement agencies responsible for antiterrorist operations. They conclude that:

> Ultimately . . . the only truly effective counter-weapon is intelligence. That means -- in the United States -- giving the F.B.I. the legal and scientific tools it needs, plus public understanding and support for their aggressive use. It means spies, networks of paid informers, wiretaps, bugs, computerized dossier systems -- the whole spectrum of clandestine warfare so necessary to the cause, yet so vulnerable to attack by civil-libertarian extremists.
>
> Congress should immediately authorize the F.B.I. to use wiretaps and bugs -- forbidden at present -- for anti-terrorist intelligence collection.[18]

Strother and Methvin went on to suggest that such intelligence gathering should be overseen by a bipartisan Congressional committee to prevent abuses of power by the F.B.I.[19] The potential and the temptation for authorities to employ extraordinary means and assume extraordinary powers will be a reoccurring theme throughout this section on policy choices. Repressive countermeasures often appear to be the easiest to implement and the most effective to use, particularly by governments that feel frustrated by their legal constraints or are prone to blame the constraints for their own ineffectuality in antiterrorist operations. In any case, the temptations to abridge civil liberties and to use extralegal means will be evident in the discussions of the other modes of response as well.

Obstruction

A wide variety of obstacles may be erected by governments to deter international terrorist activity within their jurisdictions. Although deterrence is not likely to be entirely successful, to some extent the terrorists can be denied the means of launching violent attacks and targets can be made less vulnerable to the attacks that do occur.[20]

Denial of means can be achieved by isolating the terrorists from their support structures (e.g., public support, potential recruits, supplies, weapons, and communication and transportation media) and by increasing pressure on the terrorist core group to reduce its remaining resources.[21] By definition, terrorist groups are relatively small and have limited resources. They are dependent on outside sources for their weapons and ammunition, supplies, food, and other logistical support. If a government can effectively control terrorist access to domestic munitions supplies and cut off terrorist support from outside of the country, the terrorist violence can be reduced substantially.[22]

Critical financial resources from and sanctuaries in foreign states can also be limited to some extent by cooperative agreements with the foreign states involved and by increasing border security. If the foreign government is not supportive of the terrorists and has the capacity to deny the terrorists their supply and escape routes and staging areas or is willing to let the target government employ preemptive strikes within its territory, terrorist resources can be further reduced.[23] If, however, the foreign government is not sympathetic to the target government's efforts, other measures may be used to induce its cooperation or to circumvent its refusal to cooperate. Sanctions can be levied against the uncooperative government or preemptive and punitive strikes against terrorist training and supply bases can be launched without the foreign governments' permission.[24]

The reduction of terrorists' material and personnel resources within the responding government's territory can be accomplished by several means. In the course of armed conflicts, ammunition and explosives, financial resources, food and medical supplies, and personnel are consumed, spent, or captured. Escape routes and sanctuaries are exposed and neutralized. Weapons are damaged and lost. These are resources that terrorist organizations can ill-afford to lose.

Aggressive government actions can hasten the attrition of terrorist resources. The evocation of emergency powers may be employed to facilitate law enforcement operations. The passage of the Northern Ireland (Emergency Provisions) Act in 1973, for example, enables the British army to conduct searches without a warrant, question suspects for up to four hours without having to justify their being detained, collect personal data on citizens at random ("P-tests"), and conduct "head-checks" to determine the whereabouts of possible terrorists. In 1974, the fruits of those efforts included the arrest of several high-ranking P.I.R.A. leaders, the detention of numerous other P.I.R.A. operatives, and the confiscation of 1260 guns and 26,120 pounds of explosives.[25] To varying degrees, the same sorts of counterterrorist operations may be used by other governments experiencing extensive terrorist activity.

Less controversial measures may be adopted to increase the defenses of potential targets. Strengthened law enforcement and security measures, with or without special grants of power to the agencies involved, can insure that the terrorists have to invest more of their resources in each operation and take greater risks in order to penetrate target defenses. Thus, the likelihood that more of the terrorists will be killed or captured will increase. Additionally, by increasing the certainty that the terrorists who escape will be apprehended, punished, and prevented from participating in further violence (or killed), the government can strain the personnel resources of the terrorist organization. Experienced, skilled, and dedicated terrorist operatives are hard to replace.[26]

To some extent, fugitive terrorists can be subdued by means of formal extradition arrangements or informal agreements with foreign governments, but in some cases target governments have resorted to clandestine abduction or assassination operations.[27] The latter course has been used by Israel to eliminate Palestinian terrorist leaders, as well as to seize Nazi war criminal Adolf Eichmann.[28]

While legal, moral, and ideological debates may question how far governments should go to impose sanctions on terrorists, the effectiveness of at least some of the counterterror measures is not disputed. There are still questions about the advisability of using capital punishment to preclude terrorist operations to secure the release of captured comrades, the ethics of using vigilante-type counterterrorist groups to track down and kill or capture known terrorists, and the potential dangers inherent in the evocation of emergency powers to facilitate law enforcement operations (to mention but a few of the most controversial measures that have been suggested).[29]

Much less controversy attends the task of reducing the vulnerabilities of potential targets, except when the freedom of movement or communication of the general public is lessened. Although all potential targets cannot be absolutely protected (or, indeed, identified),[30] the technology and expertise exists or is being developed to provide at least minimum security for a wide variety of potential targets. Sensors of numerous types, metal detectors, alarms, and other security devices,[31] including less exotic applications of commonplace security tools like closed circuit television cameras, are being utilized increasingly.

The apparent successes of antiterrorist precautions that have been employed at airports and in airliners suggests that security technology may reduce the likelihood of at least some types of terrorist operations. The redesigning of buildings and airplanes to obstruct terrorist operations, the positioning of guards and surveillance cameras, the implantation of security precautions are but one possibility for "hardening" potential targets. The other possibility is the implementation of psychological precautions, including making potential victims aware of the dangers that they may face and preparing them for the rigors of captivity and the opportunities for escape and evasion.[32]

The modification of procedures and routines may also reduce vulnerabilities, such as requiring that police work in groups if there is a chance that they might be attacked,[33] avoiding routines in daily activites that might facilitate terrorist kidnappings or murders, centralizing the living accommodations of diplomatic personnel to permit closer surveillance, and escorting potential targets between secure areas.[34] The range of possibilities is quite broad, limited only by the breadth of information concerning the types of violent attacks that may be expected, the weapons that may be used, the targets that may be chosen, and by the technology and imagination of the defenders.

Containment

Terrorism is essentially a two-step process, the first being the commission of the violence and the second being the communication of the terrorists' messages, i.e., the threats and the propaganda. Because it is a two-step process, it is necessary to contain both the physical damage and the message in order to limit its impact. Short of acts of mass destruction, the actual physical damage caused by the violence is generally less significant than are the social, economic, and political ramifications, i.e., the secondary effects.

In any case, the initial step is to contain the physical effects of the violence by (1) cordoning off the immediate areas of the event;[35] (2) evacuating civilians and nonessential personnel; (3) laying siege to any terrorists still within the area, disposing of unexploded bombs, or otherwise acting to prevent further destruction; (4) removing injured and dead civilians, government agents, and terrorists;[36] and, (5) at the conclusion of the event, restoring normal activity as soon as possible.[37] Containment of the physical effects is a fairly clear task, but containment of the secondary effects of the violence is more difficult and more important.

The "preeminent goal," according to Kupperman and Trent, "is to 'decouple' secondary effects from the primary incident."[38] That task is facilitated by the containment of the physical damage, but it also requires that the process of communication be interrupted (or counteracted) to lessen the shock value of the violence. This can be achieved by government actions to "blacken out" news reports of the events, censor reports to limit the information disclosed, issue false reports, supplement regular reporting with legitimate negative publicity about terrorist actions and intentions, or distort regular news reports with "black propaganda."[39] The news media can also be encouraged to exercise voluntary restraint in their reporting, individually or by means of some special media body.[40] The recognition of the need to do something to inhibit terrorist manipulation of the news media is evident from the number of journalists that are now expressing concern and suggesting controls.[41]

As well as controlling or influencing the dissemination of information about terrorist activities, governments can limit the psychological impact of the violence by promoting public confidence in the government's counterterrorist operations and reducing the public fear and uncertainty that accompanies the violence. The most direct means of increasing confidence and decreasing fear is for the government to demonstrate that it can provide a defense against terrorism or, at least, that it is winning the battle and is not weak or inept.[42] As stated by Samuel Huntington: "Whichever side can convince the target group that it is winning is in fact winning."[43] In other words, the government does not have to be winning; it has only to convince the public that it is. The claims of success must be credible, however.[44]

Very much related to the process of containing the psychological impact of terrorist violence is the process of counteracting the content of terrorist messages. The two processes are intertwined.

Counteraction

To counteract the content of terrorist challenges first requires that the responding government determine what the terrorists hope to gain by their violence. A strategy must be formulated then to contain, as much as possible, the projected threats and the propaganda messages and, then, to counteract what is not or cannot be contained.

Counteracting the terrorists' intimidatory messages necessarily entails reducing the credibility of their threats and is best served by providing sufficient security to reduce the violence to a tolerable level. Failing that, governments may attempt to deny their failures by claiming victories over the terrorists or denying the successes (or even the violent activities themselves) of the terrorists.[45] The objective, in any case, is to reassure the public. A large part of that task is to maintain a "business as usual" atmosphere, preserving the usual social, economic, and political routines and functions, as well as treating the terrorist violence in the same manner as common criminal activities as long as possible.[46]

One of the advantages of treating terrorists like common criminals is that it permits the government to deny the political nature of their violence. Indeed, to argue ideology or policy with the terrorists would imply recognition of their political motivations and, perhaps, acceptance of their political dissent,[47] As "criminals," terrorists have no claim to represent legitimate authority and, thus, they can be isolated from the general public more easily.[48] Their causes become irrelevant. Their violence alone defines their status as "outlaws."

To the extent that being branded "outlaw" may effectively discredit terrorist causes, governments may also attempt to manipulate the activities of terrorist groups to increase the likelihood that their domestic and foreign support will be alienated. One such possibility is the use of <u>agents provocateurs</u> to provoke the terrorists into counterproductive operations, such as stimulating less discriminant violence that will be more threatening to potential supporters.[49] If the government cannot infiltrate the group, government agents, vigilantes, or other terrorist groups may be used to commit violence and attribute it to the group being discredited. The most effective means of discrediting the group, however, may be to increase security efforts and law enforcement to make the terrorists more desperate and, thus, more careless.

Of course, terrorist groups with legitimate grievances are much more difficult to discredit. For that reason, governments may find it more expedient and efficacious to accommodate legitimate and compatible terrorist objectives. Ideally, this would involve divorcing the accommodation from the violence to deny that the terrorists precipitated the reforms. If the separation can be made effectively, it will make it more difficult for the terrorists to justify further violence.

However, many analysts deny the usefulness and efficacy of such accommodations, particularly if they can be perceived to have been enacted under duress. Those arguments can be illustrated better within the context of the function of answering terrorist demands.

<u>Answering</u>
The range of responses thus far considered have

involved government manipulations of the relationships among the primary actors, including the communication media and the audiences, and of the processes of terrorism. In the cases of hostage incidents and other incidents in which terrorist demands are articulated fairly clearly, the government is obliged to address directly the terrorists' objectives (usually their ideological or tactical objectives, rather than their strategic ones).

Under these circumstances, the terrorists state their demands and, generally, the price of noncompliance; and, the government reacts to the ultimatum. The range of possible responses is indicated in Figure 6.

FIGURE 6: AN ELEMENTARY TYPOLOGY OF DIRECT RESPONSES AND SOME VARIATIONS

Response	Variation
1. Compliance	Abdication of power Reform of Policy Tactical Concession
2. Negotiation	Partial Compliance Counteroffer (Delaying Tactic)
3. Noncompliance	Refusal to Negotiate Siege Armed Attack
4. "Nonresponse"	Deference to Another Government's Response Passive Containment

International terrorist incidents may complicate the

communication of demands and the governments' answers somewhat. In incidences of spillover terrorism the host government may simply serve as a conduit for the projection of terrorist demands and threats to the target government. Although the host state is not itself a party to the basic conflict, it can elect to respond or not to the terrorist demands. Inversely, external terrorism (against a government's constituents or property located in another state) requires that the injured state base its response on the opportunities afforded by the host state, i.e., cooperation or minimum interference. Integrated internal terrorism is generally handled by the host state, but here, too, the host may pass on the demands to the target government or the target may respond without the host state's cooperation.

In brief, the government that ultimately does respond has the options to (1) comply with the terrorists' demands, whether they require complete abdication of power or some lesser concession; (2) mitigate the demands through negotiation; (3) refuse to comply and to seek other means of resolving the crisis; or, (4) permit an outside agency or government to respond. Negotiation may also be used as a delaying tactic to permit the responding government to marshall its forces for a military action or to test the resolve of the terrorists before complying with their demands. In some cases, governments may feign compliance in order to catch the terrorists off-guard. Similarly, passive containment, "nonresponse," may be a means of delaying action until other options become practicable. In other words, a mixed strategy may be used.

Whether by preference or by necessity, governments will ultimately choose one or a combination of the responses in Figure 6 in order to resolve terrorist incidents and answer specific terrorist demands. The choice may be predetermined by policy commitments, such as the U.S.'s "no bargaining, no concessions" policy, or chosen on an ad hoc basis dependent on the terrorists involved, the types of acts or demands, the vagaries of government decision-making, or some other factors. In any case, there is no consensus on which response will be the most effective in the short- or long-terms in reducing the incidence of international terrorism, and government objectives may differ as well.

Media of Response

The processes of preparing for, obstructing, containing, counteracting, and answering terrorist challenges require governments to designate or establish agents to implement their responses. Generally, the first lines of defense and response are the law enforcement agencies that were developed to protect public order from common criminal disruptions. But, when the police agencies have been unable to cope with terrorist violence, the military has inherited part or all of the task of subduing the terrorists. Increasingly, however, governments are creating special task forces and antiterrorist units and developing specialized technology and tactics to counter persistent threats of both international and domestic terrorist violence. Moreover, in a few cases, governments are employing clandestine, extralegal antiterrorist forces. But, at present, traditional police and military forces, more functionally specific antiterrorist forces, and their coordinating, administrative, and logistical support structures are performing the tasks of counterterrorist response for most states.

There is still great variance in the response agents that have been established. Most states still rely heavily on their conventional police apparatuses. Indeed, many analysts conclude that antiterrorist operations are more properly within the purview of the police function,[50] principally because the police mission is more restrained[51] and the police are generally more imbedded in the civilian population than are the military.

When the police cannot maintain order, the military forces become the logical second line of defense. But, several analysts have expressed concerns that the military is ill-suited to the function of internal security, except as a last resort.[52] According to Wilkinson:

> There are very strong reasons why governments of liberal states should only employ troops for internal security purposes with the very greatest reluctance, and why

they should seek to withdraw them at the earliest opportunity. First, in any conflict of this scale it may be assumed that the belligerent faction or factions enjoy at least some support or sympathy in sections of the general population. Hence an unnecessarily high military profile may merely serve to escalate the level of violence by polarizing pro- and anti-government elements in the community. Second, internal security duties under the strict limits imposed in a constitutionalist liberal democratic system conflict fundamentally in many respects with the professional instincts, traditions and ethos of the military.[53]

Wilkinson went on to suggest that the military normally is not accustomed to situations where the enemy is indistinguishable from the general population, the enemy "soldiers" are supposed to be captured and tried (if possible) rather than killed, and the community may be hostile to the security forces. The danger of an overreaction would be greatly increased by the unfamiliar mission and environment and the temptation to resort to familiar tactics.[54] The temptation to use prior training and experience might also be stimulated by terrorists seeking to "militarize" the situation, to give more credence to their claims to be "soldiers" fighting a "war."[55]

Because of the disparities between law enforcement and military missions, more specialized agents of response are being created by many states. More than a dozen nations now have national antiterrorist forces and many local governments also have antiterrorist-type units, such as the S.W.A.T. teams that have become popular with American police departments.[56] The proliferation of such units has also provided opportunities for cooperation and cross-fertilization in antiterrorist operations. For example, the British Special Air Services (S.A.S.) regiment and the Israeli General Intelligence and Reconnaissance Unit 269 (that conducted the rescue at Entebbe) reportedly provided advice and assistance to the West Germany Border Protection Group 9 (G.S.G. 9) during the Mogadishu rescue in 1977.[57]

The development of antiterrorist technology and the creation of specialized units at national and local levels, as well as the demand for increased allocations of monies for those activities, have necessitated the growth of coordinating and control bureaucracies. The coordination of intelligence gathering and utilization, training, planning, and operations has made centralized decision-making essential, and the nature of the phenomenon of international terrorism has increased the demand for political input from national government leaders.[58]

In the U.S., for instance, the jurisdictional disputes that might arise from terrorist incidents make coordination necessary. As a consequence of that and other factors, the U.S. Security Council formed a special coordinating committee to act as liaison with the planning and operating agencies and other involved departments, including the State Department's Office for Combatting Terrorism (that has an ambassador-rank director), and created several command posts to monitor and direct operations. In 1978, President Carter also added the Federal Emergency Management Agency (through Reorganization Plan No. 3) to the program to assist in containing the physical impact of terrorist violence.[59] There have also been suggestions that the coordinating bodies arrange for cooperation and assistance from the news media, crucial participants in international terrorist events.[60]

It must also be mentioned that the official media of response may be supplemented or replaced by extralegal agents. Particularly when the regular police forces have failed to reduce the incidence of violence and when there are no other specialized antiterrorist forces available, governments may resort to using clandestine forces. For example, "death squads" have been employed or, at least, permitted to operate with little interference by the governments in Columbia, Guatemala, Brazil, Uruguay, Argentina, and the Dominican Republic to eliminate or intimidate opponents (some terrorist and some not) of those regimes.[61] Clandestine agents have also been used to eliminate terrorist personnel outside of the responding governments' jurisdictions. The encouragement or support of such counterterrorist operations is clearly an option for some governments, albeit a less common choice that the legally constituted media of response.

Apart from the possibility that governments may react to the phenomenon of international terrorism on the basis of a humanitarian desire to liberate genuinely oppressed peoples or to discourage the use of violence against innocent persons, the level of response that governments might adopt will be dependent on their perceptions of what regime and societal values and structures the terrorists threaten. Certainly human lives and property are threatened regardless of the other values that might be involved. A singular focus on the acts of violence themselves, emphasizing the need for security precautions to limit damage and casualties, might then be taken to be an implicitly low assessment of the terrorist challenge to authority. Similarly, evidence of great concern about the process of terrorism, particularly the containment of the communication of terrorist threats, might mean that the regime and/or society being attacked is perceived to be vulnerable to disruptive pressures, that they are institutionally weak. Moreover, an emphasis on the content of the terrorists' propaganda might indicate ideological or consensual weaknesses in the society-regime relationship. The preparations made in anticipation of or in response to international terrorist activity may reflect any or all of those concerns.

It is not likely, however, that the level of response chosen will be so clearly defined or so exclusive of all others. Variables other than the government's perceptions of value conflicts and systemic vulnerabilities also will have an impact on the foci of government response policies. Nevertheless, the determination of the level or levels of response that a government adopts may provide a valuable indicator of its perception of the threat to social and political order inherent in the terrorist activity.

The implementation of one or more of the first four modes of response (i.e., preparation for, obstruction, containment, and counteraction of terrorist challenges) will reflect varying degrees of repression. Governments may employ a diffuse strategy, whereby the terrorists' movement and communication are restricted by limiting the general movement and communication of large segments of the population, or a focused strategy, whereby restrictions are placed only on those segments of society that are most likely to be or to harbor terrorists. Each strategy may be based on applications of normal police powers, legally derived extensions of power (e.g., emergency, "state of siege," or martial law powers), or extralegally assumed powers. The imposition of the more repressive countermeasures is likely due to intolerably high levels of violence.

The decision to comply with, negotiate, or refuse to comply with terrorist demands may be predetermined by prior policy commitments or based on the responding government's perception of a specific terrorist event or terrorism in general. To some extent, the decision may be determined by the government's tolerance for terrorist violence, but it is primarily a reflection of the government's willingness to deal with any terrorists or a particular terrorist organization.

In implementing those measures and actions, the government can make use of regular law enforcement agencies, regular military forces, specialized police and/or military anti-terrorist units, and various bureaucratic decision-making and support structures, as well as clandestine agents. The degree of sophistication and complexity of the counterterrorism agencies will likely reflect the government's experience with terrorist violence and its assessment of the seriousness of the terrorist challenge.

In summary, then, the approaches that governments take, the methods that they adopt, and the agencies that they employ to resist international terrorist violence may vary widely. The configurations of a government response will be influenced by a multiplicity of factors, including the government's perception of, experience with, tolerance for, assessments of and apprehensions about terrorist activity. Policy will be shaped by the unique circumstances of the terrorist events and the context of the responding government's domestic and international environments and by the government's assumptions about the efficacy of general or specific modes and agents of response.

Theories of Response[62]

Even a cursory examination of the options available to governments in their efforts to resist international terrorist violence reveals that there is little consensus on the most effective means of combatting terrorist activity. That lack of consensus is readily apparent from the wide variety of actions and programs that governments have employed to counteract terrorism. Although resistance to international terrorism has taken many forms, the policy configurations do share some common elements. Each policy draws from a relatively narrow range of assumptions about the most effective means of deterring and combatting international and domestic terrorism.

First, however, it is necessary to reiterate briefly what is meant by an "effective" response. The previous formulations of response objectives have indicated that to protect public order and regime legitimacy governments should attempt to (1) provide security for their constituents, agents, and foreign nationals within their jurisdiction (and their property); (2) reduce the impact of terrorist violence to minimize interference with the normal processes of social, political, and economic interaction; and (3) define the nature and status of the terrorist challenge to regime authority.

In pursuing those objectives, governments implement policies and programs to increase the risks and the costs of terrorist activity and/or to deny terrorists the rewards and benefits that they seek. Both courses of action may be approached domestically or internationally and in differing ways and degrees, but the process of deterrence involves those basic elements. Because there is still much disagreement concerning the efficacy of the methods used to achieve each task, we will consider first the major views on how to increase terrorists' costs and risks ("deterrence by punishment") and, second, the views on how to deny terrorists' objectives ("deterrence by denial").[63]

1. Deterrence by Punishment

The creation of obstacles to violent activity, designed to increase the consumption of the terrorists' organizational resources and the likelihood that the terrorists will be killed or captured, is a primary element of deterrence. Such a plan of action raises serious questions, however, when it necessitates the implementation of extraordinary, repressive measures.

It is common for governments, when faced with intense or widespread violence, to resort to strong repressive measures to restore order.[64] Normally a government's first line of defense is its regular law enforcement and criminal justice system. Unless the violence is unusually intense or extensive, police forces generally are capable of responding adequately within the bounds permitted by their legal mandates. International and domestic terrorism, however, frequently overload the system, exceed the capacity of the police to respond within the law. In such a case, the government generally resorts to extraordinary means to control the violence. The assumption of emergency power, declarations of "states of siege" or marital law, and imposition of curfews are a few illustrations of extraordinary responses. Other governments have resorted to extralegal agents and methods of response, i.e., "state terrorism," to counteract terrorist violence. In short, governments' antiterrorist responses may be derived from legally constituted authority (including special grants of power) or from extralegally assumed powers.

Throughout the literature on domestic and international terrorism there are expressions of concern about and injunctions against overreactions to terrorist violence. The resort to extralegal, diffuse or focused, repression is viewed as counterproductive in terms of its real value as a deterrent to terrorism[65] and as dangerous to the institutions and freedoms that it is supposed to protect. The lesson of Uruguay has not been lost on most analysts, officials, and commentators.

Just the same, it is extremely difficult to determine just how much repression is necessary in particular circumstances. Analysts do admit that at least an initial recourse to repressive counterterrorist operations may be necessary, but it should be selective, focused, rather than diffuse.[66] Popular support for the authorities may be jeopardized by the use of seemingly indiscriminate repression. Indeed, that might be exactly what the terrorists hope will happen.[67]

If the government has already lost popular support or maintains its authority through high levels of coercion already, the situation is different. Broad applications of government intimidation and more intrusive social control measures may be advisable. Anthony Burton, for example, has concluded that "[i]n countries where there are few civil liberties their suspension in the face of terrorism is necessary if the government is to survive . . . and failure to act ruthlessly would lead inevitably to further outbreaks."[68] Similarly, Harry Eckstein has determined that repression is more effective in preventing widespread violence in the least democratic societies, ones which probably have greater capacity for coercion than liberal democratic societies.[69]

In general terms, the use of repressive countermeasures by regimes, pluralistic or otherwise, needs to be commensurate with the dangers that the measures are supposed to overcome. According to Eckstein:

> Repression can be a two-edged sword. Unless it is based upon extremely good intelligence and unless its application is sensible,

ruthless, and continuous, its effect may be quite opposite to those intended. Incompetent repression leads to a combination of disaffection and contempt for the elite. Also, repression may only make the enemies of the regime more competent in the arts of conspiracy . . .

. . . Repression is of course least likely to prevent internal war in societies which, unlike totalitarian regimes, have a low capacity for coercion. In such societies, adjustive and diversionary mechanisms seem to check revolutionary potential far better. Indeed they may in any society.[70]

It must be noted, however, that international terrorism seldom offers the same degree of challenge to government authority that domestic terrorism does. As a consequence, the imposition of broadly repressive antiterrorist measures would be less justifiable and, probably, less effective. It is more likely that governments will be tempted to employ more selective coercion, aiming at the most likely supporters and sanctuaries of terrorists. To the extent that normal law enforcement agencies cannot cope with the violence, repression of international terrorist activity may manifest itself as abridgements of the civil rights of apprehended or suspected terrorists and their supporters;[71] extralegal extensions of government power to apprehend and punish suspected terrorists (e.g., kidnappings, killings, and lesser intimidation of suspects by government agents or tacitly approved vigilante organizations); or, illegal surveillance and harrassment of potential terrorists or terrorist supporters.[72]

The potential for the abuse of government authority when officials are permitted or assume extraordinary powers raises basic questions about how far governments should go in their efforts to protect public order and regime and societal values. The relatively low levels of violence associated with international terrorism would not seem to justify high levels of government coercion, unless the violence is sustained at high levels or over a prolonged period of time, such as in Northern Ireland and Israel.

In terms of "theories" of response that can be extrapolated from the preceding discussion of repression, there are several. The major view is that reliance on normal, but aggressive, law enforcement and criminal justice procedures should be the preferred course of action, but that extraordinary (but legally derived) structures and procedures should be implemented if normal processes fail. No government has openly chosen, nor do reputable analysts suggest, the use of extralegal agents or methods. The appropriate response, based on the majority view, would depend on the dangers perceived in the violence. The choice of means, including extralegal, would be greatly affected by the inherent coerciveness (repressiveness) of the government's "normal" law enforcement processes. In essence, then, the use of extraordinary repressive countermeasures by responding governments may be deemed necessary if the level of violence is intolerable or if such coercion is not entirely alien to the society and regime involved. The major question, however, is at what point does the cure become worse than the disease.

The other "theories" that can be identified in the domestic repression context involve more specific techniques of response, such as the deterrent effect of the death penalty (including the value of public hangings and beheadings that have been used in the Middle East to eliminate terrorists), the efficacy of gun control laws in limiting terrorist access to weapons, the effectiveness of stricter immigration and visa requirements to restrict the movement of terrorists across borders, and so on.

As a substitute for or supplement to these domestic measures, governments may also seek international commitments and responses. Because international terrorism has become so widespread and terrorist organizations have developed international links and support structures, many view the violence as fundamentally an international problem -- a "common danger" -- requiring international or, at minimum, regional action. The proponents of this view argue that international terrorism should be recognized as an international crime and each terrorist as <u>hostis generis</u>

humani (an enemy of humanity).[73] Given that recognition, the United Nations or some other international body could appropriately act to discourage support for international terrorist organizations, including the application of sanctions against states that support terrorist activities.

To insure compliance with an international mandate to refrain from supporting and to eliminate terrorist activities, state jurisdictions and responsibilities would have to be clarified and broadened.[74] Apprehension of terrorists would be the responsibility of every state and punishment would be meted out by an international criminal court,[75] the state whose nationals or property were victimized, the state having jurisdiction over the location of the violence, or any state exercising its responsibility to apprehend the terrorists (universal jurisdiction). Extradition or punishment of the terrorists would be viewed as a responsibility of every state under the principle of aut punire aut dedere.[76]

Some commentators go so far as to suggest that an international police force be organized to respond to international hostage incidents in much the same way as the Israeli force did at Entebbe.[77] That suggestion, however, apparently finds little support among most analysts because few consider an international force to be a realistic alternative.

The preceding synthesis of major views on how the international community could respond collectively to international terrorism illustrates the response choice preferred by many analysts, particularly those having an international law-perspective of the issue. However, a more pessimistic view is shared by many other analysts. They find that, despite the limited successes to-date in reaching an international consensus on the need to protect particularly vulnerable terrorist targets (e.g., airline flights and diplomatic personnel[78]). This middle-range approach puts greater emphasis on the efficacy of bilateral and more limited international agreements to secure the extradition and punishment of terrorists[79] and on the feasibility of international commitments to protect specific targets. Sanctions against uncooperative states would be more limited, relying primarily on reductions in diplomatic contacts, tightened immigration laws, economic boycotts, and other nonviolent protestations,[80] but also permitting self-help actions under the provisions of Article 51 (self-defense) of the United Nations Charter to resolved terrorist crises.[81]

This approach places the burden of response on the target government while, at the same time, encouraging the pursuit of international consensus and support to supplement the responding government's own antiterrorist actions.

The primary "theories" of "deterrence by punishment," then, are based on: (1) a sliding scale of domestic repression, dependent on the perceived seriousness of the threat to government authority and the government's coercive capacity and experience, to obstruct terrorist operations; (2) a reliance on international sanctions against terrorists and supporting states to discourage the use of violence; and, (3) a mixed strategy of government repression supplemented by bilateral, regional, and international cooperation when practicable. All three include the implementation of general security measures within the state to reduce the vulnerabilities of potential terrorist targets and the mobilization of internal security agencies to contain the violence and resolve the crises.

2. Deterrence by Denial

Effective security, apprehension, and punishment may serve to deny the terrorists the benefits that they seek by making those benefits too costly for the terrorist organization to afford. However, governments may also adjust the other side of the equation as well. If terrorists can be effectively denied the objectives of their violence, the violence itself may become much more difficult to justify and support. The idea that terrorist violence must produce results or it will dissipate has been considered earlier.

To the extent that the benefits sought by the terrorists include disruption of the social, economic, and political life of the target state, the containment of the physical impact of the violence can deny the terrorists at least a portion of their goals. But, the containment (denial) of the projected threats and propaganda messages can severely curtail terrorist effectiveness. To that end, many analysts suggest that the news media be restrained, voluntarily or involuntarily. One method suggested is to create a mass media council, made up of media executives, to determine when and what information should be withheld (temporarily) to prevent interference with government antiterrorist operations.[82] That and similar suggestions indicate a concern about restraining the media as a short-term, tactical maneuver, but there are also concerns about the long-term effects of unrestrained media coverage, the "amplification effect" as Neil Hickey calls it,[83] which gives the violence publicity disproportionate to its real importance. Relatively low-level violence is sensationalized in the media. Part of the problem is that the press often do not witness the terrorist violence itself, only the police response; thus, the police may be depicted in a worse light than are the terrorists.[84] As a consequence of this and other difficulties that are caused or exacerbated by the free publicity accorded terrorists by the media, experts have suggested that the media minimize the "how-to" information in their reports, omit or downplay the names of the terrorist groups, restrict "live" coverage of hostage events, give "proper emphasis to the inhuman and barbarous aspects" of the violence (do not glamourize it), have no interviews with terrorist leaders, give air time appropriate to the importance of the events, emphasize the low success rate, and make a policy of airing dissident views to preempt terrorist causes.[85]

These suggestions, to varying degrees, reflect concerns among journalists and officials about the role of the media in international terrorist violence and the impact of the media on the long-term success or failure of the governments to eliminate the threat. The suggestions may also reflect a concern that, if the media do not restrain themselves, the governments will.[86]

Control of the media or, at least, manipulation of the news is one "theory" of how to interrupt the process of terrorism and deny terrorists the benefits, the publicity, they seek. A more direct denial of benefits can be evidenced in government responses to specific terrorist demands.

When presented with terrorist demands, governments have the option to comply, seek a negotiated settlement, refuse to comply, or decline to respond to the demands. It is generally not suggested that governments comply with terrorist demands without attempting to mediate the demands through negotiation, nor is it suggested that governments not respond to the violence. The major views, "theories," presently receiving the most support among analysts and governments revolve around the question of whether governments should negotiate and bargain with terrorists or whether they should refuse.

Proponents of the "no bargaining-no concessions" policy, including officials of the U.S. government, advise that capitulating to terrorist demands will increase their expectations of success and will only lead to more and greater demands. Moreover, they argue, concessions undermine the authority of the state. Paul Wilkinson has concluded that, "nothing so rapidly undermines the authority and power of a constitutional government as an apparent readiness to treat and bargain with those who have openly abused the constitution."[87] Wilkinson also warned that the assumption that negotiation can result in a viable solution when revolutionary terrorists are involved is dangerous and that governments should not confuse the terrorists' "short-term tactical demands for their strategic objectives" because the latter are not negotiable.[88]

In terms of dealing with the terrorists' tactical demands during the course of a bargaining situation (i.e., a hijacking, skyjacking, kidnapping, or hostage-barricade situation), the tactical options of the responding government that adheres to a "no concessions" policy are to use force (e.g., direct assault, sharpshooters, or chemical agents) or a siege technique to resolve the crisis. Some success has been achieved with a "freezing out" technique used in recent years in Holland, Ireland, and England.[89] The procedure is to surround the site (containing the violence physically), send in food to the hostages and terrorists, and wait for the terrorists to give up or for an opportunity to use force with minimum casualties.

Since the Entebbe rescue, there also has been a decided tendency for governments to resort to the use of force outside of their borders, as evidenced by the successful West German action at Mogadishu and the ill-fated Egyptian action in Cyprus and U.S. action in Iran.[90]

Whatever the tactical measures taken, the view that terrorism can best be combatted by means of a firm "no concessions" policy is presently the guiding force behind the antiterrorism policies of at least two states, the U.S. and Israel. The U.S. position was expressed by former Secretary of State Henry Kissinger in a Vail, Colorado, speech in August of 1975. Kissinger stated that:

> The problem that arises in the case of terrorist attacks on Americans has to be seen not only in relation to the individual case but in relation to the thousands of Americans who are in jeopardy all over the world. In every individual case, the overwhelming temptation is to go along with what is being asked.
>
> On the other hand, if terrorist groups get the impression that they can force a negotiation with the United States and an acquiescence in their demands, then we may save lives in one place at the risk of hundreds of lives everywhere else.

Therefore it is our policy . . . that American Ambassadors and American officials not participate in negotiations on the release of victims of terrorists and that terrorists know that the United States will not participate in the payment of ransom and in the negotiation for it.[91]

It must also be noted that several analysts have expressed concerns that the "no concessions" approach will become untenable if a government is faced with a credible threat of mass destruction or some other exceptional threat.[92]

To other analysts, officials, and commentators, the reliance on a "hardline" approach seems callous or, in some cases, a sign that the government is helpless. The major argument for a more flexible policy toward terrorist demands, however, is that flexibility affords a responding government more alternative actions to resolve individual crises with minimum losses of life.[93] Generally, the core of this argument is that hostage negotiations have been successful, particularly those conducted by the New York City Police Department's Hostage Negotiating Team. The Bolz-Schlossberg technique used by the N.Y.C.P.D. team involves the stabilization of the situation (containment of the violence), calming the hostage-takers, and, then, increasing pressure on the hostage-takers to convince them to give up.[94] The process involves a support group of psychologists to evaluate the state of mind, the resolve, and the vulnerabilities of the hostage-takers to facilitate response. It is not assumed that this type of negotiation will always prevent casualties, however.[95]

Negotiation is also used as a delaying tactic to permit the police forces to evaluate alternative responses on the basis of the information gathered during the initial stages of the seige. While concessions do not necessarily follow from the negotiations, "tactical" concessions may be made to insure the safety of the hostages without greatly increasing the prestige or bargaining position of the terrorist group.[96]

The major "theories" of "deterrence by denial," then, involve the containment of terrorist threats and messages and the answering of terrorist demands. The interruption of the communication process is controversial in the sense that it would necessarily involve the restriction or manipulation of press freedoms; and, the response to specific demands is controversial in the sense that there are differing opinions as to the efficacy of "hard-line" policy commitments as well as more flexible approaches.

The "theories of response" identified in the preceding discussions by no means exhaust the views concerning which responses are the most effective in combatting international terrorism in the short- or long-term. Nonetheless, they do illustrate the major approaches to antiterrorist resistance: implementation of repressive domestic measures to reduce opportunities for terrorists to commit violent acts; pursuit of an international consensus against the phenomenon of international terrorism and assistance in combatting it; interruption of the communication of terrorist threats and propaganda to reduce their impact and effectiveness; and, direct responses to the content of terrorist challenges (their ideological and tactical objectives).

Policy Constraints and the Value Dilemma: A Summation

Throughout the preceding discussions there have been references to the constraints on government policy choice and the value dilemmas inherent in policy selection. It is apparent that international terrorism presents special difficulties to responding governments, particularly when the choice of responses involves a valuation of the immediate effects of the violence on the lives of hostages and potential victims and the long-term effects of the violence on the society and regime.

The configurations of government response policies and programs are dependent on the unique circumstances of the society and regime in which they are made. The levels of response assumed, the modes adopted, and the media employed will be determined by the resources and freedom of action afforded by the responding government's domestic and international environments, as will the more specific antiterrorist measures implemented. All governments do not have the same capabilities. Influences differ. Orientations change and may or may not be realistic given the dangers inherent in the terrorist violence.

It is not possible to identify all the constraints on policy choice, but it is likely that the impacts of a responding government's social, economic, military, and political resources are crucial factors in policy choice. The available resources have a tremendous impact on government abilities to cope with domestic and international political violence, but the determining factor in response effectiveness is the regime's ability to utilize its resources. That ability will be tremendously affected by the authorities' experience with terrorist and other disruptive crises, leadership skills,[97] administrative abilities,[98] and capacities to apply coercive countermeasures in critical situations.[99]

The methods adopted, such as intelligence gathering and restrictions on public movement, and the media used will also be constrained by the legal restrictions placed on government exercises of authority. The rights and freedoms accorded all citizens will also impact the government's freedom of action, limiting policy choice. Repressive techniques that are available to an authoritarian regime are not available to a liberal democratic regime in all cases.

Similarly, the policy commitments of the regime vis-a-vis terrorist violence will constrain policy choice. The "no negotiation-no concession" policy stance taken by the U.S. and Israel, for example, will limit response alternatives. Even when a compromising position is taken, the prior policy commitment may inhibit flexibility. For example, Israel decided to offer concessions to terrorists when a large group of children (and some adults) were taken hostage at Maalot in May of 1974. But, the agents and techniques of negotiation were so underdeveloped that the adjustment in policy did not work. As a consequence, twenty-nine persons were killed, including twenty-one children and three terrorists.[100] Policy commitments, the training of personnel, planning, and all the other preparations made prior to action are based on assumptions about the contingencies that may arise. When the contingencies are different from expectations, problems arise.[101]

Interest group pressures, too, may restrict the choice of responses. Certainly the segments of society that benefit from the maintenance of the status quo, and those most vulnerable to the terrorist attacks will attempt to influence the decision-making process.[102] The American Foreign Service Association's Committee on Extraordinary Dangers, for instance, has influenced the U.S. State Department and Congress to invest more money and planning in the security of diplomatic facilities.[103]

Public opinion also has to be considered in terms of its impact on decision-makers and on the context of the violent activity. The force of public outrage and frustration may precipitate actions, particularly if the officials that are responsible for formulating responses feel pressure to follow popular preference.[104] More importantly perhaps, the tolerance, or intolerance, of societies for political violence has had a tremendous impact on how governments (and, indeed, terrorist groups) have responded. Tolerance of terrorism and "permissive" societies have been blamed for the failure of national and international antiterrorist efforts.[105] In fact, the high level of tolerance for terrorist violence perceived by many analysts has been blamed for causing terrorism. Sympathy for national liberation movements,[106] historical traditions of revolutionary development,[107] and the contemporary "fashion" of rebellion[108] have all been cited as reasons for the tolerant attitudes toward terrorism. Antiterrorist policymaking has undoubtedly been affected by that general climate of tolerance.

Similarly, the high levels of tolerance for terrorist violence within the international community has greatly affected national efforts to find a general solution to the terrorism dilemma. There has been some evidence that the tolerance is decreasing, such as the assistance given West Germany in 1978 to apprehend terrorists in Bulgaria and Yugoslavia, but there are still several regimes that routinely give aid and sanctuary to terrorists.[109] Moreover, the failure to reach a general consensus on what is to be done to combat terrorism has limited the number and value of international agreements and conventions to limit or eliminate international terrorism.[110]

As well as the international climate of tolerance which has perpetuated the support and sanctuary given violent pretenders to power, responding governments have had to wrestle with the difficulties and constraints engendered by jurisdiction problems, foreign involvements in internal conflicts, pressure from international organizations and interest groups, and the responding government's own status perceptions and imperatives.

International law does not provide clear guidelines for government responses that extend beyond national boundaries. The Israeli rescue at Entebbe, for example, has raised considerable controversy concerning the applications of Article 51 of the U.N. Charter and the principle of "protective jurisdiction" (i.e., the assumption of jurisdiction over crimes and persons outside of the state when the acts are directed against the security, territorial integrity, or political independence of the responding state).[111] Even if a government decides that it can justifiably respond to external violence, there are constraints on its freedom to act. The logistical and tactical constraints have been noted earlier and so have the political necessities to seek the cooperation of foreign states close to the events or persons. Other constraints might include fear of exacerbating already strained relations with the other states in the region, fear of being criticized for "attacking" a weaker state,[112] or fear of failure and the resultant loss of prestige.

Those problems and constraints become much more complex when the government having jurisdiction over the acts or persons sympathize with the terrorists or when there are other governments involved. The political context in which the response is made will not only affect the action's mechanics, but it will also affect its probability of success.

As well as constraints that may restrict aggressive action, there may be strong international pressures to act forcefully rather than nonviolently to resolve terrorist crises. Attacks on foreign nationals and property, in particular, may result in strong pressures from the affected government to deal harshly with the terrorists or to give greater consideration to the lives of hostages (i.e., pay ransoms or issue other compromises to secure hostage releases).[113] In some cases, pressures may be brought to bear by international interest groups rather than governments. The recently enacted anti-skyjacking conventions, for example, were due in large measure to the pressures of the International Federation of Airline Pilots Associations and its threats to terminate air service until strong actions were taken.[114]

Finally, the status perceptions of the responding government itself may have a decisive impact on the response chosen. Desires to defend national honor, to reassert the authority of the state, or to salve wounded pride may have a great impact on decision-making. Frederick Hacker, for example, concludes that:

> Self-righteous impatience, national pride, and curiously archaic concepts of courage often have greater influence on decision making (or drift into violence because it comes naturally) than concern for the preservation of human lives.[115]

Hacker feels that greater emphasis should be put on the safety of hostages and other potential victims, rather than on the immediate punishment of the terrorists. Whether his view is right or wrong, there is probably some truth in his statement. The phenomenon of terrorism elicits a variety of responses. Indeed, the terrorists may hope for an irrational and violent reaction, rather than sympathy. To remain objective about the violence, to eliminate the pressures of pride and senses of honor, or to resist the temptation to react emotionally may be an impossibility.

J.K. Zwodney suggests that the violence is antithetical to the Judaic-Christian tradition and contrary to the American "code of manly conduct" which is more sympathetic to violence committed in self-defense and face-to-face.[116] Therefore, Americans would be more inclined to react emotionally. In fact, the U.S. is one of the relatively few countries that refuses to negotiate with terrorists (or, at least, has a public commitment not to negotiate). Brian Crozier, too, has suggested that the tolerance with which terrorist activites are received in the Western states is a sign of the moral crisis in the West and that the tolerance is a kind of "intellectual pacifism." Crozier's political orientation is amply clear in his suggestions that the Western countries need a "moral reconstruction" and a return to some kind of a "public philosophy," as well as a less tolerant attitude toward challenging ideologies and philosophies.[117]

The question that is important here is not whether one or another of those views is more valid, rather it is which view is guiding the decision makers in their selection of a response policy. It is obvious from the contrasting positions taken by Hacker and Crozier that the attitudes and prejudices of the decision-makers are very important variables and will be constraints on policy choice.

The choice of a response policy is a value-laden endeavor. Aside from the imperatives to maintain public order and regime authority, which are based on the value judgment that violence (including political violence) is abnormal and to be avoided when possible, governments are faced with several major value dilemmas.

International and domestic terrorism present long- and short-term challenges and policy dilemmas. Target governments have to consider the ultimate (ideological) objectives of the terrorists and the challenge that those objectives (countervalues) represent to regime and societal objectives (values). The questions that have to be answered are whether the countervalues are incompatible with the values that the government is defending and whether a satisfactory accommodation can be made or should be made. As a rule, governments have a commitment to the values that underlie their social and political processes and institutions and, thus, are not willing to seek accommodations unless the costs of maintaining those values threaten to jeopardize the existence of the state or regime. In other words, if the costs (e.g., the deaths, the damage, and the disruption) exacted by the terrorists and by the antiterrorist policies and programs outweigh the benefits derived from the maintenance of those values challenged by the terrorists, accommodation may be advisable, otherwise it is not. That determination identifies the need to resist terrorist violence.

When terrorist activity is particularly intense or extensive, the responding government has to decide whether it is worth it to sacrifice a portion of its values, e.g., individual freedoms or economic resources, in order to reduce the violence. It is a cost-benefit trade-off. It is also possible that the costs can be manipulated by means of such measures as decreasing the vulnerabilities of particularly sensitive targets (obstruction) or increasing the likelihood that damage can be limited (containment). Similarly, the benefits can be increased if the government has even more to gain than the reduction of violence, such as the deterrent effect that successful antiterrorist operations may have on other potential challengers.

The value that has not been factored in completely, in this discussion, is that of human life. At what point does the value of human life supercede the other values that are involved in a particular terrorist event or campaign? This value dilemma is most clear in the context of a terrorist hostage situation when the demands of the terrorists are weighed against the lives of the hostages.

Responses to terrorist events, international and domestic, are predicated on the value choices being made by the responsible officials and the terrorists involved. Each party to the conflict has to make choices involving the lives of hostages or other victims. Each has to determine what sacrifices are worth making in order to realize the benefits being sought or protected. Because the focus here is on the choices being made by governments in response to international terrorism, it is necessary to consider the major hypotheses generated in the preceding discussions concerning the optimal value choices. Those hypotheses and an empirical measurement of some of the costs of government response (i.e., hostage lives) will be the subject of the next chapter.

CHAPTER V
INTERNATIONAL HOSTAGE INCIDENTS

What has been manifest in the discussions of the nature and the challenge of international terrorism and the response perspectives and options that governments may adopt is that a plethora of perceptual and situational variables may influence response policy choice. Throughout the discussions, it has been suggested that the degree of threat that international terrorist events present to the governments involved in the violence is dependent on the extent to which the attacks approximate the challenges of domestic terrorism (i.e., whether the attacks challenge regime authority and legitimacy as well as public order). It was further suggested that the perceptions of the challenges inherent in each terrorist event and the response imperatives will be or can be different for each government involved in the violence. Consequently, each government may react differently to the same event. The typology of international terrorist events was predicated on those differences in government involvement.

At this juncture, the analysis will examine more closely the impact of government involvement in terrorist events on response policy choice. In addition, the analysis will consider the impacts of terrorist demands on response choice and test some of the propositions that were posited earlier concerning the relationships between demands and challenges to authority. The final part of the analysis will focus on the immediate impact of policy choice and will examine the direct relationship between policy choice and one indicator of policy impact and the extent to which response policies mitigate the impacts of government involvement and terrorist demands on that same indicator. International hostage incidents will provide the context for the analysis and hostage safety will be the most visible and immediate indicator of policy impact.

The measurement of policy impact that is to be undertaken here is admittedly very limited. To some extent, the possible impacts of several policy choices have already been considered. For example, the short-term efficacy of repressive countermeasures such as detention of suspected terrorists in inhibiting terrorist activity and the long-term potentials for repression and media regulation to subvert democratic processes have been noted. The impacts of policy choice, however, may be much more complex. Some consequences will be consistent with the intent of the policymakers and some, like abuses of governmental power, will not.[1] For example, the restriction of public and private communications within those segments of the population in which terrorists are most likely to seek support or anonymity may be an effective short-term obstacle to terrorist activity. But, such restrictions, especially if prolonged or severe, can create an atmosphere of public distrust and secrecy that will facilitate terrorist activity and inhibit antiterrorist operations in the long-term. Fear of the police may replace fear of the terrorists and, thus, support for the terrorists may increase. Similarly, controls and regulations designed to obstruct the flow of foreign financial and material assistance to terrorists may also interfere with domestic commercial operations. Moreover, if legal restrictions are placed on the importation of materials useful to the terrorists, such supply channels may be replaced by more clandestine sources of supply that will be less vulnerable to government interruption. Legal restrictions may have to be supplemented with physical obstructions which, in turn, may have to be reinforced by even more restrictions. In short, the diffused impact of antiterrorist policies may create problems that will cancel out the intended benefits of the policies.[2] As a result of the ripple-effect of policy consequences, the selection of a response policy requires careful consideration of the situational variables that may amplify or neutralize intended policy impacts.

Due to the dilation and contraction of policy consequences, the complete determination (and ultimate prediction) of policy impacts is generally an unmanageable task.[3] Nonetheless, it is feasible to evaluate some of the major influences on policy choice. Those two tasks will be the focus of the analysis to follow. It is not expected that the analysis will lead to the construction of concrete predictors of policy choice or strong measures of policy impact. However, it is hoped that the relationships are sufficiently strong to warrant further inquiry along similar lines and that the typology of international terrorist events, in particular, can demonstrate sufficient explanatory power to justify its being included in a much more complex multivariate model of policy choice.

The data that will be utilized in the analysis were drawn from international hostage events that occurred during the ten-year period from 1968 to 1977 and include those kidnappings, hijackings, and barricade and hostage incidents in which hostages were successfully taken and demands were made by the terrorists as a precondition for their release.

Hostage Incidents and International Terrorist Violence

The selection of hostage incidents as the context for the evaluation of the typologies of international terrorism and direct response options created earlier and the consideration of policy impacts was based on three primary attributes of international hostage events, as well as the general consensus that at least some forms of terrorist hostage-taking can properly be considered international terrorism. The first reason for the selection is that hostage events afford responding governments greater opportunity to react directly and deliberately to terrorist demands than do less prolonged and dramatic events, such as bombings, in which governments simply react to <u>faits accomplis</u>.[4] The second reason is that terrorist demands and government responses are generally more public when the violence involves the taking of hostages (and, thus, there is more public information available).[5] The third reason is that the taking of hostages presents a more pronounced value dilemma for responding governments than do threats to property or to less-defined victims. The question of the consensus, however, will require some qualification.

It has been noted earlier that skyjackings committed solely for the purpose of securing political asylum cannot be considered international terrorism by most definitions. There is also some question as to whether the kidnapping of foreign business agents can properly be considered international terrorism. Unless the terrorists make political demands other than for ransom monies and direct those demands to a foreign government, such hostage events should be considered to be manifestations of domestic terrorism rather than international. To illustrate, Jorge and Juan Born of the multinational corporation Bunge and Born, Ltd., were kidnapped in September of 1974 by the Montoneros, an Argentine terrorist group. The terrorists demanded that full-page declarations be published in the <u>Washington Post</u> and four European newspapers announcing the trial of the Borns as representatives of a company guilty of "exploitation" by "multinational monopoly." The demands also included a $60 million ransom with $1 million in merchandise to be distributed to villages, factories, hospitals, and schools. Ultimately, the ransom was paid, the announcement was published, and the Borns were freed.[6] To the extent that the announcements involved an international audience in the event, the kidnapping would qualify as having an international character. But, the demands were levied against the company rather than a foreign government or people, thus the kidnapping can be classified as domestic terrorism, as can most other kidnappings of and attacks on foreign business agents.[7]

There is much more support for the inclusion of diplomatic kidnappings, "diplonapping," in the category of international terrorism, because of the international "protections" customarily granted diplomatic agents.[8] The distinction can be somewhat blurred, however, because of the unique qualities of each terrorist event. The kidnapping of Stanley Sylvester in Argentine in May of 1971 is a case in point. Sylvester was the honorary British consul in Rosario as well as the director of the Swift Company meat-packing plant there. The terrorists who kidnapped Sylvester demanded only that the company distribute $62,500 worth of food, clothing, and school supplies to the poor in Rosario.[9] The relevant question here is whether Sylvester was kidnapped because of his position as director of the plant or his post as honorary consul. The demands themselves would suggest that the violence was primarily of a domestic nature, although the terrorists may have been influenced to select Sylvester as a victim because of his semi-official post.[10]

Apart from the ambiguities in categorizing hostage events, there is general consensus that hijackings that cross national borders and kidnappings and barricade situations that involve diplomatic agents or demands levied against foreign states are international terrorist events. As such, those types of events will be the focus of this analysis.

But first, to put those and related events into perspective, it is useful to note that hostage incidents represent only a relatively small percentage of the total number of international terrorist events. According to Central Intelligence Agency figures for the 1968-1979 period, most terrorist attacks have involved bombings, with 47.6% of the total number of events being explosive bombings and 13.7% being incendiary bombings. The remaining events, in order of frequency, were: kidnappings (7.9%), assassinations (7.4%), armed attacks (5.5%), letter bombings (5.5%), hijackings (3.0%), thefts and break-ins (2.3%), barricade and hostage incidents (2.2%), sniping (2.1%), and other forms of violence (2.6%).[11] Based on those figures, hostage incidents represented only about 13% of the total number of international terrorist events during the 1968-1979 period. Similarly, Jenkins, Johnson, and Ronfeldt estimated hostage-taking to be an attribute of about one-fifth of the total number.[12] Methodological differences probably account for the relatively slight (7%) disparity between the two figures. In any case, it is amply clear that hostage-taking is not the most frequent manifestation of international terrorism.

It also must be noted that the preferences for particular types of hostage-taking operations among terrorists change over time. The changes that took place during the 1968-1977 period are illustrated in Table I. The table indicates a general decline in the number of hijackings since 1970. That decline is likely due to increased airport and aircraft security since 1970-1972, as well as the decisions by some terrorist organizations to direct their violence against other targets.[13] While hijacking incidents have decreased, kidnappings and barricade and hostage incidents have increased, although both appear to have peaked in 1975.[14]

Given the relationships between international hostage incidents and other forms of international terrorism and the fluctuations in the frequency of each type of hostage-taking, the final consideration should be the relative low-risk that terrorists face when they engage in such violence. More often than not, the terrorists escape without retribution.

TABLE I
INTERNATIONAL HOSTAGE INCIDENTS, 1968-1977[15]

	Forms		
Years	Kidnapping	Barricade-Hostage	Hijacking-Aerial and Non-aerial
1968	1	0	3
1969	3	0	11
1970	32	5	21
1971	17	1	9
1972	11	3	14
1973	37	8	6
1974	25	9	8
1975	38	14	4
1976	30	4	6
1977	22	5	8

Source: U.S. Central Intelligence Agency, National Foreign Assessment Center, International Terrorism in 1977 (Washington, D.C.: U.S. Central Intelligence Agency, RP 78-10255U, August 1978), p. 10

Brooks McClure, for instance, estimates that 80% of the politically-motivated kidnappers go unpunished. Thus, kidnapping is a "low-risk, high-return activity,"[16] as hijackings of aircraft have been.[17] Barricade and hostage incidents, on the other hand, involve much greater risk because the terrorists involved are themselves captives, protected only by their capacity to do harm to their hostages. Nonetheless, in most cases of hostage-taking, there is little risk to the terrorists and, for that reason, it can be expected that hostage-taking will continue to be a tool of terrorist coercion.

On the whole, then, the phenomenon with which this analysis will deal is one that is less common than many other forms of terrorism, tends to run in cycles, presents few risks to the terrorists, and is likely to continue. With those aspects of the phenomena in mind, the relationships among hostage events, government responses, and policy impacts can be brought into sharper focus. Those relationships will be the subject of the analyses to follow.

The Propositions

During the course of the previous discussions, numerous relationships among the types of international terrorism (based on the relationships of the responding governments to the victims, terrorists, and locations of the events), the perceptions of the threats that terrorists pose to regime authority, the response options and constraints, and the policy choices were posited. A considerable number of testable propositions could be drawn from among the associations suggested. The task here was to select a few hypotheses that would provide a means of applying the typologies of international terrorism and direct response options (the former in particular), while at the same time focusing on the larger questions of why governments choose to adopt the policies that they do and what impact those policies have on terrorist events.

To a large extent, the nature of events data precludes the measurement of a wide range of situational and perceptual variables.[18] But, several direct relationships among primary concepts were indicated in the analysis, and it is from those that the following sets of hypotheses were extrapolated.

The first set of propositions postulate a relationship between types of international terrorism and government responses. Throughout the discussions of the typology of international terrorist events created in this study, it was suggested that the closer that the international events approximate domestic terrorism, the greater would be the likelihood that the government will respond to it harshly. First, it was suggested that responding governments will deal more harshly with terrorist violence when it is committed within their territorial jurisdictions and when their constituents are intimately involved in the violence as either victims or terrorists (i.e., integrated internal terrorism). It was further indicated that responding governments will tend to deal less harshly and be more accommodating when the violent acts are extensions of foreign conflicts to which the responding governments and their constituents are not parties (i.e., spillover terrorism). Finally, it was proposed that, because violent attacks on a government committed outside of its jurisdiction pose fewer dangers to regime authority and public order than do internal events, responding governments may be more inclined to adopt compromising positions and negotiate terrorist demands in those cases (i.e., external terrorism). The four posited relationships, in more testable terms, are that:

> 1.0 Government responses to terrorist demands are related to the type of international terrorism that is committed.
>
> 1.1 Responding governments will tend to refuse to comply with terrorist demands that result from acts of integrated internal terrorism.
>
> 1.2 Responding governments will tend to comply with terrorist demands that result from acts of spillover terrorism.
>
> 1.3 Responding governments will tend to comply with terrorist demands that result from acts of external terrorism.

Because of the precedent established by the Entebbe and Mogadishu rescue operations, proposition (1.3) must be somewhat qualified. Increasingly, it is to be expected that target governments will attempt to rescue hostages when they are being held outside of the target governments' territorial jurisdictions, particularly when there is reasonable expectation of success. In most cases, the expectation that rescue operations can be effective will be raised when the government having jurisdiction over the event or a neighboring government is cooperative and the responding government's antiterrorist units and logistical support structures are perceived to be adequate to the task, although there may be other extenuating factors which would dissuade external response. In any event, we might expect the fourth relationship stated above to have changed since 1977.[19]

The second and third sets of propositions concern the relationship between the threats posed by terrorist organizations to regime authority and government responses to terrorist demands. It was suggested that government responses to international (and domestic) terrorism would be greatly influenced by the responding government's perceptions of the dangers inherent in the violence. In large measure, the government's perceptions of the threats should be a function of the nature of the responding government's involvement in the violence, as postulated in the first set of hypotheses. But the perception of the threats should also be a function of what the responding government believes the terrorists are attempting to achieve (their objectives) and are capable of achieving (their strengths, limitations, and potentialities). That is not to say that there will be no other factors involved, such as government biases toward certain types of terrorist ideologies or terrorism in general or government commitments to certain policy courses, however. It is to say that the level of threat, the credibility of the threat, to regime authority will be a major influence on policy choice.

It has been indicated earlier that the long- and mid-range objectives of the terrorists may not be readily apparent because of intentional and unintentional distortions in the communication of terrorist objectives, differences in the objectives sought by the members of the terrorist organizations, or simply the absence of clear, long-term objectives. The objectives that are generally the easiest to identify are the short-term, tactical ones; those that are enumerated as demands in the course of terrorist attacks, particularly hostage events. For that reason, only the lowest level of terrorist objectives are to be considered here, measured in terms of terrorist demands.

The issue raised in the discussions was whether responding governments will be more receptive to some demands than to others. In particular, it was suggested that specific demands for publicity (e.g., the publication or broadcast of terrorist declarations or other propaganda messages) are generally less threatening to regime authority than are demands for ransom or the release of captured terrorists. As a consequence, the likelihood that responding governments will accede to demands for publicity should be greater than for other demands. Demands for the release of captured terrorists, on the other hand, involve a challenge to the law enforcement and judicial processes that detained or imprisoned the terrorists; thus, the challenge to authority is much more direct than that of publicity demands. Demands for ransom, too, pose greater challenges in that the responding government is being coerced into submitting to demands that will contribute to an escalation of the level of violence.

The relationships between terrorist demands and government responses, then, can be stated as:[20]

> <u>2.0</u> Responding governments will tend to comply with terrorist demands for publicity.
>
> <u>2.1</u> Responding governments will tend to refuse to comply with terrorist demands that include demands for ransom.
>
> <u>2.2</u> Responding governments will tend to refuse to comply with terrorist demands that include demands for the release of prisoners.

Demands for political asylum or safe passage to a sympathetic country may accompany one or more of the other demands, but it is not expected that government responses will be affected by the inclusion of either, except to the extent that safe passage may be granted to terrorists in order to resolve hostage incidents.[21] The cases in which those demands were the only demands made do not conform to the definition of international terrorism used here and were factored out of the analysis.

The second measure of the threat to regime authority, terrorist capabilities, also presents perceptual difficulties. Although government assessments (perceptions) of terrorist capabilities may not be realistic, it is likely that they will not be entirely inaccurate in most cases. For that reason, equating government assessments of terrorist capabilities and more objective measures should be practicable.

The measurement of terrorist organizational capabilities was suggested by Miller and Russell in their hierarchy of terrorist tactics based on levels of organizational competence (Figure 4, p. 97). They indicated that the capabilities of terrorist groups will be reflected in their tactics; that is, that there will be a relationship between the terrorists' levels of organizational competence (e.g., their weapons, leadership skills and experience, and sophistication) and the tactics that they employ in seeking to realize their objectives. The hierarchy included, in descending order based on competence: mass destruction, mass (national) disruption, kidnapping, hijacking, assassination, attacks on facilities and barricade and hostage events, and bombing. While some reservations were noted concerning the first two tiers in the hierarchy and it was suggested that the preferences for one tactic over another may have more to do with what the terrorists perceive to be the most appropriate tactic rather than with what they are competent to carry out, the hierarchy may have some utility in the context of international terrorist events in which hostages have been selected as the medium of exchange for the terrorists' demands.

Kidnappings, for example, generally require that terrorists have both the operational competence necessary to effect the capture of their intended victims and the underground organizations necessary to support the movement and detention of hostages without detection by security forces and while negotiations are being conducted for the release of the hostages. In many cases, the clandestine detention of hostages requires at least a minimum of popular support for the terrorist organization. Hijackings, on the other hand, do not require the domestic support that kidnappings do. They do require substantial operational sophistication if the group is to overcome the security obstacles around the intended victims and to effect an escape with hostages. Airport and aircraft security, in particular, presents obstacles that require considerable competence to overcome in most cases. The hijacking of international flights also requires that terrorists be familiar with the capabilities of the aircraft being used and be able to maintain effective control over the aircraft while conducting negotiations. This means that the terrorists need to have some knowledge of aircraft navigation and be able to speak English, the primary language of international flight control. By contrast, barricade and hostage incidents generally require only enough operational sophistication to effect the take-over of a facility and to capture the intended victims (or at least some hostages). Frequently, barricade and hostage events result from unsuccessful operations in which the terrorists' escape routes are cut off and the terrorists themselves are trapped. Therefore, terrorist organizations that utilize barricade and hostage events should present less danger to regime authority than those who use kidnapping and hijacking tactics.

In general terms, then, it can be concluded that the choice of kidnapping, hijacking, or barricade and hostage tactics will be a reflection of the capabilities of terrorist organizations. Because responding governments are expected to be influenced in their choices of replies to terrorist demands by their assessments of the capabilities of the terrorist groups making the demands, it can be stated that:

> 3.0 Responding governments will tend to comply with terrorist demands that result from international barricade and hostage events.
>
> 3.1 Responding governments will tend to refuse to comply with terrorist demands that result from international hijacking events.
>
> 3.2 Responding governments will tend to refuse to comply with terrorist demands that result from international kidnapping events.

The final set of propositions will be concerned with policy impact. Hostage safety, as the most visible indicator of policy impact, will be correlated with government responses and the major influences on response policy choice suggested in the previous sets of propositions. Hostage safety is a crucial consideration in the arguments for and against more flexible, compromising responses to terrorist demands. Whether negotiation leads to complete or partial compliance with terrorist demands or to noncompliance, those in favor of maintaining a pragmatic position contend that flexibility is the best means of minimizing the danger to hostages. The arguments for a firm, no compromising and nonnegotiating position, on the other hand, are based on the belief that lives will be saved in the long-run if it is demonstrated that the terrorists have nothing to gain by their violent acts. The "hard-line" position accepts the possibility that lives will be lost due to refusal to negotiate, but expects to reduce the number of casualties from terrorist violence over the long-term.

Each view is predicated on a valuation of the lives that terrorists threaten, consequently an assessment of the probabilities that lives will be lost in a given hostage situation would be a valuable decision-making tool. Basic to such an assessment are the questions of whether acceding, wholly or partially, to terrorist demands will, in itself, insure hostage safety; and, conversely, whether refusing to comply will increase the likelihood of hostage casualties. Logic dictates that both propositions will be true, but it is not at all certain to what extent refusals to negotiate will affect hostage safety. It is not uncommon for terrorists to surrender their hostages when it becomes apparent that there is nothing to gain from a continuation of their threats and violence. In such cases, firm, "hard-line," positions would appear to have been effective in the short-term as well as the long-term. For that reason, the measurement of the immediate impact of government responses on hostage safety will be useful and that relationship is reflected in the following hypotheses:

> <u>4.0</u> Complying with terrorist demands will decrease the likelihood that hostages will be killed or injured.
>
> <u>4.1</u> Refusing to comply with terrorist demands will increase the likelihood that hostages will be killed or injured.

In addition to the four sets of primary hypotheses, the analysis will also include supplementary evaluations of the impacts of event locations and terrorist and hostage nationalities (i.e., the components of the international terrorist events typology) on response choice and hostage safety and the impacts of terrorist demands and tactics (types of hostage events) on hostage safety. By disassembling the terrorist events typology, it can be determined to what extent the variables from which the typology was derived contribute to its explanatory power. Moreover, the component variables are dichotomous and will permit a higher level of analysis to be used. The location, nationality, demand, and tactic variables will also provide benchmarks against which the impacts of government responses on hostage safety can be measured. As no direct relationships are being suggested between these variables and government responses or hostage safety, the supplementary propositions will be understood to be null hypotheses.

Given the four sets of primary propositions and the supplementary propositions, the next step is to specify the parameters of the concepts and the measures that will be used in the analysis.

Concepts, Measures, and the Analytical Design

The final steps before testing the propositions enumerated in the previous section are to define the concepts, identify the measures, and describe the analytical design that will be used in the analysis to follow. To a certain extent, the conceptualizations will be redundant as most have been considered elsewhere in the study in terms that were designed to facilitate operationalization. It also must be noted that the definition of international terrorism being utilized here is essentially the same as the one constructed by Edward Mickolus. Although the distinction that Mickolus makes between international and transnational terrorism is not critical to this analysis, virtually all (if not all) of the cases represented in the data conform to his definition of transnational terrorism.

Concepts and Measures
Terrorist Demands (Tactical Objectives)

Terrorist demands are simply the specified conditions and concessions sought by the terrorist in the course of a terrorist event. Generally, the demands are for ranson, the release of prisoners being held by government authorities, the broadcast or publication of a terrorist message, or safe conduct to (including political asylum in) another state. The last three demands are fairly clear, but the demands for ransom may include monies, supplies and equipment, or such commodities as food and clothing to be distributed to the poor. In a few cases, the demands issued by terrorists during hostage events have also included ultimatums concerning specific government policies. The demands related more closely to terrorists' ideological objectives were not within the scope of this study, however.

In terms of the measurement of the demands, no attempt was made to determine the exact amounts or numbers involved in the demands (conflicting and incomplete reports would preclude that possibility in many cases anyway). Demands were simply noted as being specified or not.

Response to Demands

The responses to the demands were categorized as compliance, partial compliance, refusal to comply, and undetermined. The first two categories were then collapsed due to the difficulty of determining whether all or part of the demands were met. The categorization of responses were made on the basis of the final reports of the events to eliminate some of the influence of media conjecture and rumor and to insure that the categorizations were based on the final actions of the governments rather than on their delaying tactics.

Responding Governments

Several governments may respond to a single terrorist event. In this case, the responding government is the one to which the majority of the demands were addressed (e.g., the release of the largest number of prisoners or the payment of the largest amount of ransom), rather than the government or persons that ultimately resolved the crisis. In a few cases, the ransoms were paid by the families of the hostages, by other governments, or by nongovernmental parties rather than by the principal responding government. In those cases, the payment of the ransom was not considered to be compliance with terrorist demands on the part of the responding government.

Types of International Terrorist Events

Integrated internal terrorism involves acts of terrorist violence committed within the territorial jurisdiction of the responding government when either the terrorists or the victims are nationals of that government (and the others are not).

Spillover terrorism involves acts of terrorist violence committed within the territorial jurisdiction of the responding government when neither the terrorists nor the victims are nationals of that government.

External terrorism involves acts of terrorist violence committed outside of the territorial jurisdiction of the responding government when the terrorists, the victims, or the facilities being attacked are nationals, agents, or property of the responding government or when the demands of the terrorists are addressed to the government.

Types of International Hostage Events (Terrorist Tactics)

Hijackings involve the takeover of aircraft or some other means of transportation by terrorists. The hijackings considered here are those in which effective control of the vehicles was achieved by the terrorists and demands were issued stating preconditions for their relinquishing of control of the vehicle and their releasing of the hostages. The distinguishing characteristic of this type of hostage taking is that the event is mobile; that is, the terrorists can change the venue of the event themselves, in most cases.

Kidnappings involve the seizure of one or more government agents or civilians and the forcible detention of those captives in a clandestine location for purposes of exacting a ransom or other concessions in exchange for their release.

Barricade and hostage situations involve the seizure of one or more government agents or civilians and the forcible detention of those persons in a public place for purposes of exacting a ransom or other concessions (generally including safe passage to a sympathetic state) in exchange for the release of hostages. Barricade and hostage situations characteristically are sieges, with the terrorists using their hostages as shields to prevent the authorities from using force to resolve the crises. Essentially, the terrorists are captives themselves. For purposes of categorization and measurement, the kidnappings that turned into barricade and hostage situations (when the locations of the terrorists and hostages became known) were considered to be the latter.

Hostage Safety

Hostage safety simply means whether hostages were killed or injured, either from the actions of the terrorists or the authorities attempting to rescue the hostages. To account for the possibility that relatively minor injuries might affect the determination of the level of hostage safety, only those cases in which there were reports that one or more hostages were wounded as a result of terrorist or government actions were counted. The operative word in that clarification is "wounded." The deaths and injuries that resulted from the initial seizures of the hostages also were not included in the determination of hostage safety.

Nationality

The determination of whether terrorists and hostages were nationals of the responding government or foreigners was based on the perspective of the responding government. Israel, for example, generally does not consider the Palestinian terrorists to be nationals of Israel, although some undoubtedly were born in Israel and resided there most of their lives. The distinction is frequently difficult to make, even given the responding governments' own interpretations. When there was some doubt about the nationality of terrorists or hostages and whether the nationality differed from that of the responding authorities, a determination was made on the basis of the terrorist organization involved (whether it was indigenous to the responding state). When more than one nationality was evident among the terrorists or hostages, the dominant one was selected or the group was determined to be "international." When more than one terrorist group were involved in an event, the group with the largest number of representatives among the terrorists or for whom the terrorists appeared to be acting (based on their demands and their apparent target) was selected as the determinant of terrorist nationality.

The Analytical Design

The data to be used in the analysis represent ninety-one international hostage incidents that occurred between January 1, 1968, and December 31, 1977.[22] All the data being used are dichotomous, with the exceptions of the types of international terrorist events and the types of hostage events. Therefore, after the initial consideration of each of the two typologies, the level of analysis and measurement will be metric.

The analysis will be conducted in three parts. The first section will include a measure of association between the types of international terrorist events and government responses. After that initial consideration of the typology, dummy variables will be created to permit multivariate analysis of the relationships between each type of event and government responses. Regression analysis will be used to determine the strengths and directions of those relationships and the relative impact of each event type on response choice. The supplementary propositions will be similarly tested.

The second section will deal with the impact of the level of terrorist challenge to regime authority on government responses to terrorist demands, the second and third sets of propositions. Using regression analysis, the relationships posited in the second set of propositions will be tested to determine their strengths and directions, as well as the relative impacts of each on government responses. The third set of relationships will be tested using simple bivariate analysis (Pearson's product-moment correlation) to determine the direct relationships between each type of hostage event and government responses.

The third section will consist of a simple bivariate analysis (Pearson's product-moment correlation) to determine the direct relationship between government responses and hostage safety; three multiple regression analyses to determine the relative impacts of terrorist demands, types of international terrorist events, and types of hostage events on hostage safety; and, a partial correlation analysis to determine the extent to which government responses mitigate the impacts of the demands and event variables on hostage safety. This last portion of the analysis is essentially the policy impact analysis.

Analysis of Data

Types of International Terrorist Events and Government Responses

The measure of association (Cramer's V) indicated in Table II, below, reveals that the relationships between the types of international terrorist events and government responses is a very slight one (if it exists at all). While the probability of error is too high to justify drawing conclusions about the relationships with any confidence, it should be noted that the table does suggest that responding governments tend to refuse to comply with terrorist demands resulting from acts of integrated internal terrorism and to comply with demands resulting from acts of spillover terrorism.

As the figures in Table II indicate, the number of cases of spillover terrorism included in the analysis was very small and that probably affected the statistical analysis. In fact, the regression analysis with terrorist event dummy variables resulted in the spillover terrorism cases being deleted from the analysis altogether because of the low tolerance-level that it reflected. The results of that analysis are shown in Table III. The relationships between integrated internal and external terrorism and government responses were determined to be very weak. Moreover, there were no indications that those relationships might be nonlinear (based on the plots of the standardized residuals).

TABLE II

TYPES OF INTERNATIONAL TERRORIST EVENTS AND GOVERNMENT RESPONSES (PERCENTAGES)

Responses to Demands	Types of International Terrorist Events		
	Integrated Internal Terrorism	Spillover Terrorism	External Terrorism
Whole or Partial Compliance	46	83	52
Refusal to Comply	54	17	48
N =	52	6	33

Total N = 91

V = .18

P greater than .05

TABLE III

TYPES OF INTERNATIONAL TERRORIST EVENTS AND
GOVERNMENT RESPONSES (REGRESSION ANALYSIS)

Variables	Simple R	R^2	R^2 Change	Beta
External Terrorism	-.023	.0005	.0005	.307
Integrated Internal Terrorism	.112	.0354	.0349	.379
Spillover Terrorism	-----	-----	-----	----

The results of the multiple regression analysis of the relationships between the components of the typology of international terrorist events (event locations and terrorist and hostage nationalities) and government responses are depicted in Table IV. In none of the cases was a relationship substantiated. The coefficients of determination (R^2) reveal very slight relationships between those variables and government responses. Moreover, the plot of the standardized residuals gives no indication that the relationships might be nonlinear.

TABLE IV

GOVERNMENT RESPONSES WITH EVENT LOCATIONS
AND TERRORIST AND HOSTAGE NATIONALITIES
(REGRESSION ANALYSIS)

Variables	Simple R	R^2	R^2 Change	Beta
Terrorist Nationality	-.090	.008	.0081	-.089
Hostage Nationality	-.028	.008	.0005	-.028
Event Location	.001	.009	.0002	-.016

Challenges to Regime Authority and Government Responses

For purposes of clarity, government responses to specific terrorist demands (tactical objectives) are illustrated in Table V, and the results of the regression analysis of the posited relationships between terrorist demands and government responses are shown in Table VI. The strongest relationship revealed in the regression analysis is that between demands for the release of captured prisoners. Although that correlation is not a particularly strong one (-.267), it does reveal that responding governments are less likely to comply with terrorist demands that include releases or prisoners. The relationship between the other demands and government responses are uniformly weak, and the residuals for all four relationships do not suggest a nonlinear relationship.

Despite the lack of a strong correlation between any of the demands and government responses, the responses to each of the demands as indicated in Table V do conform to the relationships as posited in the second set of propositions, except that it was expected that demands for ransom would be less acceptable to responding governments.

The relationships between the types of hostage events (terrorist tactics) and government responses are illustrated in Table VII. While the responses to each type event do conform to the directions suggested in the propositions, the correlation coefficients are uniformly weak, particularly that between hijacking events and government responses.

TABLE V

GOVERNMENT RESPONSES WITH TERRORIST DEMANDS

(TACTICAL OBJECTIVES)   (PERCENTAGES)

Terrorist Demands (Tactical Objectives)

Responses to Demands	Asylum or Safe Passage	Publicity	Ransom	Release of Prisoners
Whole or Partial Compliance	62	60	52	43
Refusal to Comply	38	40	48	57
N per demand	39	20	33	68
Total N	90	90	91	91

TABLE VI

GOVERNMENT RESPONSES WITH TERRORIST DEMANDS
(TACTICAL OBJECTIVES) (REGRESSION ANALYSIS)

Variables	Simple R	R^2	R^2 Change	Beta
Release of Prisoners	-.267	.071	.0714	-2.67
Asylum or Safe Passage	.184	.105	.0331	.196
Publicity	.095	.116	.0117	.108
Ransom	.006	.117	.0009	.030

TABLE VII

GOVERNMENT RESPONSES WITH TYPES OF HOSTAGE
EVENTS (TERRORIST TACTICS) (PERCENTAGES)

Responses to Demands	Types of Hostage Events (Terrorist Tactics)		
	Barricade and Hostage	Hijacking	Kidnapping
Whole or Partial Compliance	61	50	41
Refusal to Comply	39	50	59
N =	29	38	23
R =	.13	.00	.12

Government Responses and Hostages Safety

The bivariate analysis of the relationship between government responses and hostage safety reveals a moderate correlation between the two (Pearson's r=.48). That relationship is illustrated in Table VIII. The table also indicates that, while compliance with terrorist demands generally assures that hostages will be released safely, noncompliance does not necessarily mean that the hostages will be killed or injured. In fact, in most cases, the hostages were released safely despite the responding governments' refusals to comply with terrorist demands.

TABLE VIII

HOSTAGE SAFETY WITH GOVERNMENT RESPONSES (PERCENTAGES)

	Government Responses		
Hostage Safety	Whole or Partial Compliance	Refusals to Comply	N
Hostages Released Safely	96	56	69
Hostages Killed or Injured	4	44	22
N =	46	45	

r = .48
p less than .001
Total N = 91

The regression analysis of the relationships between terrorist demands and hostage safety yielded uniformly weak correlations as can be seen in Table IX. Here, too, the plots of the standardized residuals did not reveal the presence of a nonlinear relationship. Of the three relationships tested, the greatest amount of association was found between the demands for the release of prisoners and hostage safety. That negative relationship appears to be similar to the negative relationship found between demands for the release of prisoners and government responses noted earlier.

TABLE IX

HOSTAGE SAFETY WITH TERRORIST DEMANDS
(TACTICAL OBJECTIVES) (REGRESSION ANALYSIS)

Variables	Simple R	R^2	R^2 Change	Beta
Release of Prisoners	-.155	.024	.024	-.149
Asylum or Safe Passage	.080	.030	.006	.082
Ransom	.057	.031	.001	.034
Publicity*	----	----	----	----

*Not computed because of an unacceptable probability of error.

As Table X reveals, there were no substantial relationships between the types of hostage events (terrorist tactics) and hostage safety, nor was a nonlinear relationship suggested by the plot of the standardized residuals. The impact of the kidnapping events were not figured in the analysis because of a high probability of error, however.

TABLE X

HOSTAGE SAFETY WITH TYPES OF HOSTAGE EVENTS (TERRORIST TACTICS) (REGRESSION ANALYSIS)

Variables	Simple R	R^2	R^2 Change	Beta
Barricade and Hostage Events	.082	.077	.077	.098
Hijacking Events	-.015	.008	.001	.034
Kidnapping Events*	----	----	----	----

*Not computed because of an unacceptable probability of error.

Table XI gives the results of the regression analysis of the relationship between event locations and terrorist and hostage nationalities and hostage safety. No appreciable association was found. In both cases, the coefficients of determination (R^2) are quite low, and the residuals do not suggest a nonlinear relationship.

Table XII lists the relationships between all of the supplementary concepts and hostage safety, with government responses used as a control variable. In all cases, the relationships are extremely weak. The slight association between demands for prisoner releases and hostage safety noted earlier was reduced significantly when the influence of government responses was controlled. While a few of the correlations increased with the control variable introduced, the probabilities of error are so high (P greater than .05) that little significance can be attached to the changes.

TABLE XI

HOSTAGE SAFETY WITH EVENT LOCATIONS AND
TERRORIST AND HOSTAGE NATIONALITIES
(REGRESSION ANALYSIS)

Variables	Simple R	R^2	R^2 Change	Beta
Hostage Nationality	.105	.011	.0110	.099
Terrorist Nationality	.078	.016	.0051	-.071
Event Locations	.070	.017	.0005	-.025

Conclusions

According to the analysis of the relationships between the types of international terrorist events and government responses, Hypothesis 1.0 cannot be substantiated. While Table II does reveal a tendency for governments to refuse to comply with demands resulting from acts of integrated internal terrorism (Hypothesis 1.1) and to comply with demands resulting from spillover terrorism (Hypothesis 1.2), neither relationship can be substantiated by the data being used in this analysis. Both relationships, however, should be investigated further to determine whether the associations can be increased by increasing the number of spillover terrorism cases. The focus on primary responding governments in this study eliminated many of the responses by governments to acts of spillover terrorism. The broadening of the data base to include multiple responses to single events of terrorism might alleviate the problem. The posited relationship between government response and demands resulting from external terrorism acts (Hypothesis 1.3) also was not substantiated. The responses to external acts were about evenly divided between compliance and refusals to comply.

TABLE XII

HOSTAGE SAFETY WITH EVENT LOCATIONS, TERRORIST AND HOSTAGE NATIONALITIES, TERRORIST DEMANDS AND TYPES OF TERRORIST EVENTS BY GOVERNMENT RESPONSES (PARTIAL CORRELATION ANALYSIS)

Dependent Concept: Hostage Safety
Control Concept: Government Responses to Terrorist Demands

Dependent Concepts	Partial Correlation Coefficient	Zero Order Partials
Event Locations	-.064	-.070
Terrorist Nationality	-.040	-.078
Hostage Nationality	.118	.105
Demands for Ransom	.062	.057
Demands for Prisoner Releases	-.033	-.155
Demands for Asylum or Safe Passage	-.008	.080
Demands for Publicity	-.060	-.007
Hijacking Events (Tactics)	-.017	-.015
Kidnapping Events (Tactics)	-.132	-.060
Barricade & Hostage Events (Tactics)	.160	.082

The analysis of the impacts of terrorist demands (tactical objectives) on response choices also did not reveal strong associations. The strongest correlation (-.267) was between demands for the release of prisoners and government responses, with the negative correlation indicating that governments tend to refuse to comply with demands for prisoner releases. While that was the hypothesized direction of the relationship, the correlation coefficient is too low to substantiate the hypothesis (2.2). Similarly, the other two posited relationships between demands and responses cannot be substantiated because of low correlation coefficients. While Table IV did reveal a slight tendency for governments to comply with terrorist demands for publicity, as indicated in Hypothesis 2.0, the probabilities of error prevent that conclusion from being drawn with any confidence. The expected response to demands for ransom indicated in Hypothesis 2.1 was not substantiated by the correlation or suggested in the table. Responding governments appeared to accede to ransom demands as frequently as they refused them. Because the demands or terrorist tactical objectives were not discrete variables, but rather were components of sets of demands, it is difficult to determine exactly what the impact of each demand is on government response. A possible alternative approach to the relationships analyzed here would be to develop a means of separating the demands and considering government responses to each, rather than to focus on one response to each set of demands.

The analysis of the relationships between the types of hostage events also did not reveal any substantial correlations. Nonetheless, the percentages of each response shown in Table VII do conform to the directions of the posited relationships, with the exception of the responses to hijacking events. Governments did comply more with the demands that resulted from barricade and hostage events than they did with the demands resulting from the other types of events, but Hypothesis 3.0 cannot be substantiated on the basis of this analysis. Similarly, governments did refuse to comply with demands resulting from kidnapping events more so than they did with demands resulting from the other events, but, here too, the correlation revealed was too low to substantiate the hypothesis (3.2). There appeared to be no difference in government responses to demands resulting from hijackings, compliance was as frequent as noncompliance, so that hypothesis (3.1) cannot be substantiated either.

The analysis of the impacts of government responses, terrorist demands (objectives), types of hostage events (terrorist tactics), event locations, and terrorist and hostage nationalities on hostage safety only revealed one moderately strong correlation. That was between government responses and hostage safety. Of all the relationships that were suggested in the hypotheses, this one would have been selected as the most probable. The product-moment correlation of .48 indicates a fairly strong association between the two concepts, but it is still insufficient to substantiate the two hypotheses (4.0 and 4.1). Just the same, there is strong reason to believe that the relationship exists.

The analyses of the impacts of terrorist demands, types of hostage events, event locations, and terrorist and hostage nationalities on hostage safety, particularly when government responses were controlled for, did not reveal any substantial relationships. In fact, none were expected. It was hoped, however, that at least moderate relationships would be revealed so that the impact of government responses could be more clearly defined.

On the whole, the analysis did not uncover any strong relationships among the concepts that were correlated. The direct relationships that were indicated in the four sets of hypotheses were not substantiated, although the one that was expected to be the strongest, between government responses and hostage safety, did evidence a moderately strong degree of association. There were other encouraging results as well. While the analysis did not produce large correlation coefficients, the weak correlations generally conformed to the directions hypothesized. The weak relationships revealed between the types of international terrorist events and government responses undoubtedly was affected by the small number of cases of spillover terrorism. Even so, the relationships between terrorist demands resulting from integrated internal acts of terrorism and from spillover acts and government responses were consistent with the hypotheses. The contingency table (Table II) also suggested that governments tend to refuse to comply with terrorist demands when their own nationals are involved in the events as hostages or as terrorists (i.e., integrated internal and external terrorism).

The differences between the responses to terrorist demands or tactical objectives indicated in Table V also suggest that it may be possible to develop a more precise ranking of terrorist tactical objectives, based on the degrees of challenge that they present to regime authority. It has already been suggested that demands for political asylum or safe passage and for publicity are less threatening than the other demands. The table suggests that demands for ransom may be less threatening than those for prisoner releases, as well. If that difference can be substantiated by further research, a rank-ordering of terrorist tactical objectives may be feasible and, in conjunction with the Miller-Russell hierarchy of terrorist tactics, an index of terrorist threats to regime authority may be possible. That is a good many "maybes," but the rank-orderings of both demands and tactics are certainly promising.

As an exercise in determining the major influences on policy choice and in measuring policy impact to a limited degree, the analysis had mixed results. Several potentially fruitful associations among the concepts included in the analysis were suggested, although not confirmed by the analysis. Whether the typology of international terrorist events has utility as a tool for response policy study has not been resolved. It did not demonstrate a high level of explanatory power in this analysis, but the extenuating circumstances of skewed data recommend that the construct not be rejected out of hand. The data problem, as noted earlier, could be alleviated by the factoring in of some form of multiple response. In fact, the unit of analysis might be changed from terrorist events to government responses to allow for the inclusion of government responses that do not directly involve terrorist demands (which is the kind of response generally given to terrorists when their violence spills over into other states).

In any event, the analysis does provide a starting place for further research on why governments choose the response policies that they do and what impact those policies have. The inclusion of more concepts in the analysis, as well as a larger data base, would certainly provide greater potential for explaining policy choice and impact.

CHAPTER VI

CONCLUSIONS: AN OPTIMAL RESPONSE TO INTERNATIONAL TERRORISM?

In his book, <u>Internal War</u>, Harry Eckstein described "internal war" as "one of the great synthetic subjects of social science"[1] and that is no less true of the related phenomenon of terrorism. This study brings together a diverse body of literature on international terrorism (and similar forms of political violence) and presents a sample of the interpretations of the problem by international law analysts, law enforcement analysts and agents, government analysts and policymakers, United Nations officials, journalists, social commentators, and scholars. Because international terrorism is such a broad subject, the implicit intent of this study was to synthesize the major approaches to, definitions of, and solutions for the problem that were expressed in the diverse corners of the literature.

More specifically, the intent of the analysis was (1) to define the initial parameters of the international terrorism problem, including the nature of the phenomenon and government relationships to the violence; (2) to identify and define the objectives and capacities of terrorist organizations and how those aspects of the terrorist threat conflict with the basic authority maintenance functions of the state; (3) to define the environment of government policymaking in terms of the range of policy options from which governments may choose, the major "theories" concerning which policy options will be effective, the major constraints on policy selection, and the major value dilemmas and tradeoffs inherent in policy choice; and, (4) to test some of the propositions developed in the previous discussions concerning why governments choose the responses that they do and what impact those choices have in the resolution of international terrorist (i.e., hostage) events. The last objective, by way of summation, is to consider the question of whether there is an "optimal" response to international terrorism. In short, the analysis is designed to describe the policy problem and the policymaking environment and to develop some expectations concerning the relations between those two factors and response policy choice and impact.

To a large extent, the first objectives of the study were met. The nature of international terrorism was defined and examined and a typology of international terrorist events was constructed which should offer some utility as a framework for terrorism-related policy studies. The typology permits the examination of terrorist events on the basis of how governments are involved in the violence, and it is dynamic in the sense that it can accommodate multiple and evolving relationships between governments and individual events.

The examination of the challenge of international terrorism included the development of a three-part categorization of the levels of terrorist objectives that expanded on those that have been suggested in the literature; and, an expansion and synthesis of the mid-range, strategic objectives that have been suggested. The consideration of the options available to responding governments also included a categorization of the modes of response which represents a significant expansion of the general response categories that have been suggested by law enforcement and security analysts. The consideration of the major "theories" of response was somewhat limited because of their diverse nature, but the superimposition of the deterrence model conceptualizations provided a means of tying the "theories" together.

In terms of the typologies and other constructs included in the analysis, then, the study should provide a useful framework for similar policy-oriented studies.

The analysis itself was predicated on a number of primary relationships among the central concepts. Chief among those was the proposition that government responses to international terrorism are based on the extent to which the violence threatens regime authority, in particular, and public order, in general. This hypothesis represents the central theme of the study.

The corollary propositions were that government responses to international terrorist events will be greatly influenced by (1) the nature of the government's involvement in the events and (2) the degree of challenge to regime authority inherent in what the responding government perceives to be the terrorists' objectives and their capacities to realize their objectives. These two hypotheses were the core of the statistical analysis dealing with why governments chose the policies that they do.

The concept of government involvement in terrorist events was developed within the context of the nature of international terrorism. The crucial factors included: the relationships between the affected government and the principal actors in the events (the terrorists and the victims), the relationship of the affected government and the target of the violence, the impact of jurisdictional constraints on government responsibility in and responses to the events, and the impact of proximity on the perceptions of terrorist violence. In short, the assumptions were that governments will react differently to terrorist violence if their own nationals are involved and if the violence is committed within their jurisdictions. While the analysis did not provide strong support for these relationships, it did indicate that governments do react differently in those circumstances. In fact, despite the inadequacies of the data in some cases, there was an indication that governments react more harshly to acts of integrated internal and external terrorism, which involve the government's own nationals, than to acts of spillover terrorism, which do not. The jurisdictional influence was not apparent in the analysis, however.

The concept of challenge to regime authority was similarly approached. The initial theoretical discussion indicated that terrorist organizations can have a variety of objectives which can generally be categorized as: (1) ideological (long-range), (2) strategic (mid-range), and (3) tactical (short-range) objectives. The assumptions are that terrorists do not necessarily seek the same ends and, for that reason, some terrorists' objectives will be more compatible with regime and societal values than will others. Moreover, even if the terrorist organizations' objectives are incompatible with regime and societal values (especially regime authority and public order), not all of the organizations are or ever will have the capacity to achieve their objectives. Terrorist organizations, then, have different strengths, limitations, and potentialities.

Based on the differences in terrorist objectives and capabilities, the challenges to regime authority offered by terrorist organizations will vary considerably and the defensive needs (response imperatives) of the governments affected by the violence will also vary considerably. Each of those two variables were considered in the analysis as components of the terrorist challenge.

When tested, the impact of terrorist objectives on government responses was generally as predicted. Despite low correlation coefficients, the data generally supported the propositions that terrorist objectives contain different levels of threat to authority or were at least perceived by the responding governments to carry less danger. The analysis itself dealt exclusively with the lowest level of terrorist objectives, most frequently manifested in their demands, but the differences in the responses to each objective followed the hypothesized pattern for the most part. Unfortunately, the higher order objectives are not amenable to statistical analysis. But, if the examination of the lower level objectives can be taken as an example, governments should weigh the challenges inherent in terrorist objectives before responding to the violent events.

The examination of the second component of the terrorist challenge, terrorist capabilities, was based on a measure of the organizational competence of terrorist organizations, as reflected in the tactics that they chose to employ. Here, too, only very weak correlation coefficients were produced, but the data did indicate a pattern of responses consistent with the proposition that governments will respond more harshly when the terrorist organization is perceived to have a higher capacity for sophisticated operations and, thus, poses a greater threat to government authority.

On the whole, then, while the analysis did not produce strong evidence to support the specific propositions, it did offer substantial support for the general ones. For the most part, the data conformed to the general patterns that were expected.

The analysis of the impact of government responses on hostage safety, however, did uncover a moderately strong correlation. More importantly, the analysis revealed that government decisions to refuse to comply with terrorist demands do not necessarily mean that the hostages involved will be injured. In other words, the implicit trade-off in the decision not to comply with terrorist demands has to be qualified to account for the possibility that the response will have no effect on hostage safety. The trade-off only involves an increased probability that there will be casualties. On the basis of the evidence revealed in this study, the probability of casualties when demands are complied with is almost nil and when demands are not complied with it is about fifty percent. A more convincing study will be necessary before that probability can be evaluated more precisely, however.

In terms of the value of the analyses to policymaking, the identification of the fundamental differences between terrorist objectives should indicate that all terrorist organizations may not seek to violate the authority maintenance imperatives of the government in whose jurisdiction their violence is committed. Additionally, not all organizations are capable of offering credible threats to government authority; some are not serious threats to public order, either. Those factors and the results of the policy impact analysis should sensitize policymakers to the variabilities in the trade-offs that are involved in policy choice. That is, responses to terrorist demands do not always involve a zero-sum game. What the terrorists seek to achieve may not be a crucial value for the responding government or it may be very crucial. The important distinction is that the values may change for every terrorist conflict, and it will mean that the trade-offs are different. If the responding government is interested in making the best "deal" for itself and its constituents, it should be aware of what it is giving away and what it is getting in return. A particular response may be cost-effective in one circumstance and not in another. Quite apart from the necessity of eliminating terrorist violence, there is a need to deal with it effectively.

In terms of other policymaking uses, the study gives clear guidelines for the selection of a response to international terrorist violence, including the major processes of:

>   1. Determining the government's involvement in the violence; that is, whether it is internal or external and whether the violence is directed against the government and its constituents or against another government or people.

>   2. Assessing the challenge offered by the terrorists: including their ideological, strategic, and tactical objectives; their capacities to realize their objectives or to escalate the level

of violence; and, their organizational vulnerabilities and limitations, as well as the limitations and advantages of terrorist violence itself.

3. Assessing the risks to regime authority and public order, as well as to other values, including the risks to particularly vulnerable facilities or unstable social, economic, or political conditions.

4. Evaluating the response alternatives, including: the options that might be possible, the "theories" concerning which policies are the most effective or should be avoided, the constraints on policy choice that may prevent the implementation of a specific policy or program or may neutralize its impact and create undesirable side-effects, and the value dilemmas or trade-offs inherent in the policies under consideration.

That is, by no means, a comprehensive guide to selecting a response to international terrorist events, but it does offer a means of systematizing the process and sensitizing policymakers to the trade-offs that their decisions entail and to the options that are available.

Now that the utility of the conceptualizations, typologies, approaches, and analyses have been considered, it is time to consider the question of response.

The first considerations in determining whether there is an "optimal" response to international terrorism is to determine just what "optimal" means and what an "optimal" response would look like. In general terms, "optimal" can be taken to mean "best." It has been determined in the analysis that the best response is one that accomplishes the goals of protecting the regime's agents and constituents, reducing or eliminating the violence, and minimizing interference with normal social, political, and economic activities by the terrorists or the antiterrorist forces. The best response was also determined to be one which is commiserate with the level of terrorist violence, not an overreaction or an underreaction. The injunction against overreacting is important because it means that an appropriate response to international terrorism in some cases may be a very simple and inexpensive task, like the repositioning of a security guard to dissuade terrorist violence from occurring at a particular place. In most cases, however, the process is much more complex and expensive.

When the threat of disorder and violence is great, an "optimal" response would be one that manages in a deliberate, but inobtrusive, manner to prepare for, obstruct, contain, counteract, and answer the terrorists' actions and threats. In short, the "optimal" response is one adequate to the task of applying minimum force for the resolution of violent conflicts.

In most cases, the agents of government response would be the police, with assistance from specialized antiterrorist units when the violence becomes frequent or intense. The response would also not be repressive, unless domestic order and regime authority are severely threatened and even then the repressive countermeasures would be focused on the terrorists or on a relatively narrow segment of society that is supporting the terrorists or within which the terrorists are hiding.

The use of extralegal countermeasures or media of response by the government would be prohibited. There would be no extralegal intelligence gathering or detention of suspects. Extranormal countermeasures, like media restraints, would also be avoided. Ideally, the public would not be inconvenienced unless absolutely necessary. Above all, a "business as usual" atmosphere would be maintained to reassure the public.

Of course that description is very incomplete because without a context, i.e., without the threat of violence, there is no reference point against which to measure the need for a response. The first question that has to be answered is what kind of problem does the violence represent? Even a relatively small sample of the responses would reveal that it is a humanitarian, an international law, a law enforcement, a military, and a political problem. Those that see the problem as a humanitarian one suggest that it can only be resolved when governments and peoples recognize that terrorism violates the human rights of its victims and ignores the sanctity of life. Those that see it as a problem of international law suggest that, while it may not be resolved altogether, it can be significantly reduced once it is recognized and defined in law and effective international sanctions against terrorists and supporting states are implemented. Those that see it as a law enforcement problem suggest that it can be reduced by the implementation of increased domestic security, enhanced police powers to facilitate detection and apprehension, and more severe domestic legal sanctions against convicted terrorists. As well as those approaches to the problem, there are still some vestiges of the post-World War II period's orientations toward terrorist violence in the literature. Those early analysts based their suggested responses on their observations of or experiences in the post-war independence struggles in Asia and Africa and view the problem of terrorism and, to some extent, international terrorism as a military problem, albeit with generally recognized political aspects.

The diversity of those perspectives on the problem of international terrorism illustrates the difficulties that would be encountered in trying to apply one solution to a very amorphous problem. Those perspectives on international terrorism did not even include all the possibilities, such as the views that international terrorism may be an economic or social problem. The problems are simply not viewed in the same way by everyone involved. Indeed, terrorist violence itself may not be the same for all the parties involved. Terrorists seek different objectives and have different capacities to realize their objectives. Governments have different imperatives (values to defend) and different vulnerabilities. That an "optimal" response will be found to provide a panacea for all the problems of international terrorism is unlikely. That is not to say, however, that there cannot be enough similarities among government imperatives or perceived problems to suggest using a particular type of response in different circumstances. Nor is it to say that a combination of general response policies and programs will not provide an "optimal" response for a variety of events.

While this study sampled the diverse approaches to the problem of international terrorism and considered them as options that governments may adopt, the analysis relied primarily on those studies and commentaries that approached the issue as a political problem involving a fundamental value conflict.[2] Viewed as a political problem, international terrorism is generally approached from several perspectives, based on the recognition that conflicting political values limit the efficacy of humanitarian and legal (international and domestic) approaches and the acceptability of military approaches. Many of the political analysts, therefore, suggest that a combination of responses are necessary and that a single "magic formula" solution to the problem is not possible. Their general recommendation is for the problem of international terrorism to be approached in terms of the necessities both for increased security, including improved crisis management techniques and structures, and for the recognition and alleviation of legitimate grievances. Wilkinson calls this approach a "two-front war."[3]

Despite the general consensus on the need to consider the causes of international (and domestic) terrorism, as well as the security precautions necessary to reduce the frequency and limit the impact of the violence, proponents of the "two-front" approach do not agree on which "theory" or "theories" of response will be the most effective. Few, however, suggest that the implementation of broadly repressive countermeasures or the use of regular military forces should be done, except as a last resort. The greatest disagreement concerns the advisability of adopting a firm, "no negotiations and no compromise" policy toward terrorist demands or a flexible, negotiation policy. While giving credence to the political motivations of terrorists by showing a willingness to try to alleviate the antecedent conditions for political violence, proponents of both the "hard-line" and "two-front" policies do not recognize the merits of terrorist grievances in the resolution of individual terrorist events. As a sanction against the users of terrorist violence, the terrorists' demands are not recognized. The proponents of negotiation, on the other hand, are willing to consider the political grievances of terrorists during the resolution of violent events.

The point is that the selection of a response to international terrorism involves trade-offs, as well as the interaction of a complex array of perceptual and situational variables, and the perceptions of the values that are being traded will determine whether a government thinks of its response policy as being the "optimal" one. The selection of the policy involves a tremendous amount of uncertainty. That is one of the reasons why a large number of analysts support the policy of negotiating for the release of hostages. By negotiating, the uncertainty can be reduced through the assessment of the process of negotiation itself and the conduct of the hostage-holding. The terms of the trade-offs are better assessed.

An "optimal" response, then, is one in which the government feels that it received the greater benefit for its costs.

All that is certain about the phenomenon of international terrorism is that it presents special problems for policymakers, as well as its victims, and there are no "magic formula" cures for it. What appears evident about the phenomenon is that it is not likely to go away. Despite the fact that the absolute number of international terrorist incidents has been on the decline, the absolute number of casualties has been on the increase. Moreover, the evidence that lives are getting cheaper gives impetus to questions and concerns about the possibility of a terrorist group resorting to mass destruction to achieve its aims. Certainly that possibility cannot be ignored.

There are other ominous trends as well, such as the emergence of new types of terrorist groups that do not conform to the patterns of behavior that have come to be expected of terrorists. Rather than being motivated by national liberation or traditional ideological causes, the new terrorists are more nihilistic and more violent, thus they are much more unpredictable. Because the causes of their violence are unknown, little can be done to prevent the eruption of violence. What this means for policymakers is that the context of the policy environment is changing. The assumptions that the old responses to international terrorism were based on may no longer hold true in a few years; the trade-offs will have been rearranged.

- End -

REFERENCES

References -- Chapter I

1. "Statement by United States Representative Ambassador Anthony Quainton Before the Ad Hoc Committee on International Terrorism; March 21, 1979," U.S. Department of State. (Mimeographed).

2. James N. Rosenau, "Internal War as an International Event," in International Aspects of Civil Strife, ed. James N. Rosenau (Princeton: Princeton University Press, 1964); excerpted in Struggles in the State: Sources and Patterns of World Revolution, ed. George A. Kelly and Clifford W. Brown, Jr. (New York: John Wiley and Sons, Inc., 1970), p. 200. Rosenau was primarily addressing the likelihood of foreign interventions in internal wars, but also considered the morbid curiosity or attraction that people have for such extreme violence, a curiosity fed by the press coverage of such events. There is also a growing body of literature expressing concern about the "symbiotic" relationship between the news media and terrorists. This concern will be investigated later in conjunction with the policy implications of restricted press coverage of terrorist events. Also see: John C. Novogrod, "Internal Strife, Self-Determination, and World Order," in International Terrorism and Political Crimes, ed. M. Cherif Bassiouni (Springfield, Ill.: Charles C. Thomas, 1975), p. 98.

3. Jordan J. Paust, "A Survey of Possible Legal Responses to International Terrorism: Prevention, Punishment, and Co-operative Action," Georgia Journal of International and Comparative Law 5 (1975): 432.

4. Henry Tanner, "German Troops Free Hostages on Hijacked Plane in Somalia; Four Terrorists Killed in Raid," New York Times, 18 October 1977, p. 1. Subsequent reports of the West German rescue operation indicate that three terrorists were killed and one wounded. Some accounts of the rescue also indicate that

eighty-six hostages were freed instead of the eight-five initially stated in the Tanner article.

5. Laurie Johnston, "News Agencies' Cooperation Sought," New York Times, 18 October 1977, p. 12. An excellent treatment of the "causes of terrorism," psychological and otherwise, can be found in: Martha Crenshaw, "The Causes of Terrorism," Comparative Politics 13 (July 1981), pp. 379-99. Professor Creshaw summarizes the "common wisdom" and offers several suggestions concerning how individual motivations may carry over into organizational objectives, as well as the difficulty in differentiating between the two.

6. "For Tough West German Force, Feat Capped Years of Training," New York Times, 19 October 1977, p. A14.

7. "13 Nations Training Commandos to Save Air-Hijacking Hostages," New York Times, 22 October 1977, p. 7; and, U.S. Central Intelligence Agency, National Foreign Assessment Center, International Terrorism in 1977: A Research Paper, RP 78-10255U, August 1978, p. 4.

8. U.S. Department of State, "Department Spokesman Released the Following on 10/18/77," Washington, D.C. (Mimeographed).

9. International Terrorism in 1977, p. 4. This C.I.A. study indicates that the establishment of anti-terrorist units may increase the propensity of governments to use them, even in cases for which they are inappropriate. The Reagan administration reaffirmed the U.S. policy not to pay ransoms or to negotiate with terrorists in June of 1981.

10. See Lt. John A. Cully, "Defusing Human Bombs -- Hostage Negotiations," FBI Law Enforcement Bulletin, October 1974.

11. The policy implications of much of the research on revolution and violence, and development and change for that matter, suggest a reformist point of view.

12. See Paul Hofmann, "German and Italian Radicals Linked," New York Times, 20 December 1977, p. 4; and, David Binder, "Palestinian Group Linked to Terrorists of 14 Nations," New York Times, 26 June 1978, p. A10, for journalistic accounts of the cooperative efforts by terrorist organizations. The types of linkages among terrorist groups are discussed by Jillian Becker in Hitler's Children: The Story of the Baader-Meinhof Terrorist Gang (Philadelphia: J.B. Lippincott Company, 1977), pp. 15-18, and other analysts of terrorist groups and individuals. A broader treatment of this phenomenon, including some of the implications for efforts to combat terrorism, can be found in David L. Milbank, International and Transnational Terrorism: Diagnosis and Prognosis (Washington, D.C.: U.S. Central Intelligence Agency, PR76-10030), April 1976). By far the most comprehensive treatment can be found in: Claire Sterling, The Terror Network (New York: Holt, Rinehart and Winston, 1981).

13. D. V. Segre and J. H. Adler, "The Ecology of Terrorism," Encounter 40 (February 1973): 17-18, as quoted in Albert Parry, Terrorism: From Robespierre to Arafat (New York: The Vanguard Press, 1976), p. 537.

14. Parry, Terrorism, p. 538, and Lester A. Sobel, ed., Political Terrorism (New York: Facts on File, Inc., 1975), pp. 52-53.

15. There have been several recent projections that international terrorism is leveling off or declining. Walter Laqueur of the Center for Strategic and International Studies Georgetown University, has stated that international terrorism is on the decline globally. However, he also warned that terrorist activity might expand in terms of the technology, destructive capability, accessible to the terrorists (i.e., nuclear, biological, or chemical weapons), despite the decline in the absolute number of terrorist incidents. "World Terrorism Said Declining," Tupelo (Miss.) Daily Journal, 15 May 1978, p. 25. A 1976 U.S. Central Intelligence Study has indicated that terrorist activity has leveled off. The study did not suggest that terrorist activity would decrease significantly or

disappear in the next decade; instead, it stated that the threat "is not only likely to persist for at least the next several years, but also to evolve in ways that could pose a more substantial threat to U.S. interests -- and, under certain circumstances, to world order -- than in the recent past." Milbank, *International and Transnational Terrorism*, p. 32. Subsequent studies done by the Central Intelligence Agency have indicated a continuing decline in the absolute number of terrorist incidents and an apparently growing preference among terrorist groups for low risk attacks, such as bombings and murders of individuals. Higher risk hostage incidents are on the decline, according to the National Foreign Assessment Center (Central Intelligence Agency) studies: *International Terrorism in 1977* and *International Terrorism in 1978: A Research Paper* (Washington, D.C.: U.S. Central Intelligence Agency, RP 79-10149 March 1979).

16. "A Reassessment of Axiomative Models in Policy Studies," in *Policy Analysis and Deductive Reasoning*, ed. Gordon Tullock and Richard E. Wagner (Lexington, Mass.: Lexington Books, 1978), p. 6. Similar statements indicating the need for more theory and value considerations can be found in: Phillip M. Gregg, "Problems of Theory in Policy Analysis," in *Problems of Theory in Policy Analysis*, ed. Phillip M. Gregg (Lexington, Mass.: Lexington Books, 1976), p. 2; and Ira Sharkansky, "The Political Scientist and Policy Analysis," in *Policy Analysis in Political Science*, ed. Ira Sharkansky (Chicago: Markham Publishing Company, 1970), p. 2.

17. Thomas R. Dye, "A Model for the Analysis of Policy Outcomes," in *Policy Analysis in Political Science*, pp. 24-25.

18. Jack R. van der Silk, *American Legislative Processes* (New York: Thomas J. Crowell Company, Inc. 1977), pp. 328-329; Robert L. Lineberry, *American Public Policy: What Government Does and What Difference it Makes* (New York: Harper and Row, 1977), pp. 85-86; and, as a cost-benefit approach, George C. Edwards III and Ira Sharkansky, *The Policy Predicament: Making and Implementing Public Policy*

(San Francisco: W.H. Freeman and Company, 1978), pp. 170-198.

19. This use of policy impact analysis is suggested in: Lineberry, American Public Policy, p. 93.

20. "An Antidote for Apology, Service, and Witchcraft in Policy Analysis," in Problems of Theory in Policy Analysis, p. 23.

References -- Chapter II

1. J. Bowyer Bell, "Terror: An Overview," in International Terrorism in the Contemporary World, ed. Marius H. Livingston (Westport, Conn.: Greenwood Press, 1978), p. 36.

2. Franco Salomone, "Terrorism and the Mass Media," in International Terrorism and Political Crimes, ed. M. Cherif Bassiouni (Springfield, Ill.: Charles C. Thomas, 1975), p. 44; and, Brain Crozier, A Theory of Conflict (London: Hamish Hamilton, 1974), p. 28.

3. Rosenau, "Internal War as an International Event," pp. 201-202.

4. Parry, Terrorism: From Robespierre to Arafat (New York: The Vanguard Press, 1976), pp. 21-30. Parry summed up his view by stating that: "At all times the root of the terrorists' so-called idealism is a psychological disturbance. Naturally, this does not mean that all people who do not agree with the majority are psychologically disturbed. But we emphatically include among the psychologically disturbed those dissidents who are violent, who try to prove their nonconformity by bombings, killings, skyjackings, and kidnappings" (pp. 23-24). Parry vacillated later by saying that " . . . not all such political terrorists are insane or mentally disturbed, but most are" (p.35).

5. For example, see the discussions of terrorist violence as rational behavior in: Bell, "Terror: An Overview," p. 37; and Jenkins, "International Terrorism: A New Mode of Conflict," p. 15.

6. Wilkinson, *Terrorism and the Liberal State* (New York: John Wiley and Sons, 1977), p. xiii. Walter Laqueur concurs with Wilkinson's conclusion that a comprehensive definition is extremely difficult at best and goes on to suggest that a general theory is "hopeless." Laqueur, *Terrorism: A Study of National and International Political Violence* (Boston: Little, Brown, and Company, 1977), pp. 5-6. Also see: Yonah Alexander, "Introduction," in *International Terrorism: National, Regional, and Global Perspectives* (New York: Praeger Publishers, 1976), p. xi.

7. Bell, *Transnational Terror* (Washington, D.C.: American Enterprise Institute for Public Policy Research, 1975), preface. Bell went on to specify some of the major difficulties with research in this area in his statement that: "Many spectacular terrorist deeds are of uncertain motive, hectic in orchestration, and of mixed results. There are so many variables, so few available articulate terrorists, and such a miasma of outraged indignation and shoddy rationalization surrounding the whole topic that there is seldom any valid analysis" (p. 19).

8. What amounts to a bibliographic essay on international terrorism can be found in the introductory narrative in Robert A. Friedlander, *Terrorism: Documents of International and Local Control*, Vol. 1 (Dobbs Ferry, N.Y.: Oceana Publications, Inc., 1979). More general treatments of the literature on terrorism and international terrorism can be found in: Walter Laqueur, *Terrorism: A Study of National and International Political Violence* (1977) and Paul Wilkinson, *Political Terrorism* (London: Macmillan Press, Ltd., 1974).

9. Thornton, "Terror as a Weapon of Political Agitation," in *Internal War*, ed. Harry Eckstein (New York: Free Press, 1964), p. 71.

10. Alexander Dallin and George W. Breslauer have contended that "just as some violence involves no terror, some terror (e.g., intimidation) requires no violence." See Dallin and Breslauer, *Political Terror in Communist Systems* (Stanford, Calif.: Stanford University Press, 1970), p. 2. The solution to this

conflict may be explained by the phenomena of "residual terror" and "latent terror" within the Communist societies studied by Dallin and Breslauer. The memories of past violence may remain with the members of a society for many years, improving the credibility of any sort of threat and reducing the need for terrorists to actually use violence. This hypothesis can be found in: Peter R. Knauss and D.A. Strickland, "Political Disintegration and Latent Terror," in The Politics of Terrorism, ed. Michael Stohl (New York: Marcel Dekker, Inc., 1979), p. 85.

11. This definition was mentioned by Chalmers Johnson as one given by a participant in a U.S. State Department conference on terrorism held March 25-26, 1979. The author was not mentioned by name, however. See Johnson, "Perspectives on Terrorism," in The Terrorism Reader: A Historical Anthology, ed. Walter Laqueur (Philadelphia: Temple University Press, 1978), p. 268.

12. For example, see the selections written by Carlos Mariguella in Laqueur, The Guerrilla Reader: A Historical Anthology (New York: The New American Library, Inc., 1977), pp. 219-228.

13. Walter, Terror and Resistance: A Study of Political Violence With Case Studies of Some Primitive African Communities (New York: Oxford University Press, 1969), p. 5. Walter also realized that a state of terror could be triggered unintentionally, and he confined his study largely to what he called "intended terrorism" (pp. 8-9). That qualification is also implicit in this study.

14. Ibid., p. 6.

15. Ibid., pp. 6-7. Similar conceptualizations of earlier vintage can also be found, such as: Thornton, "Terror as a Weapon of Political Agitation," pp. 71-73. Thornton called the first form "enforcement terror" (when used by the powerholders or authorities), and the other form "agitational terror" (when used by those aspiring to power). Thornton also referred to similar comceptualizations antecedent to his own, including those of Brian Crozier in his seminal work, The Rebels:

A Study of Post-War Insurrections (Boston: Beacon Press, 1970). Crozier's dichotomy was between "terrorism" and "counter-terrorism" (p. 159). Both Crozier and Thornton discuss terrorism within the context of internal war and it is for that reason that Walter's conceptualizations have been used here. The relationship between terrorism and internal wars is to be explored later.

16. Wilkinson, Political Terrorism, p. 32. Wilkinson also found Walter's terminology to be somewhat ambiguous (pp. 34-35).

17. The distinction becomes less ambiguous in the context of international terrorism when the determination, in many cases, is made by a third party.

18. Wilkinson, Political Terrorism, pp. 36-40. It is not necessary at this point to differentiate between "revolutionary terrorism" and "subrevolutionary terrorism," except in very general terms. The objectives of the terrorists, or at least the affected government's perceptions of those objectives, will become more important later in the analysis. In any case, Wilkinson devotes a large portion of his book, Political Terrorism, to such a differentiation. While the use of the concept of "revolutionary terrorism" is common in the literature, the definitions vary as to the specific types of violence that may be involved. Nonetheless, the ultimate objectives of the violent acts or campaigns are generally considered in much the same way as has been done by Wilkinson. See, for example: Martha Crenshaw Hutchinson, "The Concept of Revolutionary Terrorism," Journal of Conflict Resolution 16 (September 1972): 383-396; Harry R. Targ, "Societal Structure and Revolutionary Terrorism: A Preliminary Investigation," in The Politics of Terrorism, pp. 119-143; and J. Bowyer Bell, Transnational Terror, pp. 15-19 (in particular).

19. Gurr, "Some Characteristics of Political Terrorism in the 1960s," in The Politics of Terrorism, p. 23. Also see: Michael Stohl, "Myths and Realities of Political Terrorism," in The Politics of Terrorism, pp. 3-4.

20. Dallin and Breslauer, Political Terror in Communist Systems (Stanford, Calif.: Stanford University Press, 1970), p. 1. It is obvious that Dallin and Breslauer were primarily confining their definition to the predominant form of terrorist violence within communist societies, but, as will be evident later in the analysis, revolutionary terrorism may not be entirely unknown in those societies.

21. Wilkinson, Political Terrorism, p. 40. The concept of "repressive terrorism" is also similar to Feliks Gross' concept of "mass terror," some aspects of J. Bowyer Bell's "authorized terror," and the uses of "state terror" or "official terror" which appear in many of the recent studies, as well as Walter's "regime of terror" and Thornton's "enforcement terror." See: Gross, "Political Violence and Terror in the 19th and 20th Century Russia and Eastern Europe," in Assassination and Political Violence: A Report to the National Commission on the Causes and Prevention of Violence, ed. James F. Kirkham, Sheldon G. Levy, and William J. Crotty (Washington, D.C.: U.S. Government Printing Office, 1969), p. 428; Bell, Transnational Terror, pp. 13-14; and, Edward Mickolus, "Transnational Terrorism," in The Politics of Terrorism, p. 149. It is often argued by the supporters of political groups that use terrorist violence in their challenges to government authority that they are in fact combatting the application of repressive terrorism by the authorities.

22. Wilkinson, Political Terrorism, p. 40.

23. Bell, Transnational Terror, pp. 14-15. Also see: Michael Stohl, "Myths and Realities of Political Terrorism," p. 10.

24. For example, see: Mary B. Welfling: "Terrorism in Sub-Sahara Africa," in The Politics of Terrorism, p. 260; Raymond R. Corrado, "Ethnic and Student Terrorism in Western Europe," in The Politics of Terrorism, p. 191; Yonah Alexander, in the introduction to International Terrorism: National, Regional, and Global Perspectives, p. xi; Thomas Thornton, "Terror as a Weapon of Political Agitation," pp. 75-80, 91; and, Gaston Bouthoul, "Definitions of

Terrorism," in <u>International Terrorism and World Security</u>, ed. David Carlton and Carlo Schaerf (New York: John Wiley and Sons, 1975), p. 51.

25. Wilkinson, <u>Political Terrorism</u>, pp. 37, 39. Wilkinson found that terrorists working alone or in very small groups were characteristic of subrevolutionary terrorism. He did not consider the nature of vigilante groups, however.

26. Bell, "Terror: An Overview," p. 38.

27. Hyams, <u>Terrorists and Terrorism</u> (London: J.M. Dent and Sons, Ltd., 1975), p. 9.

28. L.C. Green, "Terrorism -- The Canadian Perspective," in <u>International Terrorism: National, Regional, and Global Perspectives</u>, p. 4. Brian Jenkins has suggested that the expansion of the zone of combat and the concomitant narrowing of the range of "innocent bystanders" can be attributed to the post-World War II colonial struggles where the populations of the colonial powers became party to the conflicts overseas. See: Jenkins, <u>High Technology Terrorism and Surrogate War: The Impact of New Technology on Low-Level Violence</u> (Santa Monica, Calif.: Rand Publications, P-5339, January 1975), p. 4. Michael Waltzer takes the idea a step further by suggesting that now there are no innocent by-standers. See: Waltzer, "The New Terrorists: Random Murder," <u>New Republic</u> (August 30, 1975), p. 13.

29. Thornton, "Terror as a Weapon of Political Agitation," pp. 49-80.

30. Ibid., p. 79.

31. This was the working definition given in the preface of <u>Legal Aspects of International Terrorism</u>, ed. Alona E. Evans and John F. Murphy (Lexington, Mass.: Lexington Books, 1978), p. xv. The editors indicated later that: "International terrorism may also be engaged in by private individuals who are serving as government agents." But, the broad category of repressive or state terrorism was not considered.

32. Kelly and Miller, "Internal War and International Systems," in <u>Struggles in the State: Sources and Patterns of World Revolution</u>, p. 230. The relationship between terrorism and internal war is to be explored more fully later.

33. United Nations, General Assembly, Report of the Ad Hoc Committee on International Terrorism, General Assembly Official Records: 28th Session, Supplement No. 28 (A/9028) 1973 (as quoted in Brian M. Jenkins, "International Terrorism: A New Mode of Conflict," pp. 21-22.

34. United Nations, General Assembly, Report of the Ad Hoc Committee on International Terrorism, General Assembly Official Records: 32nd Session, Supplement No. 37 (A/32/37) 1977, as reprinted in Friedlander, <u>Terrorism: Documents of International and Local Control</u>, Vol. 1, p. 379. By contrast, the definition offered by the "nonaligned" states in the 1973 Ad Hoc Committee report included "acts of violence and other repressive acts by colonial, racist, and alien regimes against peoples struggling for their liberation . . .; tolerating or assisting by a State the organization of the remnants of fascists or mercenary groups whose terrorist activity is directed against other sovereign countries; acts of violence committed by individuals or groups of individuals which endanger or take innocent human lives or jeopardize fundamental freedoms providing this definition does not affect the inalienable right to self determination and independence of all peoples under colonial and racist regimes and other forms of alien domination . . .; acts of violence committed by individuals or groups of individuals for private gain, the effects of which are not confined to one state." See: Jenkins, "International Terrorism: A New Mode of Conflict," p. 22.

35. Jenkins, "International Terrorism: A New Mode of Conflict," p. 20.

36. Ibid.

37. Ibid., p. 14.

38. That reservation can be found in Article 5 of the convention and is explained in the attached Explanatory Report. See: Yonah Alexander, et al., Control of Terrorism: International Documents (New York: Crane and Russak, 1979), pp. 88, 103-104. It is also interesting to note France's statement of reservations which included reference to its own constitution's provision for the granting of political asylum (p. 94). The "loophole" giving the signatories some flexibility in issues of extradition and prosecution of political offenders was identified by the U.S. Department of State as being the chief problem with the European Convention. See: U.S. Department of State, "Terrorism: Summary of Applicable United States and International Law: (Washington, D.C.: U.S. Department of State, n.d.), pp. 12-13.

39. Fields, "Terrorism and the Rule of Law: Society at the Crossroads" (Keynote Address at the Symposium on Terrorism and Social Control, 19-20 January 1979, Ohio Northern University College of Law, Ada, Ohio) (Washington, D.C.: U.S. Department of State, n.d.) (Mimeographed).

40. Quainton, "Government Policy and Response in a Terrorist Crisis Situation" (Address before the Chicago Association of Commerce and Industry, September 26, 1978) (Washington, D.C.: U.S. Department of State, n.d.) (Mimeographed).

41. Milbank, International and Transnational Terrorism: Diagnosis and Prognosis (Washington, D.C.: U.S. Central Intelligence Agency, PR 76-10030, April 1976), p. 1.

42. Ibid.

43. Ibid., p. 9.

44. The origin of the exact terminology used in that dichotomy is uncertain. The earliest reference to the "transnational" character of revolutionary terrorism found in this study was in" J. Bowyer Bell, "Contemporary Revolutionary Organizations," in Transnational Relations and World Politics, ed. Robert O. Keohane and Joseph S. Nye, Jr. (Cambridge:

Harvard University Press, 1973), pp. 153-168. Bell subsequently authored Transnational Terror (1975).

45. Ibid., p. 44. Similar discussions can also be found in: Mickolus, "Transnational Terrorism," in The Politics of Terrorism, pp. 147-190.

46. This is not to suggest that Milbank did not consider those aspects of terrorism, rather it means that Mickolus brought them more closely together in his definition.

47. Bishop, "The Role of Political Terrorism in the Palestinian Resistance Movement: June 1967-October 1973," in The Politics of Terrorism, p. 328.

48. Garcia-Mora, International Responsibility for Hostile Acts of Private Persons Against Foreign States (The Hague: Martinus Nijhoff, 1962), p. 153.

49. The "protective" theory of jurisdiction will be dealt with later within the context of the restraints on and arguments for government responses to terrorism outside their own borders.

50. The "single-phase" and "dual-phase" dichotomy has been ascribed, by Ernest Evans, to Martha Crenshaw Hutchinson from a paper entitled "Transnational Terrorism as a Policy Issue" delivered at the annual meeting of the American Political Science Association in 1974. See: Evans, Calling a Truce to Terror: The American Response to International Terrorism (Westport, Conn.: Greenwood Press, 1979), p. 9. This also excludes those cases in which requests for extradition is the appropriate response by the affected government.

51. This conceptualization is essentially the same as that of Ronald D. Crelinsten, Danielle Laberge-Altmejd, and Dennis Szabo in Terrorism and Criminal Justice: An International Perspective (Lexington, Mass.: Lexington Books, 1978), p. 10. They treat the phenomena as acts of domestic terrorism, however.

52. Sobol, Political Terrorism, p. 25.

53. Ibid., pp. 64-65.

54. Ibid., p. 276.

55. William Mathewson, "Bitterness Surrounding Dutch Train Hijacking Lingers a Year Later," Wall Street Journal (January 6, 1977), p. 1, reprinted in The Struggle Against Terrorism, ed. William P. Lineberry (New York: H.W. Wilson Company, 1977), pp. 62-69. There was a train hijacking at about the same time as the attack on the embassy. The May 1977 hijacking was mentioned in the editor's note following the article.

56. Sobol, Political Terrorism, p. 17.

57. Ibid., p. 266.

58. Ibid., pp. 274-275.

59. Ibid.

60. Ibid., pp. 240-241.

References -- Chapter III

1. Wilkinson, Terrorism and the Liberal State, p. 82.

2. Ibid.

3. Crozier, The Rebels, p. 159. Also see: David Fromkin, "The Strategy of Terrorism," Foreign Affairs (July 1975), reprinted in At Issue: Politics in the World Arena, 2nd ed., ed. Steven L. Spiegel (New York: St. Martin's Press, 1977), p. 131; and, David C. Rapoport, Assassination and Terrorism (Toronto: Canadian Broadcasting Corporation, 1971), pp. 54-55.

4. Brian Jenkins found that in the more than 700 international terrorist incidents between 1968 and mid-1975 only about 700 persons were killed and 1700 wounded or injured, less than the U.S. murder rate per annum and less financially costly than shoplifting losses per annum in the U.S. See: David Anable,

"Coming to Grips with World Terrorism," Christian Science Monitor (19 December 1975), p. 3, reprinted in The Struggle Against Terrorism, p. 42.

5. Laqueur, "The Futility of Terrorism," Harper's Magazine (March 1976), reprinted in The Struggle Against Terrorism, p. 140.

6. See: Jenkins, "International Terrorism: A New Mode of Conflict," p. 25; Mickolus, "Transnational Terrorism," p. 165; and, Rapoport, Assassination and Terrorism, p. 55.

7. Livingston, in the Preface to International Terrorism in the Contemporary World, p. 20.

8. Gurr, "Some Characteristics of Political Terrorism in the 1960s," p. 29.

9. Hyams, Terrorists and Terrorism, p. 9.

10. Crozier, The Rebels, pp. 160, 179.

11. Rapoport, Assassination and Terrorism, p. 46.

12. Edward Weisband and Damir Roguly have a somewhat related differentiation that they call the movement's "operational strategy," including "three interrelated phenomena: the general normative or ideological framework of common faiths or generalized principles that unifies a movement, the actions themselves, and the verbal strategy used to justify specific actions in the context of broader norms." See: Weisband and Roguly, "Palestinian Terrorism: Violence, Verbal Strategy, and Legitimacy," p. 280. The components of the "operational strategy" suggest that the terrorists' ideological objectives must be related to the lower-level objectives, or at least that has been the case among Palestinian Terrorist organizations.
Paul Wilkinson has noted the need to distinguish between an organization's "long-term political objectives and strategies and their military strategies." See: Wilkinson, Terrorism and the Liberal State, p. 106.

13. Weisband and Roguly, "Palestinian Terrorism: Violence, Verbal Strategy, and Legitimacy," p. 258.

14. See, for example: Thornton, "Terror as a Weapon of Political Agitation," p. 76; and, Evans, Calling a Truce to Terror, pp. 36-39.

15. Wilkinson, Terrorism and the Liberal State, p. 96.

16. Oran R. Young, "Systemic Bases of Intervention," in Law and Civil War in the Modern World, ed. John Norton Moore (Baltimore: The Johns Hopkins University Press, 1974), pp. 117-118. Young was primarily addressing the propensities to become involved in foreign civil wars and the forms of such involvement, but the same interventionist tendencies should also be evidenced when the civil violence is less extensive.

17. "Legitimacy potential" was one of the concepts that Chalmers Johnson mentioned as being presented at the 1976 State Department conference on terrorism. He did not identify the originator of the concept, however. See: Johnson, "Perspectives on Terrorism," p. 274. Also see: Wilkinson, Terrorism and the Liberal State, p. 107.

18. Rosenau, "Internal War as an International Event," p. 210.

19. Mickolus, "Transnational Terrorism," p. 178.

20. Gurr, "Some Characteristics of Political Terrorism in the 1960s," p. 38. According to Gurr, this was the "most striking feature" of his data.

21. Corrado, "Ethnic and Student Terrorism in Western Europe," pp. 192-195; Robert Kupperman and Darrell Trent, Terrorism: Threat, Reality, Response (Stanford, Calif.: Hoover Institution Press, 1979), p. 5; and, Jeffrey A. Tannenbaum, "For World's Alienated, Violence Often Reaps Political Recognition," Wall Street Journal (4 January 1977), p. 1, reprinted in The Struggle Against Terrorism, p. 102. Paul Wilkinson has also noted the potential for increased activity by

secessionist, autonomist, and irredentist groups in Terrorism and the Liberal State, pp. 182, 192.

22. See, for example: Crozier, A Theory of Conflict, pp. 105-106; Johnson, "Perspectives on Terrorism," p. 274; and, Peter Janke, "The Response to Terrorism," in Ten Years of Terrorism: Collected Views (London: Royal United Services Institute for Defence Studies, 1979), pp. 22-23. Somewhat different classification schemes can be found in: Wilkinson, Terrorism and the Liberal State, p. 97; Corrado, "Ethnic and Student Terrorism in Western Europe," p. 191; Jacques Ellul, Autopsy on Revolution, trans. Patricia Wolf (New York: Alfred Knopf, 1971), pp. 267-277; and, Pitirim A. Sorokin, "Fluctuations of Internal Disturbances," in Struggles in the State, p. 126.

23. Crozier, A Theory of Conflict, pp. 105-106.

24. Mickolus, "Transnational Terrorism," p. 179.

25. Wilkinson, Terrorism and the Liberal State, pp. 83-85, 107.

26. Ibid., p. 86.

27. Laqueur, "The Futility of Terrorism," p. 140. The apparent lack of success that the South Moluccans and Kurds have experienced in their efforts to attract international support is evidence of the impact of other political factors. Both of those groups lack the visibility of the Palentinian groups, and neither can evoke the same sympathies and support as can the Irish Republican Army. That is not to say, however, that they don't have the potential to increase their visibility.

28. See, for example: Thornton, "Terror as a Weapon of Political Agitation," p. 82; Jay Mallin, "Terrorism as a Military Weapon," Air University Review (January-February 1977), reprinted in International Terrorism in the Contemporary World, p. 396; Wilkinson, Terrorism and the Liberal State, p. 113; and, Stohl, "Myths and Realities of Political Terrorism," p. 14. This type of terrorism is called "organizational

terror" by J. Bowyer Bell, although there would seem to be some overlap with his concept of "allegiance terror" as well. See: Bell, Transnational Terror, pp. 15-16.

29. Wilkinson, Terrorism and the Liberal State, pp. 101-102.

30. Crozier, A Theory of Conflict, p. 129.

31. Wilkinson, Terrorism and the Liberal State, p. 111.

32. See, for example: Jenkins, "International Terrorism: A New Mode of Conflict," p. 17; Evans, Calling a Truce to Terror, pp. 26-29; Crozier, A Theory of Conflict, p. 127; Mallin, "Terrorism as a Military Weapon," pp. 395-396; Fromkin, "The Strategy of Terrorism," p. 131; and, John B. Wolf, "Terrorist Manipulation of the Democratic Process," in International Terrorism in the Contemporary World, p. 299.

33. Rosenau, "Internal War as an International Event," p. 220.

34. The competition may even be between two different terrorist groups, each trying to demonstrate their potential to wage successful campaigns against the authorities. See: Weisband and Roguly, "Palestinian Terrorism: Violence, Verbal Strategy, and Legitimacy," p. 285.

35. Mickolus, "Trends in Transnational Terrorism," p. 68; and, "Transnational Terrorism," p. 165.

36. Christopher Dobson and Ronald Payne, The Terrorists: Their Weapons, Leaders and Tactics (New York: Facts on File, Inc., 1979), p. 14. British Major General Richard Clutterbuck contends that the Munich massacre was committed solely for publicity. See: Clutterbuck, Living with Terrorism (New Rochelle, N.Y.: Arlington House Publishers, 1975), p. 25.

37. Weisband and Roguly, "Palestinian Terrorism: Violence, Verbal Strategy, and Legitimacy," p. 259.

38. See, for example: Fromkin, "The Strategy of Terrorism," p. 131; Thornton, "Terrorism as a Weapon of Political Agitation," pp. 86-87; Rapoport, Assassination and Terrorism, p. 62; Jenkins, "International Terrorism: A New Mode of Conflict," p. 17; Evans, Calling a Truce to Terror, pp. 31-32; and, P.N. Grabosky, "The Urban Context of Political Terrorism," in The Politics of Terrorism, p. 61.

39. Rosenau, "Internal War as an International Event," p. 220. According to Ted Robert Gurr, the uncertainty about the outcome of the conflict may also lead to foreign interventions or counterresponses. See: Gurr, "The Relevance of Theories of Internal Violence for the Control of Intervention," in Law and Civil War in the Modern World, ed. John Norton Moore (Baltimore: Johns Hopkins University Press, 1974), pp. 75-77.

40. Crozier, A Theory of Conflict, p. 127.

41. Wilkinson, Terrorism and the Liberal State, p. 80.

42. See: Evans, Calling a Truce to Terror, pp. 31-32; Thornton, "Terror as a Weapon of Political Agitation," pp. 83-84; and, Jenkins, "International Terrorism: A New Mode of Conflict," p. 17.

43. Thornton, "Terror as a Weapon of Political Agitation," p. 74 (also see pages 84-85).

44. Hutchinson, "The Concept of Revolutionary Terrorism," Journal of Conflict Resolution 16 (September 1972): 388.

45. Thornton, "Terror as a Weapon of Political Agitation," p. 74. Indeed, the disruption may cause the population to choose a potentially more repressive authority structure, e.g., by precipitating the election of candidates that are more inclined to abridge civil liberties in order to end the terrorism.

46. Milbank, International Terrorism in 1976, p. 4.

47. See: Crozier, A Theory of Conflict, p. 127; Jenkins, "International Terrorism: A New Mode of Conflict," p. 18; and, Stohl, "Myths and Realities of Political Terrorism," p. 14.

48. See: Crozier, The Rebels, p. 160; Thornton, "Terror as a Weapon of Political Agitation," p. 86; Mallin, "Terrorism as a Military Weapon," p. 396; and, Ernest Halperin, Terrorism in Latin America (Beverly Hills, Calif.: Sage Publications, 1976), p. 7.

49. Weisband and Roguly, "Palestinian Terrorism: Violence, Verbal Strategy, and Legitimacy," p. 285; and, Wilkinson, Terrorism and the Liberal State, p. 31.

50. Johnson, "Perspectives on Terrorism," p. 282; and, Kupperman and Trent, Terrorism: Threat, Reality, and Response, p. 37.

51. Mickolus, "Trends in Transnational Terrorism," p. 57, and "Transnational Terrorism," p. 165.

52. Rosenau, "Internal War as an International Event," p. 220.

53. Clutterbuck, Living With Terrorism, p. 29.

54. The impact of terrorism on tourist industries is discussed in: Grabosky, "The Urban Context of Political Terrorism," p. 67.

55. Milbank, International Terrorism in 1976, p. 4.

56. See, for example: Jenkins, "International Terrorism: A New Mode of Conflict," pp. 16-17; Evans, Calling a Truce to Terror, pp. 33-37; Wilkinson, Terrorism and the Liberal State, p. 112; and, Crozier, A Theory of Conflict, p. 127.

57. See, for example, the descriptions of terrorist organizations in: Gurr, "Some Characteristics of Political Terrorism in the 1960s," pp. 25, 33-35; and, Wilkinson, Terrorism and the Liberal State, p. 113. J.K. Zawodny suggests that there may be a correlation

between the size of the group and its activeness, with smaller groups being more active. See: Zawodny, "Unconventional Warfare," in Conflict Resolution: Contributions of the Behavioral Sciences, ed. Clagett G. Smith (Notre Dame, Ind.: University of Notre Dame Press, 1971), pp. 394-395.

58. Edward Mickolus suggests that terrorists may turn to international acts of violence because they do not have the necessary support structures within their own states to wage successful campaigns. See: "Transnational Terrorism," p. 179.

59. Rapoport, Assassination and Terrorism, pp. 25-26, 54-55.

60. Tannenbaum, "For World's Alienated, Violence Often Reaps Political Recognition," p. 103.

61. Mickolus has found that a few groups do possess extensive reportoires of violence, particularly the Popular Front for the Liberation of Palestine, the Jewish Defense League, the Irish Republican Army, the Japanese Red Army, Black September, and Argentina's People's Revolutionary Army. See: "Transnational Terrorism," p. 178.

62. Halperin, Terrorism in Latin America, p. 18. Also see: Thornton, "Terror as a Weapon of Political Agitation," pp. 89-90.

63. Milbank, International Terrorism in 1976, p. 8. Also see: C.I.A., International Terrorism in 1977, p. 5; and Thornton, "Terror as a Weapon of Political Agitation," p. 89. The personnel problems that small terrorist groups might encounter has been dealt with to some extent by J. Bowyer Bell. Bell suggests that terrorist organizations may exhibit what he calls "institutionalized revolutionary incompetence" characterized by "(1) the increasing assumption of responsibility by the talented to the point of overload and (2) the inherent nature of all conspiracy that hinders internal communication, often thereby guaranteeing rising incomprehension within the organization, hardening disagreement, and ultimately schism." See: Bell, Transnational Terror, p. 71. Also

see: J.K. Zawodney, "Unconventional Warfare," *The American Scholar* XXXI (June 1962), reprinted in *Problems of National Security*, ed. Henry A. Kissinger (New York: Praegar Publishers, 1965), p. 339; and, for a much broader and more theoretical treatment of internal dissension, Steve Tappis, "Factionalism in Protest Organizations," a paper presented at the annual meeting of the Midwest Political Science Association in Cincinnati on April 17, 1981.

64. Dobson and Payne, *The Terrorists: Their Weapons, Leaders, and Tactics*, pp. 4-5. Dobson and Payne identify the specific types and origins of weapons now in common use among terrorist groups. Also see: Wilkinson, *Terrorism and the Liberal State*, pp. 200-201.

65. There have been several attempts to shoot down airliners with SAMs since 1973, including one by the Popular Front for the Liberation of Palestine near Rome in 1973 and one by "Carlos" Ilich Ramiriz Sanchez at Orly Airport near Paris in 1975. See: Dobson and Payne, *The Terrorists: Their Weapons, Leaders, and Tactics*, pp. 15-16.

66. Miller and Russell, "The Evolution of Revolutionary Warfare: From Mao to Marighella and Meinhof," pp. 192-193.

67. Mallin, for instance, notes that the Cuban underground during the 1950s did not use metal in its bombs (at least in some cases) to minimize the casualties while preserving the psychological impact of the explosions. See: Mallin, *Terror and Urban Guerrillas*, p. 7.

68. The general problem and possibilities of nuclear terrorism are discussed in: Dobson and Payne, *The Terrorists: Their Weapons, Leaders, and Tactics*, p. 133; and, Grabosky, "The Urban Context of Political Terrorism," p. 8. Much more specific treatment of the issue can be found in: Brian Jenkins, *The Consequences of Nuclear Terrorism* (Santa Monica, Calif.: Rand Corporation, P-6373, August 1979); Peter deLeon, et al., *Attributes of Potential Criminal Adversaries of U.S. Nuclear Programs* (Santa Monica,

Calif.: Rand Corporation, R-2225-SL, February 1978); Mason Willrich and Theodore B. Taylor, Nuclear Theft: Risks and Safeguards (Cambridge, Mass.: Ballinger, 1974); Mason Willrich, ed., International Safeguards and Nuclear Industry (Baltimore: Johns Hopkins University Press, 1973); R.W. Mengel, "Terrorism and New Technologies of Destruction: An Overview of the Potential Risk," Appendix 2 of Disorders and Terrorism (Washington, D.C.: U.S. Government Printing Office, 1977); David Krieger, "What happens IF . . .? Terrorists, Revolutionaries, and Nuclear Weapons," The Annals 430 (March 1977): 44-57; and, the several publications of Phillip A. Karber for the U.S. Atomic Energy Commission and BDM Corporation. The Bulletin of the Atomic Scientists has also contained articles spanning the last decade that deal with numerous aspects of the potential threat.

69. Jenkins, High Technology Terrorism and Surrogate War, pp. 105-106; and, "International Terrorism: A New Mode of Conflict," p. 15. Several analysts have explained the reluctance of terrorists to use mass killing by referring to Stalin's statement, "A single death is a tragedy, a million deaths is a statistic." Indeed, the effect of the violence may be diluted when the numbers of people killed exceed the audiences' ability to conceptualize.

70. Evans, Calling a Truce to Terror, p. 56.

71. Marius Livingston, in the Preface to International Terrorism in the Contemporary World, pp. 19-20.

72. Wilkinson, Terrorism and the Liberal State, pp. 189, 203-206. Even less encouraging is the fact that there have already been threats to use nuclear devices in populated areas. Thus far, however, the terrorists or criminals attempting extortion by such means have not had access to the devices that they claim to have. Just such a scenario, although fictitious, can be found in The Fifth Horseman, by journalists Larry Collins and Dominique Lapierre, which has been a bestseller in France and was published in the U.S. by Simon and Schuster during the summer of 1980. Collins and Lapierre reveal in their book that there have in

fact been over fifty nuclear blackmail attempts in the U.S. See: "Nuclear Ransom," *Time* (March 17, 1980), p. 46. The fact that there have been attempts has been confirmed by U.S. officials. For example, see the interview with Anthony C.E. Quainton, Director of the U.S. State Department's Office for Combatting Terrorism, in: "Lessons of London's Victory Over Terrorists," *U.S. News and World Report* (May 19, 1980), p. 45. A good overview of the security problems and measures being used to protect nuclear bombs in the U.S. can be found in: Orr Kelly, "If Terrorists Go After U.S. Nuclear Bombs," *U.S. News and World Report* (March 12, 1979), pp. 43-45.

73. Roger Trinquier, *Modern Warfare* (New York: Pall Mall Press, 1964), p. 7. The need for terrorists to seek popular support is discussed in the following: John Spanier, *Games Nations Play: Analyzing International Politics* (New York: Praeger Publishers, 1972), p. 175; Crozier, *The Rebels*, p. 12, 191; and, Huntington, "Patterns of Violence in World Politics," p. 21.

74. See, for example: Brian Jenkins, *The Five Stages of Urban Guerrilla Warfare: Challenge of the 1970s* (Santa Monica, Calif.: Rand Corporation, P-4670, July 1971), p. 4; Crozier, *A Theory of Conflict*, pp. 126-127; and, Wilkinson, *Terrorism and the Liberal State*, p. 32.

75. Wilkinson, *Terrorism and the Liberal State*, p. 55. Wilkinson also suggests that the terror used during the guerrilla warfare stage is not the same as that used at the lower level of violence, i.e., terrorism (p. 58). Thornton characterizes the change as being from agitational to enforcement terror. See: Thornton, "Terror as a Weapon of Political Agitation," p. 90.

76. Crozier, *A Theory of Conflict*, p. 129; and, *The Rebels*, p. 128.

77. Weisband and Roguly, "Palestinian Terrorism: Violence, Verbal Strategy, and Legitimacy," p. 279.

78. The international status of the PLO and its impact on the organization's use of terrorist violence is discussed in: Johnson, "Perspectives on Terrorism," p. 282; Dobson and Payne, The Terrorists: Their Weapons, Leaders, and Tactics, pp. 87-88; and, Fromkin, "The Strategy of Terrorism," p. 695.

79. Dennis W. Stiles, "Sovereignty and the New Violence," Air University Review 27 (July-August 1976), reprinted in Contemporary Terrorism: Selected Readings, ed. John D. Elliot and Leslie K. Gibson (Gaithersburg, Md.: International Association of Chiefs of Police, 1978), pp. 261-267. The direct negotiation of hostage releases by foreign governments may also be a form of de facto recognition of the terrorist organization, according to Jay Mallin. See: Mallin, Terror and Urban Guerrillas, p. 7.

80. "Can Airports Be Safe from Terror Bombings?" U.S. News and World Report (January 12, 1976), p. 58.

81. See: Maynard M. Stephens, "The Oil and Natural Gas Industries: A Potential Target of Terrorists," in Terrorism: Threat, Reality, Response, pp. 200-223; and, U.S. General Accounting Office, "Key Crude Oil and Products Pipelines Are Vulnerable to Disruption," Report to the Congress, EMD-79-63, August 27, 1979.

82. Knauss and Strickland, "Political Disintegration and Latent Terror," p. 77.

83. Ibid., p. 82. The authors go on to suggest that social inertia alone may prevent complete societal collapse, as people cling to the familiar routines of their daily lives (such as happened during the civil war in Lebanon recently, when some people appeared to be oblivious to the raging conflict) (pp. 110, 89-90). The authors also draw the distinction between social breakdown and political disintegration. The latter does not always lead to the former (p. 94). Also see: Rapoport, Assassination and Terrorism, p. 44.

84. See, for example: Wilkinson, Terrorism and the Liberal State, pp. 18 - 20; Jenkins, High

Technology Terrorism and Surrogate War, p. 113; and, Knauss and Strickland, "Political Disintegration and Latent Terror," p. 81.

85. Lenin called this competition the "dual power" situation. The revolutionaries supplant state power by claiming the legitimacy of their own violence and the illegitimacy of the government's. See: Halperin, Terrorism in Latin America, p. 16.

86. See the discussions in: Wilkinson, Terrorism and the Liberal State, p. 23; Crozier, A Theory of Conflict, pp. 3-12; and, Henry Bienen, Violence and Social Change: A Review of Current Literature (Chicago: University of Chicago Press, 1968), p. 4.

87. Wilkinson, Terrorism and the Liberal State, p. 54.

88. Luis Kutner, "A Philosophical Perspective on Rebellion," in International Terrorism and Political Crimes, p. 52. More comprehensive treatment of this idea can be found in: Glenn J. Gray, On Understanding Violence Philosophically (New York: Harper and Row, 1970).

89. Crozier, A Theory of Conflict, p. 10.

90. Jenkins, High Technology Terrorism and Surrogate War, p. 113. Also see: Crozier, A Theory of Conflict, p. 5.

91. Gurr, "Some Characteristics of Political Terrorism in the 1960s," pp. 44-45.

92. Wilkinson, Terrorism and the Liberal State, p. 180.

References -- Chapter IV

1. Most of the variables mentioned above were listed in Paul Wilkinson's description of the context of terrorist campaigns. See: Wilkinson, Terrorism and the Liberal State, p. 82.

2. One or more of these possible precipitants of terrorist activity is mentioned in each of the following: Anderson, von der Mehden, and Young, Issues of Political Development, pp. 89-91; Laqueur, Terrorism, pp. 133-148; Crozier, A Theory of Conflict, p. 16; and, Rapoport, Assassination and Terrorism, p. 40. But, none of these analysts attaches much significance to such variables.

3. See, for example: Anderson, von der Mehden, and Young, Issues of Political Development, pp. 91-92; Laqueur, Terrorism, p. 134; Laqueur, in the Foreword to Kupperman and Trent, Terrorism: Threat, Reality, Response, p. xvii; and, Rapoport, Assassination and Terrorism, pp. 66-78.

4. This idea is implicit in most of the literature that deals with revolution and civil strife. Once the "causes" of political violence are identified and explained, the next step would be to eliminate them. See, for example, the theories of relative deprivation, "rising expectations," etc., in: James Chowning Davies, ed., When Men Revolt and Why (New York: The Free Press, 1971); Ivo K. Feierabend, Rosalind L. Feierabend, and Ted Robert Gurr, eds., Anger, Violence, and Politics (Englewood Cliffs, N.J.: Prentice-Hall, 1972); Ted Robert Gurr, Why Men Rebel (Princeton: Princeton University Press, 1970); and Harry Eckstein, ed., Internal War. Summaries of the theories can be found in: A.S. Cohan, Theories of Revolution (New York: John Wiley and Sons, 1975). Also see: Sloan T. Letman, "Some Sociological Aspects of Terror-Violence in a Colonial Setting," in International Terrorism and Political Crimes, pp. 33-42.

5. This is perhaps an added incentive for terrorists to operate outside of their own states. Outside they can gain access to more sympathetic news media or, at least, media that are less subject to manipulation by the target government.

6. The impact of acts or credible threats of mass destruction is an exception; it would certainly present immediate threats to government authority.

7. The complicity of both governments in the events within their jurisdictions is not difficult to determine, but the extent of their complicity is more uncertain. Whether they could have terminated the events is questionable.

8. These countermeasures are somewhat similar to those offered by Kupperman and Trent in <u>Terrorism: Threat, Reality, Response</u>, pp. 92-98. The authors give four functions of government response: prevention, control, containment, and restoration. Some of the same functions are suggested by Grabosky in his list, which includes the limitation of opportunities for terrorist violence, manipulation of the mass media (communication), and increasing of security, as well as ameliorating the conditions that cause the violence. See: Grabosky, "The Urban Context of Political Terrorism," pp. 68-70. The former special assistant to the U.S. Secretary of State and Coordinator for Combatting Terrorism, Robert A. Fearey, also suggests a process of intelligence gathering (preparation), physical security, and arrest and punishment, as well as ameliorating causes. See: "Terrorism: 'Growing and Increasingly Dangerous'," <u>U.S. News and World Report</u> (September 29, 1975), reprinted in <u>The Struggle Against Terrorism</u>, p. 52.

9. The numbering does not necessarily mean that the actions will be taken sequentially.

10. Wilkinson, for example, suggests that governments should look for clues to indicate impending terrorist violence, such as thefts of weapons, explosives, and supplies; disappearances of known revolutionaries or their meetings; and, small-scale violence. See: Wilkinson, <u>Terrorism and the Liberal State</u>, p. 125; and, Crozier, <u>A Theory of Conflict</u>, p. 12.

11. See, for example: the case study of the 1972 Munich Olympics attack in James P. Bennett and Thomas L. Saaty, "Terrorism: Patterns for Negotiation -- A Case Study Using Hierarchies and Holarchies," in <u>Terrorism: Threat, Reality, Response</u>, pp. 244-284; and, the events analyses by the C.I.A., Edward

Mickolus, David Milbank, and Brian Jenkins cited in the bibliography at the conclusion of this study.

12. See, for example: David G. Hubbard, "A Glimmer of Hope: A Psychiatric Perspective," in International Terrorism and Political Crimes, pp. 27-32; Kobetz and Cooper, Target Terrorism, pp. 119-143; and, Clutterbuck, Living With Terrorism, pp. 116-117. Hubbard's article includes his findings from interviews with fifty-two American and Canadian skyjackers. Clutterbuck describes how psychological and modus operandi profiles have permitted the U.S. government to focus its comprehensive (100%) searches of air passengers to a small percentage of the total passengers processed (.5%). The profiles have increased the likelihood that potential skyjackers will be identified while, at the same time, they have decreased the need to unduly inconvenience the majority of the passengers. This perhaps is one of the best illustrations of the utility of psychological studies in antiterrorist efforts.

13. See, for example: Gurr, "Some Characteristics of Political Terrorism in the 1960s," pp. 33-36, in particular; and Dobson and Payne, The Terrorists: Their Weapons, Leaders and Tactics, pp. 161-200. Dobson and Payne provide a lengthy listing of terrorist organizations including their origins, ideologies and aims, activities, international links, achievements, strengths, and future prospects. Group and other information can also be obtained from the increasing number of commercial consulting firms in the field. For a fee, the firms provide assessments and projections of terrorist activities to corporations conducting business outside of the U.S. Risks International, a firm based in Alexandria, Virginia, for example, provides monthly and quarterly risk assessments to subscribing corporations. It can also provide regional assessments for Europe, North America, Latin America, the Middle East-North Africa, Sub-Sahara Africa, and Asia. (This information was provided by the firm.)

14. See, for example: Paul Hofmann, "Hot Line in Europe to Fight Terrorists: 4 Nations Coordinate Their Efforts and Hope Others Will Join," New York Times (12 April 1978), p. A5; Beall, "Hostage Negotiations," pp. 230-231; Bell, Transnational Terror,

p. 85; and, Richard M. Nixon, *U.S. Foreign Policy for the 1970s: Shaping a Durable Peace* (A Report to the Congress, May 3, 1973) (Washington, D.C.: U.S. Government Printing Office, 1973), p. 223.

15. Kupperman and Trent, *Terrorism: Threat, Reality, Response*, p. 119.

16. Rapoport, *Assassination and Terrorism*, p. 61.

17. See, for example, the discussion of risk reduction in: Kobetz and Cooper, *Target Terrorism*, pp. 160-173. The authors find that planning for contingencies; surveying needs (e.g., equipment and personnel); establishing communications facilities; centralizing command and control structures; relying on team action; avoiding dangerous situations; utilizing expert advice; maintaining a low profile; and, especially, gathering intelligence can reduce significantly the risks that accompany terrorist violence.

18. Robert S. Strother and Eugene H. Methvin, "Terrorism on the Rampage," *Reader's Digest* (November 1975), p. 77. Other analysts also support a more tolerant attitude toward intelligence gathering efforts. See, for example: H.H.A. Cooper, "Terrorism and the Intelligence Function," *Chitty's Law Journal* 24 (1976), reprinted in *Comtemporary Terrorism: Selected Readings*, pp. 181-190.

19. Strother and Methvin, "Terrorism on the Rampage," p. 77. Also see: Wilkinson, *Terrorism and the Liberal State*, p. 124.

20. Denial of means and increased security are the countermeasures suggested by Kupperman and Trent. See: *Terrorism: Threat, Reality, Response*, p. 79.

21. Crozier, *A Theory of Conflict*, p. 150. Crozier concludes that efforts must be made to isolate the group from society and its supporters.

22. Mallin, *Terror and Urban Guerrillas*, p. 13.

23. An example of such cooperation is the recent F.B.I. efforts to stem the flow of financial and material support being given the Irish Republican Army by U.S. citizens. See: Bell, Transnational Terror, pp. 84-85. The value of foreign bases and staging areas in this kind of subconventional warfare is discussed in: Huntington, "Patterns of Violence in World Politics," pp. 26-27.

24. The need for internationally recognized sanctions to be used against states that aid or abet terrorist activities is discussed in: Wilkinson, Terrorism and the Liberal State, pp. 222, 225. The most clear examples of preemptive and punitive strikes are the Israeli commando raids and air strikes against Palestinian refugee camps and known terrorist personnel in Lebanon. The efficacy of the Israeli practice is questionable, however. The strikes probably do more to elicit support and sympathy for the terrorists than they do to deter it.

25. Wilkinson, Terrorism and the Liberal State, p. 154. The "cordon and search" technique and its employment in Cyprus is discussed in: Lt. Col. B.I.S. Gourlay, "Terror in Cyprus," in The Guerrilla -- And How to Fight Him, ed. Lt. Col. T.N. Greene (New York: Frederick A. Praeger, 1962), pp. 232-248; and Julian Paget, Counter-Insurgency Operations: Techniques of Guerrilla Warfare (New York: Walker and Co., 1967), p. 133.

26. The difficulty that terrorist organizations experience in replacing lost personnel probably accounts for their apparent preference for low-risk operations in recent months and the frequency of demands for the release of captured terrorists. The demands of releases may have more to do with the organizations' fear that incarcerated terrorists will reveal information to the authorities and with the need to maintain high levels of organizational morale, however. See: Wilkinson, Terrorism and the Liberal State, p. 194. Wilkinson feels that the primary reason is the replacement problem. He also suggests that the passage of the emergency powers act had much to do with the P.I.R.A.'s offer of a truce for the Christmas holidays of 1974 and the subsequent "cease-fire" the following January. With so many of its

leaders arrested or detained, the P.I.R.A. would have had difficulty mustering enough personnel for effective operations (p. 155).

27. Paul O'Higgins, "Unlawful Seizure of Persons By States," in *International Terrorism and Political Crimes*, p. 345.

28. The Israelis are, by no means, the only ones to use extralegal methods to apprehend or kill terrorists. Their activities have simply been more publicized.

29. An example of the use of extraordinary means is the recent West German action to facilitate the isolation of captured Baader-Meinhof gang members. Laws passed in 1975 and 1976 restrict the lawyer-client relationship and, among other things, prevent the use of a collective defense (presumably to help de-politicize terrorists' trials and limit terrorist communication). See: Becker, *Hitler's Children*, p. 263; Tom Wicker, "Law and Terrorism," *New York Times* (30 December 1977), p. A25; and, Craig R. Whitney, "Bonn Wasn't Eager to Extradite Abu Daoud," *New York Times* (23 January 1977), p. E2, reprinted in *The Struggle Against Terrorism*," pp. 72-76.

30. Kupperman and Trent, *Terrorism: Threat, Reality, Response*, p. 103; and, "Can Airports Be Safe From Terror Bombings?"

31. See: Clutterbuck, *Living With Terrorism*, pp. 62-64; and, Kupperman and Trent, *Terrorism: Threat, Reality, Response*, pp. 79-89. Brian Jenkins has found that with the tremendous increase in technology that is accessible to terrorists few countervailing technologies exist to protect civilian targets. See: Jenkins, *High Technology Terrorism and Surrogate War*, p. 110. The subject is also dealt with in some detail in: Kobetz and Cooper, *Target Terrorism: Providing Protective Services*.

32. Studies of hostage situations have produced a sizable body of knowledge about the course and effects of short and prolonged captivities. Especially valuable insight into the problems that hostages may face in

maintaining their physical and psychological well-being in captivity, as well as counteracting terrorist efforts to dehumanize their victims prior to carrying out physical abuse or murder, can be found in Geoffrey Jackson's account of his eight-month captivity by the Tupamaros in Uruguay. See: Jackson, Surviving the Long Night: An Autobiographical Account of a Political Kidnapping (New York: Vanguard Press, Inc., 1974).

33. Mallin, Terror and Urban Guerrillas, p. 13.

34. Clutterbuck, Living With Terrorism, pp. 54-61. Clutterbuck suggests using two-car convoys, quick reaction forces, and variations in routine to discourage kidnappings and assassinations. He finds that the use of bodyguards is of limited value because of the large number that would be required (over forty to be really effective).

35. Kupperman and Trent, Terrorism: Threat, Reality, Response, p. 112.

36. See: Martin E. Silverstein, "The Medical Survival of Victims of Terrorism," in Terrorism: Threat, Reality, Response, pp. 349-392. Silverstein assesses the types of victims, special medical (physical and psychological) problems, and numbers of victims that might result from terrorist violence and suggests a model program to provide medical rescue and care, including a national and regional plan for such emergency care responses.

37. See: Kupperman and Trent, Terrorism: Threat, Reality, Response, pp. 92-98. The authors suggest that restoration of the site is a crucial element in limiting the impact of the violence.

38. Ibid., p. 112.

39. Mickolus, "Transnational Terrorism," p. 167.

40. Ibid.; and, Franco Salomone, "Terrorism and the News Media," in International Terrorism and Political Crimes, pp. 45-46.

41. See, for example: William J. Drummond and Augustine Zycher, "The Fourth Estate: Arafat's Press Agents," Harper's Magazine (March 1976), pp. 24-30.

42. Huntington, "Patterns of Violence in World Politics," pp. 25-28; and, Crozier, A Theory of Conflict, p. 152.

43. Huntington, "Patterns of Violence in World Politics," p. 26.

44. Crozier, A Theory of Conflict, p. 152. Because of the necessity for credibility, Crozier concludes that complete censorship of the news would be unwise. Also see: Charles Roetter, Psychological Warfare (London: B.T. Batsford, Ltd., 1974). Roetter discusses some of the techniques that have been used, primarily during the Second World War, to engender public confidence and support for governments. His discussion of F.D.R.'s "fire-side chats" as a confidence building device is particularly interesting and not entirely beyond the abilities of government leaders during terrorist campaigns and other violence (Chapter 11, in particular).

45. Knauss and Strickland, "Political Disintegration and Latent Terror," p. 83.

46. Wilkinson, Terrorism and the Liberal State, p. 124, and Terrorism Versus Liberal Democracy: The Problem of Response, p. 10.

47. Crozier, A Theory of Conflict, p. 153.

48. Burton, Urban Terrorism, p. 228.

49. Grabosky, "The Urban Context of Political Terrorism," p. 60.

50. See, for example: Kupperman and Trent, Terrorism: Threat, Reality, Response, p. 128; and, Rapoport, Assassination and Terrorism, p. 64.

51. Wilkinson calls this the "constabulary" ethic. See: Wilkinson, Terrorism and the Liberal State, pp. 142-143. He also expresses concern that giving the

police increased firepower may create problems (p. 144).

52. Ibid., p. 150.

53. Ibid., pp. 150-151.

54. Ibid., p. 151.

55. Burton, Urban Terrorism, p. 220.

56. See: "13 Nations Training Commandos To Save Air-Hijacking Hostages;" Wilkinson, Terrorism and the Liberal State, pp. 140-149 (especially concerning the British antiterrorist units); Dobson and Payne, The Terrorists: Their Weapons, Leaders and Tactics, pp. 146-147; Francis A. Bolz, Jr., "Hostage Confrontation and Rescue," in Terrorism: Threat, Reality, Response, pp. 398-399 (especially the New York City Police Department's team); and, Kupperman and Trent, Terrorism: Threat, Reality, Response, pp. 153-154.

57. Dobson and Payne, The Terrorists: Their Weapons, Leaders and Tactics, pp. 146-147; and, "13 Nations Training Commandos To Save Air-Hijacking Hostages."

58. See: Wilkinson, Terrorism and the Liberal State, p. 138; and, Kupperman and Trent, Terrorism: Threat, Reality, Response, pp. 128-139.

59. See: Kupperman and Trent, Terrorism: Threat, Reality, Response, pp. 163-171; and, Darrell M. Trent, "A National Policy to Combat Terrorism," Policy Review 9 (Summer 1979): 41-53. In the second work, Trent expresses concern that the structural arrangement of the U.S. effort is not conducive to effective coordination and control. There are too many departments and agencies involved and little central control.

60. See: Sir Robert Mark, "Kidnapping, Terrorism and the News Media in Britain," in Ten Years of Terrorism, p. 85; and, Kupperman and Trent, Terrorism: Threat, Reality, Response, pp. 130-131.

61. See: Sobol, Political Terrorism, pp. 85, 123, 132-133, 143. The degree of government sponsorship and support probably varies considerably from country to country, but in each case the clandestine organization (one of which is actually called the "Death Squad") is used to reinforce regime authority. To some extent, governments may also encourage conflicts among terrorist organizations that are ideologically incompatible as a means of combatting one or more of the groups.

62. This could be more correctly stated as "Hypotheses of Response," but that would be an inescapable admission of the fragility of the arguments and the lack of hard evidence in support of each "theory." The use of "theory" here will also serve to distinguish these views from the hypotheses to follow in the next chapter.

63. This differentiation is suggested by Ernest Evans and is borrowed from the strategic deterrence literature. Evans states that "deterrence is the art of convincing an opponent that the costs and risks of a particular course of action outweigh the benefits: that C (costs) + R (risks) greater than B (benefits). Evans, Calling a Truce to Terrorism, p. 65; and, Alexander George and Richard Smoke, Deterrence in American Foreign Policy: Theory and Practice (New York: Columbia University Press, 1974), p. 48. The latter is the source cited by Evans.

64. Grabosky, "The Urban Context of Political Terrorism," p. 70.

65. See, for example, David Fromkin's assessment of the counterterror used by the French army in the "Battle of Algiers," in: Fromkin, "The Strategy of Terrorism," p. 134. Also see: Crozier, The Rebels, p. 195.

66. Crozier, A Theory of Conflict, pp. 149-150. Also see: Lindsay, "Unconventional Warfare," p. 349.

67. Crozier, A Theory of Conflict, pp. 149-150. Also see: Lindsay, "Unconventional Warfare," p. 349.

68. Burton, Urban Terrorism, p. 212.

69. Eckstein, "On the Etiology of Internal War," p. 187.

70. Ibid., pp. 186-187.

71. Examples of this type of action include the use of detentions in Northern Ireland to hold suspected terrorist operatives and the suggested use of an "offence of disguise"to permit police and British military units to detain anyone suspected of trying to conceal his or her identity. See Lord Gardiner's committee report to Parliament (January 1975) in: Friedlander, Terrorism: Documents of International and Local Control, Vol. I, pp. 415-439.

72. It has been revealed that the U.S. government engaged in such activities during the 1960s and early 1970s. Civil rights leaders and anti-war protesters were subjected to close surveillance and harrassment, in violation of their civil rights, by the F.B.I. See: Nelson Blackstock, COINTELPRO (New York: Vantage Press, 1976).

73. Friedlander, Terrorism: Documents of International and Local Control, Vol. I, p. 130.

74. See, for example: Bart De Schutter, "Problems of Jurisdiction in the International Control and Repression of Terrorism," in International Terrorism and Political Crimes, p. 383; and, Garcia-Mora, International Responsibility for Hostile Acts of Private Persons Against Foreign States, p. 175.

75. See, for example: L. Kos-Rabcewicz Zubkowski, "The Creation of an International Criminal Court," in International Terrorism and Political Crimes, pp. 519-536. Also see the suggestion of a supranational air crimes commission to prosecute skyjackers in: Peter Clyne, An Anatomy of Skyjacking (London: Abeland-Schuman, 1973), p. 166.

76. See, for example: Yoram Dinstein, "Terrorism and War of Liberation: An Israeli Perspective of the Arab-Israeli Conflict," in International Terrorism and Political Crimes, p. 165; and, Wilkinson, Terrorism and the Liberal State, pp.

221-222. Also see: Theo Vogler, "Perspectives on Extradition and Terrorism," in International Terrorism and Political Crimes, pp. 391-399.

77. See, for example: Daniel P. Moynihan, "The Totalitarian Terrorists," in Contemporary Terrorism: Selected Readings, p. 163. Robert Hotz suggests that the major nation closest to an incident should respond militarily. See: Hotz, "Israel Points the Way," Aviation Week and Space Technology (12 July 1976), p. 7.

78. The anti-hijacking conventions signed in Tokyo (1963), The Hague (1970), and Montreal (1971) have provided some guidelines for governments involved in international skyjackings, but have not effectively ended the threat of terrorist takeovers. The U.S.-Cuba accord on hijackings has had much more success. There have been no aerial hijackings between the two countries since the signing of the accord in February of 1973 (it has now expired, however). See: Friedlander, Terrorism: Documents of International and Local Control, Vol. I. p. 96.

79. Wilkinson, Terrorism and the Liberal State, pp. 217, 221-222.

80. See, for example: Evans, Calling a Truce to Terror, pp. 43-44.

81. Jiri Toman, "Terrorism and the Regulation of Armed Conflicts," in International Terrorism and Political Crimes, pp. 133-154; and, Stanley Hoffmann, "International Law and the Control of Force," in The Relevance of International Law, pp. 34-66, ed. Karl Deutsch and Stanley Hoffman (Garden City, N.Y.: Doubleday and Co., Anchor Books, 1971).

82. Salomone, "Terrorism and the Mass Media," p. 46. According to Yonah Alexander, during the course of the Mogadishu hijacking the media reported that the captain of the Lufthansa flight was passing information to the authorities on the ground via his radio messages. The captain was subsequently executed when the terrorists were apprised of his deception. See: Alexander, "Terrorism, the Media, and the Police," in Terrorism: Threat, Reality, Response, pp. 337-339.

This is not the only case in which media personnel have interferred with antiterrorist operations and jeopardized the lives of hostages and police.

83. Hickey, "Terrorism and Television: The Medium in the Middle," p. 108.

84. Drummond and Zycher, "The Fourth Estate: Arafat's Press Agents," pp. 25-26. Both authors are themselves journalists.

85. Hickey, "Terrorism and Television: The Medium in the Middle," p. 118. Also see: Sir Robert Mark, "Kidnapping, Terrorism and the News Media in Britain," in Ten Years of Terrorism, pp. 76-86; and, Mickolus, "Transnational Terrorism," p. 167.

86. There does seem to be a growing concern among the journalists themselves about their impact on the phenomenon of terrorism and the resolution of violent crises. Israel placed some limitations on press coverage of Palestinian violence in 1975, for instance. See: Drummond and Zycher, "The Fourth Estate: Arafat's Press Agents," p. 26. Also see: Sally Bedell, "Is TV Exploiting Tragedy?" TV Guide (16 June 1979), pp. 4-8; and, Arthur A. Lord, "Q: When Does the Revolution Begin? A: When Can You Get Here?" TV Guide (30 June 1979), pp. 14-18.

87. Wilkinson, Terrorism and the Liberal State, p. 118. Also see the similar statement in: Fearey, "International Terrorism," p. 94. Wilkinson was primarily considering the advisability of concessions to domestic terrorists. To the extent that domestic terrorism is directed against international targets the injunction against concessions is easily transferable.

88. Ibid., p. 180.

89. Becker, Hitler's Children, p. 17.

90. The American action resulted in the deaths of eight American servicemen without having an appreciable effect on the hostage situation, except for the dispersion of the hostages to different sites. The Egyptian action in February of 1978 at Larnaca airport,

Cyprus, was conducted without clear authority being given by the Cyprus government. When the Egyptian force began its operation, it was attacked by the Cypriot National Guard forces, and fifteen soldiers were killed. The terrorists ultimately gave up. See: Dobson and Payne, The Terrorists: Their Weapons, Leaders and Tactics, pp. 148-149.

91. Robert A. Fearey, "Introduction to International Terrorism," in International Terrorism in the Contemporary World, p. 29. The policy was announced by Nixon in 1970 and Kissinger's summary of the reasons behind the policy followed closely on the heels of a controversial initiative taken by the U.S. ambassador to Tanzania, W. Beverly Carter. Terrorists had kidnapped three students in Tanzania in May of 1975 (two of them were Americans). Carter participated in the payment of ransom using U.S. embassy personnel and facilities and the embassy's diplomatic pouch (to transport the ransom monies to Tanzania). The students were ransomed and released in July of 1975 and the Kissinger speech followed in August ostensibly as a reaffirmation of the U.S. position. See: "How Not to Combat Terrorism," National Review (12 September 1975), p. 978.

92. See: Fromkin, "The Strategy of Terrorism," p. 140; Laqueur, Terrorism, pp. 232-233; and, Kupperman and Trent, Terrorism: Threat, Reality, Response, pp. 11-12.

93. See: Kobetz and Cooper, Target Terrorism, pp. 85-86; and, Judith Miller, "Bargain with Terrorists?" New York Times Magazine (18 July 1976), p. 7, reprinted in The Struggle Against Terrorism, p. 118.

94. See: Dobson and Payne, The Terrorists: Their Weapons, Leaders and Tactics, p. 150. According to Dobson and Payne, the F.B.I. are now having personnel trained in the technique. Also see: Francis A. Bolz, Jr., "Hostage Confrontation and Rescue," in Terrorism: Threat, Reality, Response, pp. 393-404, for more information on the Bolz-Schlossberg technique.

95. There have been some indications that the P.I.R.A. is preparing its operatives to resist such techniques now. That may limit its value in the future. Also, during the South Moluccan hijacking of the Dutch train, for example, the government negotiators determined that the situation was deteriorating within the train and suggested the assault by military forces that ultimately resolved the crisis. See: Dobson and Payne, The Terrorists: Their Weapons, Leaders and Tactics, pp. 150, 155.

96. Kupperman and Trent, Terrorism: Threat, Reality, Response, p. 113. These authors suggest "tactical" concessions, such as compliance with ransom demands, to insure the release of hostages. They do not suggest giving in to demands that might have a more immediate and adverse effect on the stability of the regime or public order, i.e., "strategic" concessions. Kupperman and Trent also suggest a strategy of giving the terrorists some concessions and letting them know that their gains could be lost if they continue to use violence -- in other words, giving the terrorists a vested interest in the termination of the violence (pp. 116-117).

97. See, for example: Mosca, The Ruling Class, p. 221; and, Kupperman and Trent, Terrorism: Threat, Reality, Response, p. 118.

98. One author, for instance, finds that bureaucracies are generally ill-equipped to deal with emergencies. He suggest, therefore, that the structures designated for antiterrorist response be specialized and professionalized. See: Hubbard, "A Glimmer of Hope: A Psychiatric Perspective," pp. 29, 32.

99. Wilkinson concludes that liberal democratic governments tend to view reform and accommodation as the appropriate response to political conflict and, thus, they are hesitant to use force. Wilkinson, Terrorism and the Liberal State, p. 115.

100. Hacker, Crusaders, Criminals, Crazies, pp. 189-190.

101. Wilkinson, Terrorism and the Liberal State, pp. 117-118.

102. Kupperman and Trent, Terrorism: Threat, Reality, Response, pp. 118-119.

103. Miller, "Bargain With Terrorists?" p. 185.

104. Hubbard suggests reducing the involvement of political leaders in crisis decision-making because of their electoral pressures. Hubbard, "A Glimmer of Hope: A Psychiatric Perspective," pp. 30, 33.

105. See, for example: Zinam, "Terrorism and Violence in Light of a Theory of Discontent and Frustration," pp. 259-260; Johnson, "Perspectives on Terrorism," p. 278; and, Crozier, A Theory of Conflict, p. 200.

106. Evans, Calling a Truce to Terror, p. 18.

107. Mosca, The Ruling Class, p. 219; and, Wilkinson, Terrorism and the Liberal State, p. 95.

108. Wilkinson, "Terrorism Versus Liberal Democracy -- The Problem of Response," p. 3.

109. John Vinocur, "Brezhnev Said to Have Told Allies Moscow Will Help Fight Terrorism," New York Times (17 July 1978), p. A1.

110. L.C. Green deals with this problem in some depth in: "The Legalization of Terrorism," in Terrorism: Theory and Practice, pp. 175-197.

111. Judith Miller, for example, has suggested that the U.S. could not respond to terrorist events as Israel did at Entebbe because the U.S.'s superpower status would engender criticism for violating the territorial integrity of a much weaker state. See: Miller, "Bargain With Terrorists?" pp. 189-190. Nonetheless, the U.S. did attempt a rescue operation in Iran in 1980.

112. See, for example: De Schutter, "Problems of Jurisdiction in the International Control and Repression of Terrorism," pp. 381 - 382; and, Garcia - Mora,

International Responsibility for Hostile Acts of Private Persons Against Foreign States, p. 154. De Schutter concludes that the principle of "protective jurisdiction" is widely accepted, and Garcia-Mora concludes that it is not. The question of the legal justifications for the Entebbe action is dealt with in some detail in: Friedlander, *Terrorism: Documents of International and Local Control*, Vol. I, pp. 91-92 (in particular).

113. Judith Miller, for example, states that the U.S. pressured several Latin American countries into negotiating the releases of captive Americans during the 1970s. Miller, "Bargain With Terrorists?" p. 180.

114. John Vinocur, "U.S. and 6 Allies to Cut Air Links to Countries Sheltering Hijackers," *New York Times* (18 July 1978), p. A1.

115. Hacker, *Crusaders, Criminals, Crazies*, pp. 185-186.

116. Zawodny, "Unconventional Warfare," pp. 341-342.

117. Crozier, *A Theory of Conflict*, pp. 200-238.

References -- Chapter V

1. See, for example, the discussions of the purposiveness and predictability of policy impacts in: Van der Silk, *American Legislative Process*, pp. 328-329; and, Robert L. Lineberry and Ira Sharkansky, *Urban Politics and Public Policy* (New York: Harper and Row, 1971), p. 199. Van der Silk cited Lineberry and Sharkansky in his discussion. Also see: James S. Coleman, "Problems of Conceptualization and Measurement in Studying Policy Impacts," in *Public Policy Evaluation*, ed. Kenneth M. Dolbeare (Beverly Hills, Calif.: Sage Publications, 1975), p. 24; and, Thomas J. Cook and Frank P. Scioli, Jr., "Impact Analysis in Public Policy Research," in *Public Policy Evaluation*, pp. 101-102.

2. A discussion of the importance of spillover effects can be found in: Lineberry, *American Public*

Policy, pp. 86, 89-90. The potential for counterproductive policy impacts can be found in: Feldman, "An Antidote for Apology, Service, and Witchcraft in Policy Analysis," p. 23.

3. Lineberry, American Public Policy, pp. 86, 90.

4. Kupperman and Trent find that this attribute of hostage incidents increases the importance of developing effective crisis management structures and processes. See: Kupperman and Trent, Terrorism: Threat, Reality, Response, p. 118.

5. Skyjacking, in particular, involves public negotiations. See: Kobetz and Cooper, Target Terrorism, pp. 85-86.

6. Strother and Methvin, "Terrorism on the Rampage," p. 73; and, Milbank, International and Transnational Terrorism: Diagnosis and Prognosis, p. 14. The text of the declaration, along with the company's disclaimers, appeared in the Washington Post on June 19, 1975.

7. For arguments in favor of recognizing attacks on foreign business agents as acts of international terrorism, based largely on the international impact of the violence, see: Clarence J. Mann (of Sears, Roebuck and Company), "Personnel and Property of Transnational Business Operations," in Legal Aspects of International Terrorism, pp. 399-481. There have also been suggestions that governments outlaw the paying of ransoms by companies or families of kidnap victims to discourage such attacks. See: John B. Wolf, "Controlling Political Terrorism in a Free Society," Orbis 19 (Winter 1976): 1295.

8. See, for example: Jenkins, "International Terrorism: A New Mode of Conflict," p. 20; Wilkinson, Terrorism Versus Liberal Democracy -- The Problem of Response, p. 5; and, Baumann, The Diplomatic Kidnappings, p. 42. L.C. Green, however, suggests that diplomatic kidnappings are primarily manifestations of domestic terrorism. See: Green, "The Legalization of Terrorism," pp. 185-186.

9. Sobol, Political Terrorism, p. 85; and, Brian Jenkins, Janera Johnson, and David Ronfeldt, Numbered Lives: Some Statistical Observations from 77 International Hostage Incidents (Santa Monica, Calif.: Rand Publications, P-5905, July 1977), p. 36.

10. This particular case was included in the study of diplomatic kidnappings done by Carol Edler Baumann, despite the fact that she characterized it as a "quasi-diplomatic" kidnapping. See: Baumann, The Diplomatic Kidnappings, p. 84. Brian Jenkins, et al., also included the case in the Numbered Lives study for Rand Corporation. The case is also included in this study, albeit with some misgivings, because it is unknown what kind of protections Mr. Sylvester should have enjoyed under the British-Argentine consular arrangements.

11. The C.I.A. figures were reported in: "Anatomy of International Terrorism," U.S. News and World Report (June 16, 1980), p. 41. The relatively low numbers of hijacking incidents during those years is likely due to the factoring out of those incidents that were motivated solely by desires for political asylum. That exclusion of asylum-motivated events has been made explicit in previous C.I.A.-generated statistical analyses. See, for example, the C.I.A. report series that includes: International Terrorisn in 1976, RP 77-10034U. It is also noteworthy that the C.I.A. figures reveal a decline in the absolute number of terrorist events while, at the same time, an increase in the number of casualties (from 34 casualties in 1968 to 587 in 1979).

12. Jenkins, Johnson, and Ronfeldt, Numbered Lives, p. iii.

13. Because the U.S. has been the target of many of the terrorist attacks (about 40% according to the C.I.A. figures in "Anatomy of International Terrorism" and 36% according to Edward Mickolus in "Statistical Approaches to the Study of Terrorism," p. 225), increases in security precautions by the U.S. alone could account for much of the decline.

14. The number of kidnappings and barricade and hostage incident increased again in 1978 (over the 1976 and 1977 figures), but did not exceed the 1975 levels. See: C.I.A., International Terrorism in 1978, p. 6.

15. Similar data were presented by Mickolus in "Statistical Approaches to the Study of Terrorism," in Terrorism: Interdisciplinary Perspectives, p. 213. Mickolus, however, separated air and non-air hijackings and, evidently, included many of the asylum-motivated cases in his study. Mickolus' data were derived from the C.I.A.'s I.T.E.R.A.T.E. (International Terrorism Attributes of Terrorist Events) project, and it is probable that the C.I.A. figures cited in the U.S. News and World Report article came from the same source.

Wilkinson has noted a broader cycle of aircraft hijackings beginning with the wave of refugees from Communist countries following World War II, the wave of hijackings to Cuba during the 1958-1962 period, the lull from 1962 to 1967 when the average number of hijackings per year was four, and culminating with the new wave of political and criminal hijackings since 1968. Wilkinson concluded that the cyclic nature of the phenomenon mitigates against there being a permanent decline in skyjackings. See: Wilkinson, Terrorism and the Liberal State, pp. 209-210.

16. McClure, "Hostage Survival," in International Terrorism in the Contemporary World, p. 276.

17. Alona E. Evans deals with the apprehension and punishment of aerial hijackers in some depth in: "Aircraft and Aviation Facilities," in Legal Aspects of International Terrorism, pp. 3-147. She has determined that out of 257 hijackers of U.S. aircraft during the 1961-1977 period only 157 were ultimately apprehended (pp. 16-17). She also traces the development of terrorist demands from the primarily asylum-motivated hijackings during the 1960s to the increasing demands for ransom and prisoner releases which began around 1969. At the same time, the number of hijack-related deaths and injuries began to increase considerably (pp. 7-8).

18.   As has been noted by at least one other analyst, research on terrorist events has to rely largely on journalistic data sources that provide very little information on the decision-making processes involved in hostage negotiations or on the mechanics of government response (e.g., the preparations for deploying antiterrorist forces). Very little information is released by governments. As a consequence, most of the statistical studies of terrorism have originated from the C.I.A.'s I.T.E.R.A.T.E. project data or the Rand Corporation data. That is why the analysis in this study is restricted primarily to direct relationships between fairly precise concepts.

19.   There have been too few cases of government responses to external terrorism, like the Entebbe and Mogadishu rescues, to permit statistical analysis here. The unsuccessful operations conducted by the Egyptians in Cyprus and the U.S. in Iran have already been noted.

20.   Because most of the cases involve multiple demands, the analysis will not be able to treat each of the demands as a discrete variable, rather it will be concerned with the influence of each demand on the governments' responses to a set of demands.

21.   The best illustration of the use of safe passage as a means of resolving terrorist incidents was the response of the Thai government to the takeover of the Israeli embassy in Bangkok by members of the Black September organization in December of 1972. The Thai authorities offered the terrorists safe passage to Egypt after the Israeli government refused to comply with the terrorists' demands. The incident was resolved without casualties and the counteroffer made by the Thai government has come to be called the "Bangkok solution." See: Sobol, Political Terrorism, pp. 58-59.

22.   The data were gathered from the New York Times; Sobol, Political Terrorism; Jenkins, Johnson, and Ronfeldt, Numbered Lives; Baumann, The Diplomatic Kidnappings; Evans "Aircraft and Aviation Facilities"; and, numerous other accounts of individual events.

References -- Chapter VI

1. Eckstein, "Introduction: Toward the Theoretical Study of Internal War," p. 12.

2. Ernest Evans makes the distinction between a humanitarian issue and a political one as being the difference in whether there is broad consensual support for the definition of the issue as a problem. He contends that humanitarian issues are generally recognized as problems, although some technical questions about their resolution may remain, and that political problems do not enjoy broad consensual support. See: Evans, "American Policy Response to International Terrorism: Problems of Deterrence," in Terrorism: Interdisciplinary Perspectives, p. 111.

3. Wilkinson, Terrorism and the Liberal State, p. 116. For individual views on how that "two-front war" should be structured, see: Mickolus, "Transnational Terrorism," pp. 180-181; and, Denis Szabo and Ronald D. Crelinsten, "International Political Terrorism: A Challenge for Comparative Research," Terrorism: An International Journal 3 (1980): 343.

SELECTED BIBLIOGRAPHY

BOOKS AND REPORTS:

Allen, Francis A. The Crimes of Politics: Political Dimensions of Criminal Justice. Cambridge, Mass.: Harvard University Press, 1974.

Alexander, Yonah; Browne, Marjorie Ann; and Nanes, Allan S., eds. Control of Terrorism: International Documents. New York: Crane and Russak, 1979.

Alexander, Yonah, ed. International Terrorism: National, Regional, and Global Perspectives. New York: Praeger, 1976.

Alexander, Yonal, and Finger, Seymour Maxwell, eds. Terrorism: Interdisciplinary Perspectives. New York, John Jay Press, 1977.

Alexander, Yonah, and Kilmarx, Robert A., eds. Political Terrorism and Business: The Threat and the Response. New York: Praeger, 1979.

Alexander, Yonah; Carlton, David; and Wilkinson, Paul, eds. Terrorism: Theory and Practice. Boulder, Colo.: Westview Press, 1979.

Anderson, Charles W.; von der Mehden, Fred R.; and Young, Crawford. Issues of Political Development. Englewood Cliffs, N.J.: Prentice Hall, Inc., 1967.

Arendt, Hannah. On Revolution. New York: Viking Press, 1963.

_____. On Violence. New York: Harcourt, Brace and Jovanovich, 1969.

_____. The Origins of Totalitarianism. New York: Harcourt, Brace and Jovanovich, 1966.

Arey, James A. The Sky Pirates. New York: Schribner's Sons, 1972.

Barker, Dudley. Grivas: Portrait of a Terrorist. New York: Harcourt, Brace and Company, 1959.

Bassiouni, M. Cherif, ed. International Terrorism and Political Crimes. Springfield, Ill.: Charles C. Thomas, 1975.

Baumann, Carol Edler. The Diplomatic Kidnappings: A Revolutionary Tactic of Urban Terrorism. The Hague: Martinus Nijhoff, 1973.

Becker, Jillian. Hitler's Children: The Story of the Baader-Meinhof Terrorist Gang. Philadelphia: J.B. Lippincott Company, 1977.

Bell, David V.J. Resistance and Revolution. Boston: Houghton Mifflin, 1975.

Bell, J. Bowyer. A Time of Terror: How Democratic Societies Respond to Revolutionary Violence. New York: Basic Books, Inc., 1978.

_____. Transnational Terror. Washington, D.C.: American Enterprise Institute for Public Policy Research, 1975.

_____. The Myth of the Guerrilla: Revolutionary Theory and Malpractice. New York: Alfred A. Knopf, 1971.

_____. On Revolt: Strategies of National Liberation. Cambridge, Mass.: Harvard University Press, 1976.

_____. The Secret Army: A History of the IRA. Cambridge, Mass.: M.I.T. Press, 1974.

Beres, Louis Rene. Terrorism and Global Security: The Nuclear Threat. Boulder, Colo.: Westview Press, 1980.

Bienen, Henry. Violence and Social Change: A Review Of Current Literature. Chicago: University of Chicago Press, 1968.

Bloomfield, Louis M., and Fitzgerald, Gerald F. Crimes Against Internationally Protected Persons: Prevention and Punishment. New York: Praeger Publishers, 1975.

Bowden, Tom. The Breakdown of Public Security: The Case of Ireland 1916-1921 and Palestine 1936-1939. London: Sage Publications, 1977.

Brigham, Daniel T. Blueprint of Conflict. New York: American-African Affairs Association, 1969.

Brinton, Crane. The Anatomy of Revolution. New York: Vintage Books, 1965.

Buckley, Alan D., and Olson, David D., eds. International Terrorism: Current Research and Future Directions. Wayne, N.J.: Avery Publishing Group, 1980.

Burns, Alan. The Angry Brigade. London: Quartet Books, 1974.

Burton, Anthony. Urban Terrorism: Theory, Practice, and Response. New York: The Free Press, 1975.

Carlton, David, and Schaerf, Carlo, eds. International Terrorism and World Security. New York: John Wiley and Sons, 1975.

Carr, E.H. Studies in Revolution. New York: Grosset and Dunlap, 1964.

Carr, Gordon. The Angry Brigade: A History of Britain's First Urban Guerrilla Group. London: Housmans, 1970.

Caserta, John S. The Red Brigades. Staten Island, N.Y.: Manor Books, 1978.

Chapman, Robert D. Crimson Web of Terror. Boulder, Colo.: Paladin Enterprises, 1980.

Clark, Richard C. Technological Terrorism. Old Greewich, Conn.: Devin-Adair, 1980.

Clutterbuck, Richard. Guerrillas and Terrorists. London: Faber and Faber, Ltd., 1977.

_____. Living With Terrorism. New Rochelle, N.Y.: Arlington House Publishers, 1975.

_____. *Protest and the Urban Guerrilla.* London: Cassell, 1973.

Clyne, Peter. *An Anatomy of Skyjacking.* London: Abeland Schuman, 1973.

Cohan, A.S. *Theories of Revolution: An Introduction.* New York: John Wiley and Sons, 1975.

Cole, Richard B. *Executive Security: A Corporate Guide to Effective Response to Abduction and Terrorism.* New York: Wiley-Interscience, 1980.

Cooper, H.H.A. *Hostage Negotiations: Options and Alternatives.* Gaithersburg, Md.: International Association of Chiefs of Police, 1978.

Coser, Lewis. *The Functions of Social Conflict.* New York: The Free Press, 1956.

Crelinsten, Ronald D.; Laberge-Altmejd, Danielle; and Szabo, Denis. *Terrorism and Criminal Justice: An International Perspective.* Lexington, Mass.: Lexington Books, 1978.

Crotty, William J., ed. *Assassinations and the Political Order.* New York: Harper and Row, 1971.

Crozier, Brian. *The Rebels: A Study of Post-War Insurrections.* Boston: Beacon Press, 1960.

_____. *Transnational Terrorism.* Gaithersburg, Md.: International Association of Chiefs of Police, 1974.

_____. *A Theory of Conflict.* London: Hamish Hamilton, 1974.

Cunningham, William C., and Gross, Phillip J., comp. and ed. *Preventions of Terrorism: Security Guidelines for Business and Other Organizations.* McLean, Va.: Hallcrest Press, 1978.

Daley, William T. *The Revolutionary: A Review and Synthesis.* Beverly Hills, Calif.: Sage Publications, 1972.

Dallin, Alexander, and Breslauer, George W. *Political Terror in Communist Systems*. Stanford, Calif.: Stanford University Press, 1970.

Davies, James C., ed. *When Men Revolt and Why*. New York: Free Press, 1971.

Demaris, Ovid. *Brothers in Blood: The International Terrorist Network*. New York: Schribner and Sons, 1977.

Dobson, Christopher. *Black September: Its Short, Violent History*. New York: Macmillan, 1974.

_____, and Payne, Ronald. *The Carlos Complex*. London: Hodder and Stoughton, 1977.

_____, and Payne, Ronald. *The Terrorists: Their Weapons, Leaders and Tactics*. New York: Facts on File, Inc., 1979.

Eckstein, Harry, ed. *Internal War*. New York: Free Press, 1964.

Eggers, William. *Terrorism: The Slaughter of Innocents*. Chatsworth, Calif.: Sage Publications, 1971.

Elliot, John D., and Gibson, Leslie K., eds. *Contemporary Terrorism: Selected Readings*. Gaithersburg, Md.: International Association of Chiefs of Police, 1978.

Ellis, Albert, and Gulls, John. *Murder and Assassination*. New York: Lyle Stuart Publishers, 1971.

Ellul, Jacques. *Autopsy of Revolution*. Translated by Patricia Wolf. New York: Alred A. Knopf, 1971.

Erickson, Richard J. *International Law and the Revolutionary State*. Dobbs Ferry, N.Y.: Oceana Publications, 1972.

Evans, Alona E., and Murphy, John F., eds. *Legal Aspects of International Terrorism*. Lexington, Mass.: Lexington Books, 1978.

Evans, Ernest. *Calling a Truce to Terror: The American Response to International Terrorism.* Westport, Conn.: Greenwood Press, 1979.

Fanon, Frantz. *The Wretched of the Earth.* Foreword by Jean Paul Sartre. Translated by Constance Farrington. New York: Grove Press, 1963.

Feierabend, Ivo K.; Feierabend, Rosalind L.; and Gurr, Ted Robert, eds. *Anger, Violence, and Politics: Theories and Research.* Englewood Cliffs, N.J.: Prentice-Hall, Inc., 1972.

Friedlander, Robert A. *Terrorism: Documents of International and Local Control.* 2 Volumes. Dobbs Ferry, N.Y.: Oceana Publications, Inc., 1979.

Galula, David. *Counterinsurgency Warfare: Theory and Practice.* New York: Praeger Publishers, 1964.

Garcia-Mora, Manuel R. *International Responsibility for Hostile Acts of Private Persons Against Foreign States.* Martinus Nijhoff, 1962.

Gaucher, Roland. *The Terrorists: From Tsarist Russia to the O.A.S.* Translated by Paula Spurlin. London: Secker and Warburg, 1965.

Gellner, John. *Bayonets in the Streets: Urban Guerrillas at Home and Abroad.* Don Mills, Ontario: Collier Macmillan of Canada, 1974.

Gerassi, John, ed. *The Coming of the New International.* New York: World Publishing Company, 1971.

Gross, Feliks. *The Seizure of Political Power in a Century of Revolutions.* New York: Philosophical Library, 1958.

Groussard, Serge. *The Blood of Israel: The Massacre of the Israeli Athletes, the Olympics, 1972.* New York: William Morrow and Company, 1975.

Gurr, Ted R. *Why Men Rebel.* Princeton, N.J.: Princeton University Press, 1971.

Hacker, Frederick J. *Crusaders, Criminals, Crazies*. New York: W. W. Norton and Company, 1976.

Halperin, Ernst. *Terrorism in Latin America*. Beverly Hills, Calif.: Sage Publications, 1976.

Havens, Murray C.; Leiden, Carl; and Schmitt, Karl M. *The Politics of Assassination*. Englewood Cliffs, N.J.: Prentice-Hall, 1970.

Hodges, D.C. *Philosophy of the Urban Guerrilla: The Revolutionary Writings of Abraham Guillen*. New York: William Morrow and Company, Inc., 1973.

Horchem, H.J. *West Germany's Red Army Anarchists*. London: Conflict Studies No. 46, 1974.

Hubbard, David G. *The Skyjacker: His Flights of Fantasy*. New York: Macmillan, 1971.

Hutchinson, Martha Crenshaw. *Revolutionary Terrorism: The FLN in Algeria, 1954-1962*. Stanford, Calif.: Hoover Institute Press, 1978.

Hyams, Edward. *Terrorists and Terrorism*. London: J.M. Dent and Sons, Ltd., 1975.

Jackson, Geoffrey. *Surviving the Long Nights: An Autobiographical Account of a Political Kidnapping*. New York: Vanguard Press, 1974.

Jenkins, Brian. *The Consequences of Nuclear Terrorism*. Santa Monica, Calif.: Rand Corporation, P-6373, August 1979.

_____. *The Five Stages of Urban Guerrilla Warfare: Challenge of the 1970s*. Santa Monica, Calif.: Rand Corporation, P-4670, July 1971.

_____. *High Technology Terrorism and Surrogate War: The Impact of New Technology on Low-Level Violence*. Santa Monica, Calif.: Rand Corporation, P-5339, January, 1975.

_____, and Johnson, Janera. International Terrorism: A Chronology 1968-1974. Santa Monica, Calif.: Rand Corporationl, R-1597-DOS/ARPA, March 1975.

_____; Johnson, Janera; and Ronfeldt, David. Numbered Lives: Some Statistical Observations From 77 International Hostage Episodes. Santa Monica, Calif.: Rand Corporation, P-5905, July 1977.

_____. International Terrorism: A New Mode of Conflict. Los Angeles: Crescent Publications, 1975.

Johnson, Chalmers. Revolutionary Change. Boston: Little Brown and Company, 1966.

Joyner, Nancy D. Aerial Hijacking as an International Crime. Dobbs Ferry, N.Y.: Oceana Publications, 1974.

Joynt, Carey B., and Corbett, Percy E. Theory and Reality in World Politics. Pittsburgh: University of Pittsburgh Press, 1978.

Kellen, Konrad. Terrorists -- What Are They Like? How Some Terrorists Describe Their World and Actions. Santa Monica, Calif.: Rand Corporation, N-1300-SL, November 1979.

Kirkham, James F.; Levy, Sheldon G.; and Crotty, William J. Assassination and Political Violence: A Staff Report to the National Commission on the Causes and Prevention of Violence. New York: Bantam Books, 1970.

Kitson, Frank. Low Intensity Operations: Subversion, Insurgency, Peacekeeping. London: Faber and Faber, 1971.

Kobetz, Richard W., and Cooper, H.H.A. Target Terrorism: Providing Protective Services. Gaithersburg, Md.: International Association of Chiefs of Police, 1978.

Kuper, Leo. The Pity of It All: Polarization of Racial and Ethnic Relations. Minneapolis, Minn.: University of Minnesota Press, 1977.

Kupperman, Robert, and Trent, Darrell. Terrorism: Threat, Reality, Response. Foreword by Walter

Laqueur. Stanford, Calif.: Hoover Institution Press, 1979.

Laqueur, Walter. Terrorism: A Study of National and International Political Violence. Boston: Little, Brown and Company; London: Weidenfeld and Nicolson, 1977.

_____, ed. The Terrorism Reader: A Historical Anthology. Philadelphia: Temple University Press, 1978.

_____, ed. The Guerrilla Reader: A Historical Anthology. New York: Meridian Books, 1977.

Leiden, Carl, and Schmitt, Karl M. The Politics of Violence: Revolution in the Modern World. Englewood Cliffs, N.J.: Prentice-Hall, Inc., 1968.

de Leon, Peter, et al. Attributes of Potential Criminal Adversaries of U.S. Nuclear Programs. Santa Monica, Calif.: Rand Corporation, R-2225-SL, February 1978.

Leonard, L. Larry, ed. Global Terrorism Confronts the Nations. New York: New York University Press, 1980.

Lineberry, William P., ed. The Struggle Against Terrorism. New York, H.W. Wilson Co., 1977.

Liston, Robert A. Terrorism. New York: Thomas Nelson, 1977.

Livingston, Marius H., ed. International Terrorism in the Contemporary World. Westport, Conn.: Greenwood Press, 1978.

Lodge, Juliet, ed. Terrorism: A Challenge to the State. New York: St. Martin's Press, 1981.

McCuen, John J. The Art of Counter-Revolutionary War: The Strategy of Counter-Insurgency. Harrisburg, Pa.: Stackpole Books, 1966.

McKnight, Gerald. The Terrorist Mind. Indianapolis, Ind.: Bobbs-Merrill Co., 1974.

McWhinney, Edward. Aerial Piracy and International Law. Leiden, Netherlands: A. W. Sijthoff, 1971.

Mallin, Jay, ed. Terror and Urban Guerrillas: A Study of Tactics and Documents. Coral Gables, Fla.: University of Miami Press, 1971.

Meisel, James H. Counterrevolution: How Revolutions Die. New York: Atherton Press, 1966.

Merleau-Ponty, Maurice. Humanism and Terror: An Essay on the Communist Problem. Translated by John O'Neill. Boston: Beacon Press, 1969.

Mickolus, Edward F. Transnational Terrorism: A Chronology of Events, 1968-1979. Westport, Conn.: Greenwood Press, 1980.

_____, comp and ed. The Literature of Terrorism: A Selectively Annotated Bibliography. Westport, Conn.: Greenwood Press, 1980.

Miller, Abraham H. Terrorism and Hostage Negotiations. Boulder, Colo.: Westview Press, 1980.

Morf, Gustave. Terrorism in Quebec: Case Studies of the FLQ. Toronto: Clark Irvin and Company, 1970.

Mosca, Gaetano. The Ruling Class. Translated by Hannah D. Kahn. Edited and Revised by Arthur Livingston. New York: McGraw-Hill, Inc., 1939.

Moss, Robert. Counter Terrorism. London: Economist Brief Books, 1972.

_____. The War for the Cities. New York: Coward, McCann and Geophegan, 1972.

Mukerjee, Dilip. The Terrorists. New York: Vantage Press, 1980.

Mullen, Robert K. The International Clandestine Nuclear Threat. Gaithersburg, Md.: International Association of Chiefs of Police, 1975.

_____. The Clandestine Use of Chemical or Biological Weapons. Gaithersburg, Md.: International Association of Chiefs of Police, 1978.

Nieburg, Harold L. Political Violence: The Behavioral Process. New York: St. Martin's Press, 1969.

Norton, Augustus R., and Greenberg, Martin H. International Terrorism: An Annotated Bibliography and Research Guide. Boulder, Colo.: Westview Press, 1979.

Ochberg, Frank, ed. Victims of Terrorism. Boulder, Colo.: Westview Press, 1979.

Paget, Julian. Counter-Insurgency Operations: Techniques of Guerrilla Warfare. New York: Walker and Company, 1967.

Parry, Albert. Terrorism: From Robespierre to Arafat. New York: Vanguard Press, 1976.

Phillips, David. Skyjack: The Story of Air Piracy. London: Harrap, 1973.

Porzicanski, A.C. Uruguay's Tupamaros: The Urban Guerrilla. New York: Praeger Publishers, 1973.

Rapoport, David C. Assassination and Terrorism. Toronto: Canadian Broadcasting Corporation, 1971.

Rejai, Mostafa. The Comparative Study of Revolutionary Stragegy. New York: David McKay Company, 1977.

Roetter, Charles. Psychological Warfare. London: B.T. Batsford, Ltd., 1974.

Rothschild, J.H. Tomorrow's Weapons: Chemical and Biological. New York: McGraw-Hill, 1964.

Royal United Services Institute for Defence Studies, eds. Ten Years of Terrorism: Collected Views. London, RUSI, 1979.

Schafer, Stephen. The Political Criminal: The Problem of Morality and Crime. New York: Free Press, 1974.

Schreiber, Jan. The Ultimate Weapon: Terrorists and World Order. New York: William Morrow and Company, 1978.

Shultz, Richard H., Jr., and Sloan, Stephen, eds. *Responding to the Terrorist Threat: Security and Crisis Management.* Elmsford, N.Y.: Pergamon Press, 19.

Siljander, R.P. *Terrorist Attacks.* Springfield, Ill.: C.C. Thomas, 1980.

Sloan, Stephen. *Simulating Terrorism.* Norman, Okla.: University of Oklahoma Press, 1981.

Sobol, Lester A., ed. *Political Terrorism.* New York: Facts on File, Inc., 1975.

_____, ed. *Political Terrorism*, 2nd ed. New York: Facts on File, Inc., 1978.

Spanier, John. *Games Nations Play: Analyzing International Politics.* New York: Praeger Publishers, 1972.

Stevenson, William. *90 Minutes at Entebbe.* New York: Bantam Books, 1976.

Stohl, Michael, ed. *The Politics of Terrorism.* New York: Marcel Dekker, 1979.

Trinquier, Roger. *Modern Warfare.* New York: Pall Mall Press, 1964.

Truby, J. David. *How Terrorists Kill: The Complete Terrorist Arsenal.* Boulder, Colo.: Paladin Enterprises, 1978.

Wallace, Michael, ed. *Terrorism.* New York: Arno, 1979.

Walter, Eugene V. *Terror and Resistance: A Study of Political Violence With Case Studies of Some Primitive African Communities.* New York: Oxford University Press, 1969.

Watson, Francis M. *Political Terrorism: The Threat and the Response.* Washington, D.C.: Robert B. Luce, 1976.

Whelton, Clark. *Skyjack!* New York: Tower Publications, 1970.

Wilcox, Laird M. Bibliography on Terrorism, Assassination, Kidnapping, Bombing, Guerilla Warfare and Countermeasures Against Them. Kansas City, Mo.: Editorial Research Service, 1980.

Wilkinson, Paul. Political Terrorism. London: Macmillan Press, Ltd., 1974.

_____. Terrorism and the Liberal State. New York: John Wiley and Sons, 1977.

_____. Terrorism Versus Liberal Democracy -- The Problems of Response. London: Conflict Studies No. 67, January 1976.

Willrich, Mason, ed. International Safeguards and Nuclear Industry. Baltimore, Md.: Johns Hopkins University Press, 1973.

_____, and Taylor, Theodore B. Nuclear Theft: Risks and Safeguards. Cambridge, Mass.: Ballinger, 1974.

Wilson, Jerry, and Fuqua, Paul. Terrorism -- The Executive's Guide to Survivial. Houston, Texas: Gulf Publishing Co., 1978.

ARTICLES:

Adkins, E.H., Jr. "Protection of American Industrial Dignitaries and Facilities Overseas." Security Management 18 (July 1974): 14, 16, 55.

Aggarwala, Narinder. "Political Aspects of Hijacking." International Conciliation 585 (1971): 7-27.

Ahmad, Aqbal. "Revolutionary Warfare and Counterinsurgency." In National Liberation: Revolution in the Third World, pp. 137-213. Edited by Norman Miller and Roderick Aya. New York: Free Press, 1971.

_____. "The Theory and Fallacy of Counterinsurgency." Nation 213 (1971): 70-85.

Alexander, Yonah. "The Legacy of Palestinian Terrorism." *International Problems* 15 (Fall 1976): 57-64.

_____. "Some Perspectives on International Terrorism." *International Problems* 14 (Fall 1975): 24-29.

_____. "Communications Aspects of International Terrorism." *International Problems* 16 (Spring 1977): 55-60.

Beall, Marshall D. "Hostage Negotiations." *Military Police Law Enforcement Journal* 3 (Fall 1976).

Bell, J. Bowyer. "Contemporary Revolutionary Organizations." In *Transnational Relations and World Politics*, pp. 153-168. Edited by Robert O. Keohane and Joseph S. Nye, Jr. Cambridge, Mass.: Harvard University Press, 1973.

Bell, Robert G. "The U.S. Response to Terrorism Against International Civil Aviation." *Orbis* 19 (Winter 1976): 1326-1343.

Beres, Louis Rene. "Terrorism and the Nuclear Threat in the Middle East." *Current History*, January 1976, pp. 27-29.

Bobrow, Davis B. "Preparing for International Terrorism." *Terrorism: An International Journal* 1 (1978): 397-422.

Bolz, Francis A., Jr. "Hostage Confrontation and Rescue." In *Terrorism: Threat, Reality, Response*, pp. 393-404. Edited by Robert Kupperman and Darrell Trent. Stanford, Calif.: Hoover Institution Press, 1979.

Bonanate, Luigi. "Some Unanticipated Consequences of Terrorism." *Journal of Peace Research* 16 (1979): 197-211.

Bourne, Robert. "Terrorist Incident Management: A Canadian Perspective." *Terrorism: An International Journal* 1 (1978): 307-314.

Boyle, Kevin; Hadden, Tom; and Hillyard, Paddy. "The Facts on Internment in Northern Ireland." In Terrorism and Criminal Justice: An International Perspective, pp. 103-110. Edited by Ronald D. Crelinsten, Danielle Laberge-Altmejd, and Denis Szabo. Lexington, Mass.: Lexington Books, 1978.

Brandon, Henry. "Were We Masterful . . ." Foreign Policy 10 (1973): 158-170.

Cooper, H.H.A. "Whither Now? Terrorism on the Brink." Chitty's Law Journal 25 (6 November 1977).

———. "Terrorism and the Intelligence Function." Chitty's Law Journal 24 (1976).

Corsi, Jerome R. "Terrorism as a Desperate Game: Fear, Bargaining and Communication in the Terrorist Event." Journal of Conflict Resolution 25 (March 1981): 47-85.

Corves, Erich. "Terrorism and Criminal Justice Operations in the Federal Republic of Germany." In Terrorism and Criminal Justice: An International Perspective, pp. 93-101. Edited by Ronald D. Crelinsten, Danielle Laberge-Altmejd, and Denis Szabo. Lexington, Mass.: Lexington Books, 1978.

Crenshaw, Martha. "The Causes of Terrorism." Comparative Politics 13 (July 1981): 379-99.

Cullinane, Maurice J. "A New Era of Criminality." Terrorism: An International Journal 1 (1978): 125-146.

Davies, James C. "Toward a Theory of Revolution." American Sociological Review 27 (February 1962): 5-19. Reprinted in Struggles in the State: Sources and Patterns of World Revolution, pp. 150-167. Edited by George A. Kelly and Clifford W. Brown, Jr. New York: John Wiley and Sons, 1970.

Denton, Frank H., and Phillips, Warren. "Some Patterns in the History of Violence." In Conflict Resolution: Contributions of the Behavioral Sciences, pp. 327-328. Edited by Clagett G. Smith. Notre Dame, Ind.: University of Notre Dame Press, 1971.

Eckstein, Harry. "On the Etiology of Internal War." History and Theory 4 (1965): 133-163. Reprinted in Struggles in the State: Sources and Patterns of World Revolution, pp. 171-195. Edited by George A. Kelly and Clifford W. Brown, Jr. New York: John Wiley and Sons, Inc., 1970.

Fitzgerald, Bruce D. "The Analytical Foundations of Extortionate Terrorism." Terrorism: An International Journal 1 (1978): 347-362.

Fromkin, David. "The Strategy of Terrorism." Foreign Affairs (July 1975): 683-698.

Gourlay, Lt. Col. B.I.S. "Terror in Cyprus." In The Guerrilla -- And How to Fight Him, pp. 232-248. Edited by Lt. Colonel T.N. Greene. New York: Frederick A. Praeger, 1962.

Gurr, Ted Robert. "The Relevance of Theories of Internal Violence for the Control of Intervention." In Law and Civil War in the Modern World, pp. 70-91. Edited by John Norton Moore. Baltimore: Johns Hopkins University Press, 1974.

_____. "The Calculus of Civil Conflict." Journal of Social Issues 28 (1972): 27-27.

Hoveyda, Fereydoun. "The Problem of International Terrorism at the United Nations." Terrorism: An International Journal 1 (1977): 71-84.

Huntington, Samuel P. "Patterns of Violence in World Politics." In Changing Patterns of Military Politics, pp. 17-50. Edited by Samuel P. Huntington. Glencoe, N.Y.: Free Press of Glencoe, Inc., 1962.

Hutchinson, Martha Crenshaw. "The Concept of Revolutionary Terrorism." Journal of Conflict Resolution 16 (September 1972): 383-396.

Jenkins, Brian M. "Rand's Research on Terrorism." Terrorism: An International Journal 1 (1977): 85-96.

Kaplan, Abraham. "The Psychodynamics of Terrorism." Terrorism: An International Journal 1 (1978): 237-254.

Kelly, George A., and Miller, Linda B. "Internal War and International Systems: Perspectives on Method." Harvard University Center for International Affairs Occasional Paper No. 21, Cambridge, Mass.: Harvard University Press, August 1969. Reprinted in Struggles in the State: Sources and Patterns of World Revolution, pp. 226-260. Edited by George A. Kelly and Clifford W. Brown, Jr. New York: John Wiley and Sons, Inc., 1970.

Krieger, David. "What Happens If . . .? Terrorists, Revolutionaries and Nuclear Weapons." The Annals 430 (March 1977): 44-57.

Kupperman, Robert H. "Treating the Symptoms of Terrorism: Some Principles of Good Hygiene." Terrorism: An International Journal 1 (1977): 35-50.

Laqueur, Walter. "Interpretations of Terrorism -- Fact, Fiction and Political Science." Journal of Contemporary History 12 (January 1977): 1-42.

Leaute, Jacques. "Terrorist Incidents and Legislation in France." In Terrorism and Criminal Justice: An International Perspective, pp. 67-70. Edited by Ronald D. Crelinsten, Danielle Laberge-Altmejd, and Denis Szabo. Lexington, Mass.: Lexington Books, 1978.

Leggett, John C. "From Prodromal Conditions to Taking State Power: An Outline." In Taking State Power: The Sources and Consequences of Political Challenge, pp. 91-99. Edited by John C. Leggett. New York: Harper and Row, 1973.

Lindsay, Franklin A. "Unconventional Warfare." Foreign Affairs 40 (January 1962). Reprinted in Problems of National Strategy, pp. 344-355. Edited by Henry A. Kissinger. New York: Praeger Publishers, 1965.

Lupsha, Peter. "Explanation of Political Violence: Some Psychological Theories Versus Indignation." Politics and Society 2 (1971): 89-104.

McCormick, R.W. "Industrial Security in Europe -- A Multinational Concept." Security Management 18 (July 1974): 8-10, 13.

Mallin, Jay. "Terrorism as a Military Weapon." Air University Review, January-February 1977.

Mann, Clarence J. "Personnel and Property of Transnational Business Operations." In Legal Aspects of International Terrorism, pp. 399-481. Edited by Alona E. Evans and John F. Murphy. Lexington, Mass.: Lexington Books, 1978.

Mengel, R. William. "Terrorism in Perspective." In Prevention of Terrorism: Security Guidelines for Business and Other Organizations, pp. 7-12. Compiled and edited by William C. Cunningham and Phillip J. Gross. McLean, Va.: Hallcrest Press, 1978.

Mickolus, Edward. "Transnational Terrorism." In The Politics of Terrorism, pp. 147-190. Edited by Michael Stohl. New York: Marcel Dekker, Inc., 1979.

_____. "Negotiating for Hostages: A Policy Dilemma." Orbis 19 (Winter 1976): 1309-1325.

_____. "Statistical Approaches to the Study of Terrorism." In Terrorism: Interdisciplinary Perspectives, pp. 209-269. Edited by Yonah Alexander and Seymour Maxwell Finger. New York: John Jay Press, 1977.

_____. "Trends in Transnational Terrorism." In International Terrorism in the Contemporary World, pp. 44-73. Edited by Marius H. Livingston. Westport, Conn.: Greenwood Press, 1978.

Miller, Abraham H. "Negotiations for Hostages: Implications from the Police Experience." Terrorism: An International Journal 1 (1978): 147-168.

Norman, Lloyd. "Our Nuclear Weapons Sites: Next Target of Terrorists?" Army, June 1977.

O'Brien, Conor Cruise. "Liberty and Terrorism." International Security 2 (1977): 56-67.

Opello, Walter C., Jr. "The Social System, the Individual, and Internal War: A Conceptual Framework for the Analysis of Revolution." International Journal of Group Tensions 4 (December 1974): 455-93.

Paust, Jordan J. "A Survey of Possible Legal Responses to International Terrorism: Prevention, Punishment, and Cooperative Action." Georgia Journal of International and Comparative Law 5 (1975): 431-469.

Pierre, Andrew J. "The Politics of International Terrorism." Orbis 19 (Winter 1976).

Rosenau, James N. "Internal War as an International Event." In International Aspects of Civil Strife, pp. 45-91. Edited by James N. Rosenau. Princeton: Princeton University Press, 1964.

Rosenbaum, David M. "Nuclear Terror." International Security 1 (Winter 1977).

Russell, Charles A. and Miller, Bowman H. "Profile of a Terrorist." Terrorism: An International Journal 1 (1977): 17-34.

Seldon, Mark. Revolution and Third World Development: Peoples War and the Transformation of Peasant Society." In National Liberation: Revolution in the Third World, pp. 214-248. Edited by Norman Miller and Roderick Aya. New York: Free Press, 1971.

Shaw, Paul D. "Extortion Threats: Analytic Techniques and Resources." Assets Protection 1 (Summer 1975): 5-16.

_____. "Terrorism and Executive Protection." Assets Protection 1 (Winter 1976): 8-13.

Steinhof, Patricia. "Portrait of a Terrorist." Asian Survey 16 (1976): 830-45.

Stephens, Maynard M. "The Oil and Natural Gas Industries: A Potential Target of Terrorists." In Terrorism: Threat, Reality, Response, pp. 200-223. Edited by David Kupperman and Darrell Trent. Stanford, Calif.: Hoover Institution Press, 1979.

Stiles, Dennis W. "Sovereignty and the New Violence." *Air University Review* 27 (July - August 1976).

Sundberg, Jacob. "The Antiterrorist Legislation in Sweden." In *Terrorism and Criminal Justice: An International Perspective*, pp. 71-86. Edited by Ronald D. Crelinsten, Danielle Laberge-Altmejd, and Denis Szabo. Lexington, Mass.: Lexington Books, 1978.

Szabo, Denis, and Crelinsten, Ronald D. "International Political Terrorism: A Challenge for Comparative Research." *Terrorism: An International Journal* 3 (1980): 341-348.

Thompson, W. Scott. "Political Violence and the 'Correlation of Forces'." *Orbis* 19 (Winter 1976): 1270-1288.

Thornton, Thomas P. "Terror as a Weapon of Political Agitation." In *Internal War*, pp. 71-99. Edited by Harry Eckstein. New York: Free Press, 1964.

Trent, Darrell M. "A National Policy to Combat Terrorism." *Policy Review* 9 (Summer 1979): 41-53.

Waugh, William L., Jr. "Political Skyjackings and Hostage Safety: An Exploratory Analysis." *Southeastern Political Review* (1982, Forthcoming).

Wilkinson, Paul. "Three Questions on Terrorism." *Government and Opposition* 8 (Summer 1973): 290-312.

Wolf, John B. "Controlling Political Terrorism in a Free Society." *Orbis* 19 (Winter 1976): 1289-1308.

Wright, Quincy. "Non-Military Intervention." In *The Relevance of International Law*, pp. 14-33. Edited by Karl Deutsch and Stanley Hoffman. Garden City, N.Y.: Anchor Books, 1971.

Young, Oran R. "Systemic Bases of Intervention." In *Law and Civil War in the Modern World*, pp. 111-126. Edited by John Norton Moore. Baltimore, Johns Hopkins University Press, 1974.

Zawodny, J.K. "Unconventional Warfare." In Conflict Resolution: Contributions of the Behavioral Sciences, pp. 393-397. Edited by Clagett G. Smith. Notre Dame, Ind.: University of Notre Dame Press, 1971.

GOVERNMENT SOURCES:

Bouthol, Gaston. International Terrorism in Its Historical Depth and Present Dimensions, 1968-1975. Washington, D.C.: U.S. Department of State, 1976.

Cully, Lt. John A. "Defusing Human Bombs -- Hostage Negotiations." FBI Law Enforcement Bulletin, October 1974. Reprint by the Federal Bureau of Investigation, U.S. Department of Justice.

Deakin, Thomas J. "The Legacy of Carlos Marighella." FBI Law Enforcement Bulletin, October 1974. Reprint by the Federal Bureau of Investigation, U.S. Department of Justice.

Fearey, Robert A. "International Terrorism" (Address Before the Los Angeles World Affairs Council and the World Affairs Council of Orange County, February 19, 1976). Department of State Bulletin, 29 March 1976, pp. 394-403.

Fields, Louis G., Jr. "Terrorism and the Rule of Law: Society at the Crossroads" (Keynote Address to the Symposium on Terrorism and Social Control, 19-20 January 1979, Ohio Northern University College of Law, Ada, Ohio). Washington, D.C.: U.S. Department of State, n.d. (Mimeographed).

_____. "Terrorism: Summary of Applicable United States and International Law." Washington, D.C.: U.S. Department of State, n.d. (Mimeographed).

Karkashian, John E. "Problem of International Terrorism" (Testimony of John E. Karkashian, Acting Director, Office for Combatting Terrorism, before the Subcommittee on Foreign Assistance of the Senate Committee on Foreign Relations). The Department of State -- Statement, 14 September 1977.

Kelly, Clarence M. "Terrorism: A Phenomenon of Sickness." Res Publica, Summer 1974. Reprint by the Federal Bureau of Investigation, U.S. Department of Justice.

Mickolus, Edward F. Annotated Bibliography on Transnational and International Terrorism. Washington, D.C.: U.S. Central Intelligence Agency, PR 76-10073U, December 1976.

Milbank, David L. International and Transnational Terrorism: Diagnosis and Prognosis. Washington, D.C.: U.S. Central Intelligence Agency, PR 10030, April 1976.

_____. International Terrorism in 1976. Washington, D.C.: U.S. Central Intelligence Agency, RP 77-10034U, July 1977.

Nixon, Richard M. U.S. Foreign Policy for the 1970s: The Emerging Structure of Peace (A Report to the Congress, February 9, 1972). Washington, D.C.: U.S. Government Printing Office.

_____. U.S. Foreign Policy for the 1970s: Shaping a Durable Peace (A Report to the Congress, May 3, 1973). Washington, D.C.: U.S. Government Printing Office.

Quainton, Anthony C.E. "Government Policy and Response in a Terrorist Crisis Situation" (Address to the Chicago Association of Commerce and Industry, September 26, 1978; by Ambassador Anthony C.E. Quainton, Director, Office for Combatting Terrorism, U.S. Department of State). Washington, D.C.: U.S. Department of State. (Mimeographed).

_____. "Statement by United States Representative Ambassador Anthony Quainton Before the Ad Hoc Committee on International Terrorism (United Nations), March 21, 1979." Washington, D.C.: U.S. Department of State. (Mimeographed).

U.S. Central Intelligence Agency, National Foreign Assessment Center. International Terrorism in 1977: A Research Paper. Washington, D.C.: U.S. Central Intelligence Agency, RP 78-10255U, August 1978.

_____. International Terrorism in 1978: A Research Paper. Washington, D.C.: U.S. Central Intelligence Agency, RP 79-10149, March 1979.

U.S. Congress. House. Committee on Foreign Affairs. Subcommittee on the Near East and South Asia. International Terrorism: Hearings, 93rd Congress, 2nd session, June 11, 18-19, 24, 1974.

U.S. Congress. House. Committee on Internal Security. Political Kidnappings, 1968-1973: A Staff Study, 93rd Congress, 1st session, 1973.

_____. Terrorism: Hearings, 93rd Congress, 2d session, February-March 1974, part 1.

_____. Terrorism: Hearings, 93rd Congress, 2d session, May-June 1974, part 2.

_____.Terrorism: Hearings, 93rd Congress, 2d session, June-July 1974, part 3.

_____. Terrorism: Hearings, 93rd Congress, 2d session, July-August 1974, part 4.

_____. Terrorism: A Staff Study, 93rd Congress, 2d session, August 7, 1974.

U.S. Congress. House. Committee on Interstate and Foreign Commerce. Subcommittee on Transportation and Aeronautics. Anti-Hijacking Act of 1973: Hearings, 93rd Congress, 1st session, February-March 1973, H.R. 3858, H.R. 670, H.R. 3853, and H.R. 4287, parts 1 and 2.

U.S. Congress. Senate. Committee on Commerce. Subcommittee on Aviation. The Administration's Emergency Anti-Hijacking Regulations: Hearings, 93rd Congress, 1st session, January 9-10, 1973.

U.S. Congress. Senate. Committee on Foreign Relations. Aircraft Hijacking Convention: Hearings, 93rd Congress, 1st session, on Executive A, June 7, 20, 1971.

U.S. Congress. Senate. Committee on the Judiciary. Terroristic Activity: Hearings Before the Subcommittee to Investigate the Administration of the Internal Security Act and Other Internal Security Laws, 93rd Congress, 2d session, September 23, 1974, part 1.

_____. Terroristic Activity: Inside the Weatherman Movement: Hearings Before the Subcommittee to Investigate the Administration of the Internal Security Act and Other Internal Security Laws, 93rd Congress, 2d session, October 18, 1974, part 2.
Terrorist Activity: Testimony of Dr. Frederick Schwarz: Hearings Before the Subcommittee to Investigate the Administration of the Internal Security Act and Other Internal Security Laws, 93rd Congress, 2d session, July 5, 1974, part 3.

_____. Terroristic Activity: International Terrorism: Hearings Before the Subcommittee to Investigate the Administration of the Internal Security Act and Other Internal Security Laws, 94th Congress, 1st session, May 14, 1975.

_____. Terroristic Activity: Hostage Defense Measures: Hearings Before the Subcommittee to Investigate the Administration of the Internal Security Act and Other Internal Security Laws, 94th Congress, 1st session, July 25, 1975, part 5.

U.S. Department of Justice, Law Enforcement Assistance Administration, National Institute of Law Enforcement and Criminal Justice. Terrorism: Supplement -- A Selected Bibliography. Washington, D.C.: U.S. Department of Justice, September 1977.

_____, Law Enforcement Assistance Administration, Private Security Advisory Council. Prevention of Terroristic Crimes: Security Guidelines for Business, Industry, and Other Organizations. Washington, D.C.: U.S. Department of Justice, 1976.

_____. Facing Tomorrow's Terrorist Incident Today. Washington, D.C.: U.S Department of Justice, October 1977.

_____. FBI Uniform Crime Reports: Bomb Summary 1977. Washington, D.C.: U.S. Department of Justice, n.d.

U.S. Department of State, "Department Spokesman Released the Following on 10/18/77." Washington, D.C.: U.S. Department of State, n.d. (Mimeographed).

_____. "Bonn Declaration: Addendum to Economic Summit Conference Communique, July 17, 1978." Washington, D.C.: U.S. Department of State, n.d. (Mimeographed).

U.S. Department of State. "U.S Department of State Unclassified Bibliography on Terrorism." Washington, D.C.: U.S. Department of State, n.d. (Mimeographed).

_____. "Terrorism." GIST, August 1978.

U.S. General Accounting Office. FBI Domestic Intelligence Operations: An Uncertain Future. Washington, D.C.: U.S. General Accounting Office, GGD-78-10, 9 November 1977.

_____. Need for Uniform Security Measures in Transporting Arms, Ammunition, and Explosives (Report to the Congress). Washington, D.C.: U.S. General Accounting Office, LCD-78-237, 21 December 1978.

OTHER SOURCES:

Joyner, Nancy Douglas. "A Contemporary Concept of Piracy in International Law: The Status of Aerial Hijacking as an International Crime." Ph.D. dissertation, Florida State University, 1973.

Redlick, Amy. "The Impact of Transnational Interactions on Separatism: A Case Study of the Quebec Separatist Movement." Ph.D. dissertation, Fletcher School of Law and Diplomacy, Tufts University, 1977.

INDEX

Action Organization for the Liberation of Palestine, 57

Aden, role in Mogadishu hijacking, 8

Aerial hijacking (see specific incidents) 7-10, 12-13, 40, 42043, 46, 54-55, 108, 141, 165, 178, 187, 189-191, 199-200, 206, 214-216, 219, 222, 224

Al Fatah (see Black September organization) 102

Amtorg Trading Corporation (USSR), 1971 bombing, 61

Arafat, Yasir (See Palestine Liberation Organization) 102

Argentina, 153;
    kidnapping of Borns (1974), 187-188;
    kidnapping of Sylvester, (1971), 188-189

Baader-Meinhof gang, 8, 62

Bahrain, role in Mogadishu hijacking, 8

Begin, Menachem, 22

Bell, J. Bowyer, 25, 32-33

Bishop, Vaughn, 50

Black September Organization, 58, 64, 77

Blair, John, 15

Bolz-Schlossberg Technique, 171

Border Protection Group 9 (West Germany) 9-10, 152

Breslauer, George (and Alexander Dallin) 31

Bulgaria, apprehension of terrorists (1978) 176

Burton, Anthony, 160

Businessmen as victims, 13, 39-41, 45-46, 83, 87, 88-89, 114, 127, 187-189

Carter, President, 153

Clutterbuck, Richard, 89

Crete (Greece), role in Mogadishu hijacking, 8

Croatian terrorists, 58-59

Crozier, Brian, 73-74, 79, 82, 84, 101, 180

Cyprus, role in Mogadishu hijacking, 8;
    Egyptian rescue attempt, 170

Czechoslovakia, hijackers, 43

Dallin, Alexander (and George Breslauer), 31

"Death squads," 153-154

Diplomatic personnel as victims, 39, 40-41, 83, 141-142, 165, 175, 188-189

"Dual-phase" terrorism, 54, 64

Dubai, role in Mogadilshu hijacking, 8

Ecstein, Harry, 160-161, 228

Egypt, 73-74;
  rescue attempt in Cyprus, 170

Entebbe (see Uganda)

European Convention for the Suppression of Terrorism (1976), 45

Evans, Ernest, 98

"External terrorism," 56, 63-65, 69, 114-115, 148, 193-194, 206, 210-212, 221, 226, 231

Feldman, Elliot, 18-19

Fields, Louis G., Jr., 46, 48

"Flexible" response policies, 11, 149, 171-172, 175, 200-202, 217, 241-242

France, role in Mogadishu rescue, 8;
  definition of terrorism, 37

Garcia-Mora, Manuel R., 52

General Intelligence and Reconnaisissance Unit 269 (Israel), 152

Great Britain, 162, 169;
  attack on Washington Embassy (1973), 65;
  S.A.S., 152;
  Northern Ireland (Emergency Provisions) Act of 1973, 139

Gueverra, Che, 22

Gurr, Ted Robert, 30-31, 73, 78

Haiti, definition of international terrorism, 37

Hacker, Frederick, 179

Halperin, Ernst, 93

Hickey, Neil, 167

Ho Chi Minh, 22

Hukbalahaps or Huks (Philippines), 22

Huntington, Samuel, 144

Hutchinson, Martha Crenshaw, "revolutionary terrorism," 86

Hyams, Edward, 73;
  "direct terrorism," 33;
  "indirect terrorism," 33

Ideological objectives, 74, 75-81, 147, 232, 235

"Integrated internal terrorism," 56, 60-63, 114-115, 148, 193-194, 205, 210-212, 221, 225-226, 231

International Federation of Airline Pilots Associations, 178

Iran, role in Mogadishu hijacking, 8;
  hostage crisis of 1979-1981, 132, 170

Irish Republican Army (Provisional), 65, 139

Israel, 12, 162, 208;
  Entebbe rescue, 4, 10, 11, 64, 132, 164, 177;
  role in Mogadishu rescues, 8;
  Munich Olympics massacre (1972), 10, 83;
  Lod Airport massacre (1972), 13, 55;
  attack at Munich airport (1970), 57-58;
  bombing in Jerusalem (1968), 60-61;
  air strikes against Palestinians, 64;
  abductions and assassinations, 140;
  Maalot massacre (1974), 175

Italy, 13;
  role in Mogadishu hijacking, 8

Japan, terrorists, 13;
  Japanese Red Army, 155

Jenkins, Brian, 40-42, 43, 44, 46-47, 98, 189

Jewish Defense League, 61

Kelly, George A. (and Linda B. Miller), 36

Kissinger, Henry, 170-171

Knauss, Peter (and Darrell Trent), 143

Ku Klux Klan, 32, 74

Kupperman, Robert (and Darrell Trent), 143

Laqueur, Walter, 72

Latin America (see Specific countries), 39

"Legitimacy potential," 77

Libya, 13, 52

Livingston, Marius, 73

Lufthansa, Flight 181 - Mogadishu hijacking, 8

Majorca (Spain), Palma, 8

Maser, Steven, 15

Mau Mau (Kenya), 22

McClure, Brooks, 191

Methvin, Eugene H. (and Robert S. Strother), 136-137

Mickolus, Edward, 48-50, 79-80, 203;
  typology of terrorism, 48-49;
  definition of terrorism, 48-49;
  typology of terrorist organizations, 79-80

Milbank, David L., 46-49, 93-94

Military responses to terrorism, 5, 51-52, 114, 139, 149-152, 156, 239, 240, 241

Miller, Bowman H. (and Charles A. Russell), hierarchy of terrorist tactics, 96-97, 198, 226

Mogadishu (Somalia) rescue, 4, 5, 8-9, 51-52, 63-64, 132, 152, 194

Montoneros (Argentina), Born kidnapping (1974), 187-188

Morocco, citizen assassinated in Norway (1973), 58, 63

Netherlands, 169;
  S. Moluccan attacks, 59

N.Y.C.P.D., Hostage Negotiation Team, 171

News Media roles, 83, 143-144, 167-168, 187-188, 204-205, 238

"No Compromise, no negotiation" policies, 11, 149, 168-172, 175, 180, 200-202, 217, 241-242

Northern Ireland (Emergency Provisions) Act (1973), 139

Norway, Lillehammer assassination (1973), 58, 63, 64

Nuclear terrorism, 98-99

Ojo por Ojo (Eye for an Eye) organization (Guatemala), 32

Palestinian terrorsits, 8, 12, 55, 83, 140, 163, 208

Palestinian Liberation Organization, 13-14, 83, 102

Parry, Albert, 23

Persson, Folke, 37

Petra Schelm Command of the Red Army Faction (Rote Armee Fraktion) (West Germany) (See Baader-Meinhof gang), 62

Police Responses to terrorism, 3-4, 51, 103-104

Police responses (cont'd) 112, 113, 128, 136, 139-141, 149-152, 156, 158-159, 161, 162-163, 185, 239

Political asylum, 42, 45, 50, 187, 197, 204, 213-216, 218, 222, 226

Popular Front for the Liberation of Palestine, 57, 60

Quainton, Ambassador Anthony C.E., 2, 46-47

Rapoport, David, 74

Red Army Faction (Rote Armee Fraktion) (See Baader-Meinhof gang) 62

Roguly, Damir (and Edward Weisband), 101-102

Rosenau, James N., 23

Russell, Charles A. (and Bowman H. Miller), hierarchy of terrorist tactics, 96-97, 198, 226

"Single-phase" terrorism, 54, 64

Society Against World Imperialism, 8

Sons of Liberty (U.S.) 74

South Moluccan terrorists
 attack on Indonesian Embassy-The Hague (1975) 59;
 attack on Dutch train, (1977), 59

Special Air Services regiment (Great Britain) 152

"Spillover terrorism," 56-60, 69, 113, 115, 148, 193-194, 205, 210-212, 221, 225, 231

Strategic objectives of terrorists, 74, 81-89, 147, 230, 232, 235

Strickland, D.A. (and Peter Knauss), 109

Strother, Robert S. (and Eugene H. Methvin), 136-137

Sweden,
 defines international terrorism, 37;
 attack on Yugoslav Ambassador, 58-59

Tactical objectives of terrorists, 74, 90-91, 147, 203-204, 213-216, 218, 222, 232, 235

Territorial jurisdiction, 3, 4, 35-38, 39, 50-52, 54-55, 59, 63-66, 69, 71, 105, 177, 193-194

Third World, 121

Thornton, Thomas P., 26, 30, 34-35, 85

Trent, Darrell (and Robert Kupperman), 143

Turkey, role in Mogadishu hijacking, 8-9

Uganda, Entebbe, 4, 5, 51-52, 64, 132, 152, 164, 170, 177, 194

U.S.S.R., 13, 38

United Nations
  actions, 1, 121;
  definitions of terrorism, 2, 7;
  on aerial hijacking, 10;
  Ad Hoc Committee on International Terrorism, 1973, 36-37; 1977, 37-38;
  recognition of PLO, 83, 102-103;
  on extradition, 164;
  on jurisdiction, 177

United States, 8, 38, 39, 45, 136, 152-153, 179-180;
  U.S. Department of State, 2, 10, 153, 175;
  U.S. Draft Convention on Terrorism (1972), 7;
  U.S. policy, 6-7, 10, 149, 170-171, 175;
  Office for Combatting Terrorism (State Dept) 46, 153, 191;
  Central Intelligence Agency, 46, 189;
  bombing of Soviet Amtorg Trading Corporation, 1971, 61;
  U.S. Army, attacks in West Germany, 62;
  attack on British embassy (1973), 65;
  attacks on nuclear facilities, 99;
  Alaska Pipeline sabotage, 108;
  rescue attempt in Iran (1980), 170

Uruguay, 106-107, 153

Venezuela, 38

Walter, Eugene V., 28-29, 30, 32, 35

Weisband, Edward (and Damir Roguly), 101-102

West Germany, 43, 176;
  Mogadishu rescue, 4, 8-10, 11, 12, 13, 51-52, 132, 170, 194;
  Border Protection Group 9, 9-10, 12, 152;
  attack on El Al passengers in Munich (1970), 57-58;
  attacks on U.S. Army bases and personnel, 62

Wilkinson, Paul, 24-25, 29-33, 70-71, 80, 100-101, 110, 112, 150-151, 169, 241

Yugoslavia,
  attack on Swedish Ambassador, 58-59;
  apprehends terrorists, 176

Zwodney, J.K., 179